Edited by Carol Rutz and Mary Savina

Building Intellectual Community
Through Collaboration

College City Publications, Northfield, MN

Published by:
College City Publications / Ashmore Ink
925 Ivanhoe Drive
Northfield, Minnesota 55057
http://ashmoreink.com

**For information on ordering this volume
from the Carleton College Bookstore:**

E-mail: Carletoninfo@collegebookstore.org

Web site: http://wwwcollegebookstore.org

Phone: (507) 646-4153 or (800) 799-4148

ON THE COVER:

Twigonometry, a twig sculpture by Patrick Dougherty, was assembled
— collaboratively — on the north end of Carleton College's "Bald Spot"
in 2002. Built from willow, buckthorn, and dogwood harvested from the
Cowling Arboretum and the McKnight Prairie with the help of volunteers
from Carleton, Northfield, and southeast Minnesota, it fascinated, inspired,
and entertained faculty, staff, students, and visitors to the campus for four
years before being disassembled in the summer of 2006. (Photo by Warwick
Green.)

ISBN-10: 0-9746379-4-7
ISBN-13: 978-0-9746379-4-5

PRINTED IN THE UNITED STATES OF AMERICA

Contents

Acknowledgments

In 2004, Carleton College faculty produced a volume of essays titled *Reflections on Learning as Teachers*, a project headed by Susan Singer, professor of biology and then-coordinator of Carleton's Perlman Center for Learning and Teaching. Her vision and the center's support continue with this volume. As was the *Reflections* volume, this project also has been supported by a Faculty Career Enhancement Grant from the Andrew W. Mellon Foundation.

The essays in this book reflect the teaching and learning ethos at Carleton, enriched since 1992 by the presence of the Perlman Center. As a forum for communication about teaching, learning, assessment, pedagogical theory, faculty scholarship, and student experience, the center serves as a gathering place for people and ideas—a kind of community glue that integrates our separate experiences to produce the kinds of collegial collaborations described herein. Mary Savina, immediate past coordinator, gratefully acknowledges the contributions of the Archibald Bush Foundation, the endowment provided by Carleton trustee and alumnus Larry Perlman, and the leadership of her four predecessors as coordinator.

We thank the Perlman Center's current coordinator, Chico Zimmerman, and the administrative genius behind the scenes, Jennifer Cox Johnson. We owe extravagant thanks, too, to Nancy J. Ashmore '72, production editor and part-time muse. Without her savvy about publications and her firm—but upbeat—encouragement to meet deadlines, this book would be unformed in the most basic sense.

Finally, we thank our contributors for telling about the collaborations that matter to them as professionals, citizens, colleagues, and folks.

Carol Rutz and Mary Savina, editors

Foreword: Building Intellectual Community Through Collaboration

John C. Bean

In her introduction to this remarkable volume, co-editor Carol Rutz sees collaboration as a kind of love. Although the metaphor at first startles, her use of the *Phaedrus* to explain the eros of knowledge-seeking highlights a recurring theme in this book. Readers will find many references to eros throughout these chapters. Kristi Wermager and Susan Jaret McKinstry describe student sessions in the Gould Library's special collections as a "matchmaking" occasion intended to help students fall in love with material books. Carol Donelan, Adriana Estill, and Mija Van Der Wege—those fast-talking dames—describe the bonds of friendship that emerged during their collaboration. And literary scholar Michael Kowalewski compares himself to Shakespeare's Miranda when he marvels at the brave new disciplinary world of his colleague Gary Wagenbach, who has an office refrigerator full of frozen bugs. This is a volume about the eros of collaboration, about losing oneself in strange seas and emerging with new eyes and fresh clothes.

Like the previous volume in this series, *Reflections on Learning as Teachers* (2004), this present volume, *Building Intellectual Community Through Collaboration,* celebrates academic life at Carleton College. Although focused on Carleton, both books have much to say to other institutions and deserve a wide readership. Gathered here are stories of collaboration that would not normally appear in scholarly journals, but that are all the more vibrant and important for that very reason. What you hear in these pages are the voices of faculty writing in the relaxed atmosphere of the "essay" rather than the closed-form conventions of scholarly prose.

JOHN C. BEAN is a professor of English at Seattle University, where he serves as a "consulting professor of writing and assessment." He has an undergraduate degree from Stanford University and a PhD from the University of Washington. He is the author of *Engaging Ideas: The Professor's Guide to Integrating Writing, Critical Thinking, and Active Learning in the Classroom* and a co-author of *The Allyn & Bacon Guide to Writing.*

Consider the wonderful opening of the chapter by Deanna Haunsperger and Steve Kennedy (2007) on the national impact of Carleton's Summer Mathematics Program:

> We're not sure when it happened. It probably wasn't between the minestrone and the Caesar salad, though it may have been. ... The hubbub washed over us—we heard them talking about choosing graduate schools, choosing advisors, doing research, figuring out how to fit a family into a career, and whether to choose a sauvignon blanc or a nice pinot grigio with the grilled shrimp. (pp. 60-61)

"What is this 'it'?" readers will ask, propelled by the narrative. (I won't tell you the answer.) Or consider Kowalewski's musing about how students' crawling on their bellies to look at a grassy meadow from a mouse's perspective (a requirement in the science side of a dyad course) might have influenced their later reading of *A Sand County Almanac*.

Not only is there a collaboration of people and disciplines in this volume, but a collaboration of genres where writers are freed from the constraints of academic prose to tell us something wonderful and important about how the academic life works. I am reminded of the wisdom of my friend, Chris Anderson—a rhetorician who teaches at Oregon State University—about the academic training of foresters. Foresters, Anderson (1993) says, "should be writing essays in addition to articles because in writing them they would be forced into a stance of wonder, humility, tentativeness, attention" (p. 165). The "essay," he argues, is "the only form that can honestly and accurately reflect the complexities and the dynamics that the [ecologically oriented] New Forestry is trying to understand" (p. 165).

Likewise, it may be that the essay is the only form that conveys the complex, dynamic ecologies of the teaching life, which is at once personal and social. I am thankful to Carleton College for giving us these collections of essays about teaching.

What these essays show, in their various ways, is the creative energy of collaboration. The term "collaboration" has long been important to me. My generation of scholars in rhetoric/composition was shaped by Kenneth Bruffee's 1984 article "Collaborative Learning and the 'Conversation of Mankind,'" in which Bruffee argued that knowledge is formed in interpretive communities whose conversations students need to join. We proponents of collaborative learning placed students in groups to negotiate solutions to disciplinary problems, and we celebrated whenever the classroom buzzed with engaged, disciplinary talk. Through composition courses or the writing-across-the-curriculum movement, we taught students how to join interpretive communities by helping them learn disciplinary methods of inquiry and argument. We also knew that our own intellectual lives occurred in communities—that we as faculty also learned collaboratively—but we had little opportunity to write about these collaborations or to analyze how they worked.

At a pragmatic level, then, the essays in this volume have a special value to scholars and teachers at any institution because they take us behind the scenes into the collaborative processes that give rise to ideas, courses, and publications. As these essays teach us, collaboration works in many ways. Here are some of the recurring motifs that readers will find throughout this volume:

- Personal narratives about the experience of collaboration, often following the plot of disorientation, insight, and integration
- Stories about collaboration as community-building and friendship
- Narratives of problem-solving as a collaborators tackle together a shared problem and find that many heads are better than one
- Expositions showing how collaboration works in practice to produce scholarship
- Narratives about the creation of environments that encourage collaboration

By showing collaboration in action, the essays in this volume make an important contribution to our understanding of teaching and learning. According to a recent study of collaborative learning, there has been surprisingly little research into the impact of collaboration on faculty (Barkley, E. F., Cross, K. P., & Major, C. H., 2005, p. 24). Yet in her review of Hesburgh Award finalists between 1993 and 2001, Patricia Cross found that "a predominant feature of these cutting-edge programs was the emphasis on collaborative learning for faculty: faculty members were collaborating across disciplines and generation to share the 'wisdom of practice'" (Barkley et al, p. 24).

This volume shows us "collaborative learning for faculty" in action. The essays remind us of the creative pleasures of collaboration in our own professional lives and lead us again to the desire to create community for our students. We think again of Carol Rutz's introductory metaphor—collaboration as love.

REFERENCES

Anderson, C. (1993). *Edge effects: Notes from an Oregon forest.* Iowa City, IA: University of Iowa Press.

Barkley, E. F., Cross, K. P., & Major, C. H. (2005). *Collaborative learning techniques: A handbook for college faculty.* San Francisco: Jossey-Bass.

Bruffee, K. (1984). Collaborative learning and the "conversation of mankind." *College English*, *46.6,* 635-652.

Haunsperger, D., & Kennedy, S. (2007). Serendipity and inadvertence in the building of community. In Carol Rutz & Mary Savina (Eds.), *Building intellectual community through collaboration* (pp. 60-69). Northfield, MN: College City Publications.

Introduction:
Collaboration as a Growth Factor

Carol Rutz

WRITING TOGETHER

Planning an introduction to this collection on collaboration at Carleton College led me to reflect on the process of writing collaboratively, which was the primary means of producing this volume and its predecessor, *Reflections on Learning as Teachers* (2004). As is usual for edited collections, authors proposed chapters in response to a call for proposals. However, in an important departure from usual practice, authors then gathered several times over two weeks to read and comment on drafts in a workshop environment. Consequently, new, untenured faculty read the work of senior colleagues, learning some institutional history and conveying their own perspectives on claiming their place in this learning and teaching community. Similarly, colleagues in the humanities and the sciences asked thoughtful questions of one another about research, pedagogy, and scholarly pursuits. Some of the co-authored chapters were written by members of one department; some were not. Either way, matters of style, disciplinary convention, formality, and personality had to be negotiated. This is not to say that single authors had it easy; if anything, their responsibility to convey with one voice the intricacies of collaboration required a deft writerly touch.

A small college collects people from various disciplines for team teaching, internal reviews, scholarly projects, committee work, and other purposes, many of which are presented in detail in this collection. Those of us who wrote for the two books in this series have found that writing together offers a rich, complex set of experiences that both supplement and enact our sense of the kind of collegiality that makes a campus vital, nourishing, and healthy for its citizens.

CAROL RUTZ, lecturer in English and director of the College Writing Program, earned her B.A. degree at Gustavus Adolphus College, her M.A. at Hamline University, and her PhD at the University of Minnesota. She joined the Carleton faculty in 1997.

Clearly, this volume demonstrates that academic life encourages faculty and staff to cooperate in many ways, including as writers, yet co-authorship bears a number of complicating burdens. Successful writing collaboration requires the participants to coordinate ideas, find time to write, and agree on deadlines. Revision—well, there's another issue. As I search for a metaphor to describe the phenomenon of writing in community, I find myself considering several: A multi-headed hydra? A chain gang? Cats in need of herding? One cannot deny that writing with others can evoke conflict or the occasional headstrong impulse.

Nevertheless, to characterize collaborative writing as a more or less amicable struggle overlooks the genuine partnerships that develop through writing together. As the chapters in this volume demonstrate, collaboration is an outgrowth of relationships, and we cheat ourselves as writers and colleagues if we fail to recognize the relational work we accomplish through writing together— work that reflects the context of our larger project of learning and teaching in a small undergraduate institution.

To sort out the factors leading to successful writing collaborations, I turn to some recent cases in my own experience as a writer among writers over a period of six or seven months. First, I collaborated with a colleague on a scholarly article, which required a great deal of conversation about tone, diction, the use and display of data, specific examples, and more. The product of our first 15 drafts underwent even more revision after reviewers offered suggestions. The published result bears few traces of our detailed negotiations, but our pleasure in the accomplishment resides more in the insights achieved together than in the printed text.

A similar, but smaller project generated a panel proposal for a professional conference. Four writers from two institutions, Carleton and one on the West Coast, had to agree on an umbrella concept, program copy, and individual approaches, all within a strict word limit. The proposal was written via e-mail correspondence according to a tight deadline, and it was eventually accepted for a national conference.

A less typical example of writing with others was my service on an accreditation team for a regional university in the South. I was part of a team of 11, most of whom were strangers to one another, yet we were expected to produce a unified report with significant implications for the institution under review. The team leader insisted that all of us draft our sections of the report while we were on site, partially to prepare an oral report to key administrators and faculty. Then, to make sure a good draft of the written report was in hand for final revision by the team leader, all of us worked concurrently to revise our individual sections at least once before we dispersed to our home institutions.

Perhaps my most surprising and collegial writing experience concerned an invited article written by five Carleton faculty and administrators involved in a project sponsored by the Association of American Colleges and Universities. As we wrote, the experience of writing clarified the project, consolidated the gains, and took rhetorical form—all the while demonstrating an amazing lack of ego on the part of individual contributors. None of us could have visualized the final product when we began, yet all five were pleased with the article that appeared in print.

Extrapolating from writing experiences such as these, I find myself approaching some conclusions about writing with other people.

Successful collaboration among writers requires trust, patience, commitment, communication, respect, and a willingness to risk failure or embarrassment. This constellation of factors recalls Plato's claim for the power of dialectic as expressed in *Phaedrus*. During a lengthy discussion of the rhetoric of love, Socrates chides Phaedrus, a younger man, who takes rhetoric rather lightly: "The function of speech is to influence the soul" (Plato, 1973, section 271). Later, he elaborates: "But finer still is the serious treatment of these subjects which you find when a man employs the art of dialectic, and, fastening upon a suitable soul, plants and sows in it truths accompanied by knowledge" (Plato, 1973, section 277).

Knowledge and truth grow out of serious, cooperative searching among participants who care about the matters they discuss. In short, the dialectic process of collaborative writing enacts a kind of love—rooted in Plato's insight and further illustrated by Parker Palmer's definition of love: "the capacity to extend one's self on behalf of another person's growth" (P. Palmer, personal communication, June 8, 2005). Participation in a dialectic process employs self-disclosure for the benefit of another and yields a product that displays better thinking than either could do alone.

The components of collaborative writing include a search for and love of truth, as well as scrupulous attention to accuracy, fidelity to data, and a wish for the resulting truth to benefit humankind in some way. As humans and educators, we long to build bridges between what is and what ought to be.

There is also a yearning for cooperation toward something that one cannot do alone—a surrender of ego toward service of a larger purpose and the giving up of personal gain.

The result is a joyous, uplifting, soul-building experience. "Love" emerges from the writing. The sensibility comes from "drawing deep on our best instincts of what is needed" (Palmer, personal communication, June 8, 2005). The process of learning from one another results in warmth, pride, trust, a sense of common cause, shared values, and the nervy satisfaction of productive tension.

All of this may sound anything but academic, yet I maintain that we write out of a long tradition that honors collaboration as a means of and reason for community. As I keep telling my students, knowledge resides in people before it appears in print or on the Web or in some other medium. Sharing knowledge, therefore, depends on the honest, intentional participation of humans. The sharing produces growth in knowledge and concomitant growth in community, a convenient term for the emotional as well as geographical, intellectual, and collaborative features of Carleton as a workplace devoted to learning.

WHAT IS IN THIS BOOK

Our hope as writers in community is that this volume both promotes growth and enacts community in its pages. Three somewhat arbitrary sections treat general themes relating to collaboration in higher education.

In the first section, "Disciplines and Productive Friction," Mike Kowalewski confesses to a life-changing experience as he, a scholar of American literature, learns about field work through team-teaching stints with two environmental scientists based in biology and geology. Mike's chapter sets the tone for almost every other contribution in the book: Forget the myth of the solitary scholar, seeking truth in cloistered isolation. Perhaps academics somewhere still occupy lonely, unheated garrets and write by candlelight, but they do not teach at Carleton. The next chapter, co-written in screenplay format by Carol Donelan, Adriana Estill, and Mija VanDerWege, shows off the playful side of the struggle all young faculty work through as they write toward scholarly publication. With equal energy, Deanna Haunsperger and Steve Kennedy tell the story of their summer mathematics program, which for over 10 years has invited young women into academia as mathematicians. Working together on the notion of sustainability, Gary Wagenbach, a biologist, and Richard Strong, former director of Carleton's physical plant, describe a course that requires students to design and build an eco-friendly house. Philosopher and cognitive scientist Roy Elveton ends this section with a meditation on the development of cognitive science as a disciplinary presence at Carleton.

Our middle section, "Student-Faculty Research Collaborations," offers solid evidence that undergraduates can and do participate in real research at a small liberal arts college. Chemist Deborah Gross' chapter demonstrates how undergraduates can be vital partners in a large, multi-institutional and interdisciplinary project. From computer science, Amy Csizmar Dalal and David Musicant depict the constraints on and the benefits of designing research projects that accommodate students and simultaneously advance faculty research. Taking the long view of laboratory research, biologists Susan Singer and Catherine Reinke detail a genealogy of mentors and mentees who have acculturated one another to botanical research over several decades—mostly within the context of small liberal arts colleges. Finally, Al Montero, a political scientist, presents a model of student research conducted abroad with his supervision, contrasting the experiences of two cohorts.

The final section, "Collaboration as Inclusion and Support," shows how faculty and staff work together to offer students innovative learning experiences. Cliff Clark begins with his own reflections on teaching with faculty from other disciplines as well as his role in designing a multidisciplinary program. Susan Jaret McKinstry, an English professor, and Kristi Wermager, a librarian, write about animating courses based in British literary texts with hands-on exposure to editions available in Carleton's Gould Library's special collections. Cindy Blaha, an astrophysicist, and I write about teaching students the conventions of science writing by having them design, write, and produce magazines that simulate professional publications and involve librarians and technology experts in research and production. Classicists Clara Hardy and Chico Zimmerman tell how various campus initiatives have borne fruit in their department, from a reworking of the introductory course to a new approach to the senior capstone. Presenting an administrative point of view, Scott Bierman, dean of the college, and Elizabeth Ciner, associate dean, point toward principles of administration that foster collaboration among faculty, staff, and students.

This volume does not pretend to be a comprehensive report on collaboration at Carleton College. Nevertheless, the chapters combine to illustrate some of the ways that teaching and learning depend on and benefit from community. The community that came together to write this book enjoyed teaching and learning from one another to produce it. We hope our readers will smile upon our collaboration.

REFERENCES

Plato. (1973). *Phaedrus* (W. Hamilton, Trans.). London: Penguin.

Singer, S., & Rutz, C. (Eds.). (2004). *Reflections on Learning as Teachers*. Northfield, MN: College City Publications.

DISCIPLINES AND PRODUCTIVE FRICTION

A Rice County Almanac:
The Adventures of a Rogue Humanist in the Field

Michael Kowalewski
With Mary Savina and Gary Wagenbach

The first thing that struck me about Gary Wagenbach's office was the size of his refrigerator. It was the spring of 1996, and his office was in a then brand new biology building on campus, Hulings Hall. The new building featured large spacious walkways, multiple levels, elevators, and an airy atrium—all of which seemed somewhat exotic to a faculty member used to the busy, cramped spaces of the English Department on the second floor of Laird Hall. It was not the palatial new building space, however, but a more quotidian detail—the full-sized refrigerator in his office—that made me feel I was suddenly on terra incognita.

The English Department has a small, half-size refrigerator in the departmental office, used to store lunches, snacks, and, on occasion, a bottle of wine for a departmental social event. Gary's fridge, on the other hand, was used in his teaching and research. It was full of various living and frozen insects, vials and plastic containers with contents I couldn't identify, and plastic baggies carefully marked with felt-tip pens.

I didn't need a refrigerator in order to teach, and I certainly couldn't imagine having a refrigerator like that in my office, to be opened up with a student during office hours in order to pull out something to be spread out on a table and discussed. I felt slightly

> While I was front stage in the course, leading discussions on particular authors and themes, I was also, in some sense, always backstage as well, learning not only what but *how* ideas were framed in the sciences and attempting by indirection to find directions out.

MICHAEL KOWALEWSKI, professor of English and former director of American studies, joined the Carleton faculty in 1991 after teaching for several years at Princeton University. He earned his B.A. degree at Amherst College, and his M.A. and PhD degrees at Rutgers University.

befuddled, as if I had somehow been taken advantage of. How was I to know that my own office hours, discussing a student paper—which had previously seemed a stimulating, even important activity—might seem somewhat mundane to a student fresh from office hours that featured, say, some refrigerated South American cockroaches?

This was my first intimation that my collaboration with a biologist was going to be marked by surprise and the unexpected. Like Miranda in Shakespeare's *The Tempest*, I marveled at this brave new disciplinary world that had such (refrigerated) creatures in it.

Gary and I were meeting that spring to create a new introductory "gateway" course to the recently created ENTS (Environmental and Technology Studies) Program. The new course—to be numbered ENTS 110—was be taught in the fall of 1996. We had been given a small grant to design a fun and challenging introduction to the ENTS concentration. The course was to be taught by two faculty members: a scientist and what some of us in ENTS (unused to being defined in the negative) uneasily referred to as a "non-scientist," that is, a faculty member from the humanities or the social sciences. The intro course was to be not only interdisciplinary but cross-divisional, which is far rarer in academia than interdisciplinary teaching between allied disciplines (e.g., English and history, within the same division). This fact was verified for us by Steve Simmons, an agronomist from the University of Minnesota who sat in on several sessions of ENTS 110. "When a plant scientist and an animal scientist team-teach at the U of M," he said, "that's interdisciplinary teaching. But an English teacher and a biologist? I'd never heard of such a thing! That's why I asked to sit in on the class, so I could see for myself how this worked."[1]

Gary and I were attempting to bridge the notorious gap between the "two cultures" of science and the humanities that C. P. Snow identified nearly a half century ago. Humanistic intellectuals, particularly literary scholars, were typically antagonistic to the sciences, he claimed. "Natural Luddites," Snow called them (1959, p. 23). In some sense I was out to prove (to colleagues, to students, and to myself) that humanists actually could and did care about science and could productively collaborate with scientists, even though I had

> Upon reflection I realized that I felt connected, in a small way, to Rice County and the rural precincts we had visited in a way that I had never previously felt, though I had been living in Northfield for several years.

not had memorable experiences in my own undergraduate science classes. In my own teaching of literature, I had focused on region and "a sense of place" for several years, and there seemed to be many natural connections between my own interest in writers' imaginations of place and the light scientists might shed on such matters. Still, I had no idea what the practical pedagogical ramifications of teaching with one foot in the sciences would be. These were uncharted waters with a relative novice at the tiller.

Gary and I finally settled on a title for the course, Envisioning Landscapes. (Another ENTS faculty member had said, "Be sure it's an active title, with a verb.") In accordance with other team-taught courses I had planned, I thought the next step would involve the standard fare: extended discussions in an office or a local coffee shop about the goals of the course, the structure of the syllabus, our choice of texts, perhaps even possible suggestions about which classrooms we preferred. When I showed up in Gary's office one sunny May afternoon to discuss such matters, however, I found out that he had other plans. "Let's take a drive in the country," he said.

I couldn't imagine a team-taught English course that would have included such an invitation as a part of the intellectual structuring of the class. Gary's suggestion was tantalizing, if only as a pleasant prospect on a spring day in Rice County, but the trip turned out to be far more than a pleasure excursion. Gary took me to a number of places he hoped to incorporate into field trips in the course, from a local dairy farm with muddy milking barns to a rock quarry (I found a large fossil there that afternoon) where the air was full of hundreds of bees streaming by. We finished by stopping at a restored cabin built in 1883 that Gary had rescued from demolition and moved to his own property in order to reconstruct it, with loving dedication, in historically accurate detail.

I learned an incredible amount about local ecology and regional history that afternoon. I was tired, dusty, and my shoes were caked with mud, but I felt a deep sense of satisfaction about our explorations and was brimming with ideas for the course. Upon reflection I realized that I felt connected, in a small way, to Rice County and the rural precincts we had visited in a way that I had never previously felt, though I had been living in Northfield for several years.

Ed Buchwald, a former Carleton geologist, often said that he refused to think of Carleton as "a liberal arts college that just happened to be located in Northfield, Minnesota."[2] He said that the southern Minnesota region of maple-basswood forests and rolling cropland, studded with prairie remnants and oak savannah which surrounded Carleton was—or should be—an essential defining feature of the college as well as a rich resource for teaching and learning. I was beginning to understand what he meant. I realized that hands-on learning from a faculty colleague could be a crucial element of course design. I also realized that it was the sense of connection with and curiosity about local life, history, and ecology I had experienced (in however fledgling and tentative a way) during my field trip with Gary that I most wanted to help cultivate in students taking ENTS 110.

FIELD-BASED LEARNING & THE LIBERAL ARTS

I was involved in the founding of the Association for the Study of Literature and Environment (ASLE), which now includes over a thousand members worldwide dedicated to studying the environmental imagination in literature. Yet I would not describe myself as an "ecocritic." Neither do I think of myself as a passionate advocate for field-based learning (though I admire the work of many teachers who are, much of which is showcased in Hal Crimmel's excellent 2003 collection, *Teaching in the Field*).

I would be the first to admit that such learning is not for everyone, students or faculty. This does not mean, however, that I have any less urgent a sense of the environmental challenges now facing all of us. Like other concerned citizens, I am deeply disturbed by the catalogue of actual and potential environmental crises Glen Love (2003) reminds us of in his recent book *Practical Ecocritism*, a catalogue "so familiar as to have become dismissible" (p. 14):

> An unchecked growth of world population, tripling from 2 to 6 billion in the twentieth century and on its way to perhaps 10 billion in the next few decades, accelerating beyond the present rate of 247 new Earthlings every minute, nearly 250,000 every day, and 130 million per year. Indications of global climate warming of potentially enormous effects. The muted but still real threat of nuclear warfare. ... The overcutting of the world's remaining great forests. An accelerating rate of extinction of plants and animals, estimated at 74 species per day and 27,000 each year. The critical loss of arable land and groundwater through desertification, contamination, and the spread of human settlement. Overfishing and toxic poisoning of the world's oceans. Inundation in our own garbage and wastes. A tide of profit- and growth-driven globalization that overwhelms the principle of long-term sustainability, our best

hope for the future. At each day's end, as David W. Orr summed it up, "the Earth will be a little hotter, its waters more acidic, and the fabric of life more threadbare." (p. 14-15)

Catalogues such as these run the risk of inspiring hopelessness because of the scale of the problems. They may also seem to demand nothing less than immediate action. In the face of such massive, overwhelming challenges, anything less than passionate activism may seem like an unforgivable failure of will, a passivity, or intellectual lethargy tantamount to complicity with the very forces destroying the biosphere. Doesn't teaching literature in a wealthy, first-world country under such conditions amount to an unjustifiable leisure activity, a proverbial rearranging of the deck chairs on the Titanic?

I do not dismiss such indictments lightly, but casting the issues in this way encourages extremist thinking that reduces choice only to stark, uncompromising alternatives such as despair or militant activism. I have a strong interdisciplinary interest in the sciences, but I am also a degree-toting literature teacher and, like Love (2003), I want "to avoid the 'gotcha' manner of an eco-policeman, dragging past writers to the dock for violations of today's sense of environmental incorrectness" (p. 11).

> Science can help us measure the multiple causes and symptoms of environmental crises; literature can help us ponder the often thorny, contradictory, and entangling aspects of human nature that eventually led to those dire facts.

Some teachers are drawn to interdisciplinary study because the methods and domain of their home discipline begin to feel like bars on a cage. This has not been the case with me. I see my role as a teacher of literature—particularly the literature of place, which depends upon scientific insight—as a balancing act, with the urgency of my concern about environmental threats counterbalanced by a deep respect for the moral and artistic complexity of literature, which does not lend itself to simplification, sound bites, or quick calls to action. Productive interdisciplinary work needs to draw upon strong disciplines. Science can help us measure the multiple causes and symptoms of environmental crises; literature can help us ponder the often thorny, contradictory, and entangling aspects of human nature that eventually led to those dire facts.

GET THEE TO THE FIELD

"Up! up! My Friend, and quit your books;/ Or surely you'll grow double:/ Up! up! My Friend, and clear your looks;/ Why all this toil and trouble?"

Thus begins William Wordsworth's poem (1798/1977, p. 356) "The Tables Turned," with its famous sentiments about the competing obligations of books and nature:

> One impulse from a vernal wood
> May teach you more of man,
> Of moral evil and of good,
> Than all the sages can.

It is notable that Wordsworth includes both "Science" and "Art" in the bookish world that stands apart from nature in the poem. Notable as well is the fact that this adjuration to quit one's books comes itself from a book and not, somehow, from nature. Wordsworth is fully aware of this paradox and yet the impulse to escape the "toil" of "meddling intellect," so powerful in Romantic literature, is no less urgent or heartfelt here.

The impulse to breathe free in English meadows and woodlands actually comes not from "quitting the books" but from listening to them.[3] Wordsworth's poem, that is, arouses alternative reactions that are mutually reinforcing rather than simply self-canceling. (The poet John Hollander, 1984, p. 53, cleverly reversed Wordsworth's sentiments when he wrote, "One impulse from a vernal Book/ Taught him much more of Man/ Than any nature walk he took/ Or any risk he ran.") Wordsworth's complex sense that art, science, and nature are interfused and interdependent has been appreciated in the abstract. It has less frequently been embodied in pedagogical practice.

Teaching in the field, or "taking a nature walk," seems to strike many humanists as an example of what Mark Edmundson (1997) calls "education lite." At best it is construed by colleagues as a perhaps dubiously rewarding but picturesque attempt to escape the four-walled classroom and at worst as an example of misguided literalism or even a lavishly contrived excuse for fun and games.

Perhaps this attitude stems from the limited opportunities in which to place or extend the discussion of literature in out-of-class settings. Literature teachers frequently take students to see an out-of-class performance of a play they have read or to hear an author do a public reading. Literature classes can even be held outside in the fall or the spring, in a circle on the lawn, weather and sunscreen permitting. (Admissions brochures like to feature these occasions as a form of Socratic pastoral, one absent the background roar of grounds-crew lawnmowers and the beep of garbage trucks backing up across campus.) Beyond that, general opinion suggests, teachers and students need not venture into the field to study literature. We should all be busy close-reading and discussing texts right here in class: Please close the door.

One can understand, even concur with the reasons for this attitude and yet still find a value in spending time with literature students out-of-doors, studying natural phenomena with them. ENTS 110 was designed with an eye to helping the students see the field trips as a vital reinforcing complement rather than an escapist alternative to the on-campus "book learning" they were also required to do. Books were not all the students were using, on or off campus, in the course, which also included class discussion, research, paper writing, work with computer simulations, and time in the laboratory. ENTS 110 also involved weekly off-campus field trips: tramps through local wilderness areas, bike rides through the town of Northfield, and visits to nearby farms and wetlands.

We tried to make on- and off-campus activities seem as seamless, or at least as coherently connected, as possible. The experience of being outside, of looking hard at landscapes, of talking to local farmers, and of beginning to analyze small examples of the landscape (an "oak opening" on a knoll, a particular species of prairie tall grass, the hydrological reasons for a stream meander) was crucial to the course. But those experiences at field sites would be richer and more challenging, we felt, if they were informed and extended by on-campus book and lab learning. It was a matter of both/and, not either/or.

The act of "envisioning landscapes" in ENTS 110 required "vision" in both a metaphoric and a literal sense. To understand a particular landscape one needed to *see* it with both the eye and the mind's eye. Put another way, we wanted the students to put their "book learning" into motion, to try to make landscapes come alive within their own history, both human and non-human.

COLLABORATIVE VENTURES

The small size of a liberal arts college and Carleton's openness to collaborative teaching initiatives provided two stimulating opportunities to team-teach with natural scientists. In addition to ENTS 110 (which I taught with Gary twice, in the fall of 1996 and the fall of 1998), I also taught a "dyad" (two linked courses for entering first-year students)—Agriculture and the American Midwest: Literature and the Environment—with geologist Mary Savina in the fall of 2000.

In ENTS 110, as I have begun to suggest, we attempted to create an interdisciplinary class in which science, literature, and environmental history were integrated, not simply juxtaposed, at every step of the way. We incorporated both a vertical (temporal) and horizontal (spatial) axis in our syllabus. We used a time continuum to structure the course, asking students to think about landscapes in terms of the past, the present, and the future. Then, in relation to any one section of the temporal sections of the course, we combined local, regional, and national scales in thinking about landscapes.

For example, in thinking about the past, we asked students to read Gary Paul Nabhan's study of Native American agriculture, *Enduring Seeds*, whose examples are drawn primarily from the American Southwest. We assigned readings in environmental history that explored the origins of the "grid" land-use system in America. At the regional level, the students also read an ecological account of Minnesota meant to familiarize them with key regional differences within the state. At the local level we introduced them to some of the human and nonhuman history of Rice County (for instance, the fact that there were wild elk in the Nerstrand area at one time).

Finally, we assigned a sketching exercise in which the students were asked to imagine and draw certain views of the Carleton campus as they thought they might have existed 50, 100, and 150 years ago. We then compared their drawings with actual photographs of the campus from the Carleton Archives. We did the same kind of multiple-scale exercises in relation to the present and future sections of the course. The students received comments on their papers from both Gary and me. Literary readings included Aldo Leopold's *Sand County Almanac*, Edward Abbey's novel *The Monkey Wrench Gang*, and John McPhee's collection of essays *The Control of Nature*.

In the dyad we linked two preexisting courses (Mary's Introduction to Environmental Geology and my freshman seminar, Spirit of Place) so that the classes dovetailed in mutually enriching ways as we looked at a topic seldom taught in a liberal arts context. The dyad focused on agriculture, particularly agriculture in the Midwest. We wanted to suggest that literary scholars and scientists are both intrigued by the place of agriculture in our society but that they go about asking and answering questions about it in distinctive ways.

For instance, geologists might examine the climate of the 1930s and 1940s by studying instrumental records and comparing this period to longer-term climate records of the past. Studying the literature and films of the period (such as John Steinbeck's *The Grapes of Wrath* or Pare Lorentz's film documentary *The Plow That Broke the Plains*), historians and literary scholars might explore the cultural roots of the Dust Bowl crisis and its effect on American life. By combining these two approaches and, as in ENTS 110, by having students and both professors continually together in each other's company, in classes and in the field, we hoped to inspire more three-dimensional ways of answering questions such as, How have agricultural activities modified the landscape, soil, water, and climate of the American Midwest? What are the environmental implications of current agricultural practices and the conflicts between rural and urban land use? How has agriculture been idealized and caricatured in American culture? What are our current sources of information about agriculture?

Each of the two courses represented half of the dyad, with the students receiving separate grades in each course.

The main "geologic" topics included the geologic history of Minnesota and its influences on natural resources; ground and surface water issues; earth materials, especially soils; use of geology for land-use decisions; the Quaternary record of agriculture in the archaeological and geomorphic record; and the effects of natural disasters such as drought and floods.

In Spirit of Place, we read examples of poetry, drama, fiction, and nonfiction and focused on a broad typology of rural characters in literature, from antiquity to the present. We discussed passages from the Bible, the idealized farmers of Virgil's *Georgics*, the comic rustics of Shakespeare's *As You Like It*, the rural cider-makers and choir singers in Thomas Hardy's *Under the Greenwood Tree*, the lonely, struggling farmers of the Wisconsin coulees in Hamlin Garland's *Main-Travelled Roads*, the Bohemian immigrants in Willa Cather's

> We hoped to inspire more three-dimensional ways of answering questions such as, How have agricultural activities modified the landscape, soil, water, and climate of the American Midwest? What are the environmental implications of current agricultural practices and the conflicts between rural and urban land use? How has agriculture been idealized and caricatured in American culture? What are our current sources of information about agriculture?

My Ántonia, and the image of the displaced Joad family in the novel and movie versions of *The Grapes of Wrath*. We finished by considering examples of Seamus Heaney's poetry and contemporary essays by writers such as Paul Gruchow, Kent Meyers, and Wendell Berry, all of whom offer personal reflection and a critique of agriculture and rural life today.

The literature provided an intricate tapestry of cultural commentary on agriculture that served as a backdrop for a series of interactions between students and members of the Northfield agricultural community, including farmers, researchers, and other members of rural communities. Field trips were supplemented by in-class panels of invited guests addressing everything from memories of the Depression in Rice County to the role of new immigrant farmers in Minnesota and "Pressures on Local Farmers."

The success of these two collaborative ventures for students in these classes was not easy to assess. The students in the dyad provided a humorous account of what they had encountered in the linked courses on the commemorative T-shirt they made up for the course. The back of the shirt proclaimed the following:

THE DYAD
WE ...
... Spent 110 Hours in Class and Lab
... "Read" 2812 Pages
... Went on 11 Field Trips
... Got Back Late From 9 Field Trips
... Went to 10 Evening Presentations
... Wrote 34 Journal Entries
... "Read" 25 Articles Off Closed Reserve
... Rode 524 Miles on a School Bus
... Smelled 1 Pond o' Poop
... And Made 14 New Farmer Friends
ALL IN FALL TERM FRESHMAN YEAR

This wry attempt to quantify what the students did in the dyad displays several simultaneous emotions: pride in what they accomplished, a touch of pique at how much work they were asked to do, impish candor in admitting that they hadn't read everything assigned, and a sense of gratitude at being allowed a chance to get to know many farmers personally as well as professionally. There is also a sense of marveling disbelief that all this happened in just a ten-week term, which, for a fall-term freshman, is as much as to say, "Toto, I don't think we're in high school any more."

The students in ENTS 110 did not create a T-shirt for their class, but the sentiments expressed might have been similar. The sense that the students had been through something extraordinary and that the rewards and the demands of that experience were part of a package deal are unmistakable. Interdisciplinary courses that consist of multiple parts on- and off-campus can be daunting in terms of workload and logistics. But when readings and field observations manage to end up being mutually reinforcing, the results can be illuminating in a way that, in my experience, single-discipline courses rarely are. A few select examples of placing literature in the context of what I have dubbed "plein air pedagogy" may help suggest what I mean.

WAYS OF SEEING

As someone who has spent his professional life immersed in literary history and the workings of style, metaphor, and narrative, I tend to look to the sciences for new metaphors and models of complexity that might apply to our understanding of literature and language more generally. The interconnected nature of ecological thinking, for instance, provides a far richer, more dynamic, and responsive way of thinking about the self and community, to my mind, than do entrenched theoretical notions of "constructed" identity. I approached both the dyad and ENTS 110 not only with an eye toward what I could learn in a factual way about a particular aspect of landscape or agriculture, but also with an interest in how the imagery (say, of root systems, polycultures, watersheds, photosynthesis, or disease vectors) and analytical models of biology and geology might inspire some new thinking about literature and about place. Thus while I was front stage in the course, leading discussions on particular authors and themes, I was also, in some sense, always backstage as well, learning not only what but *how* ideas were framed in the sciences and attempting by indirection to find directions out.

In particular, I came to respect the ease with which Gary and Mary approached subjects—like the genetics of corn or hydrology—with an understanding that multiple variables and causes would most likely be at play. Both of them were open to the surprise of new findings and a flexibility of mind capable of understanding complex phenomena in rich depths of detail. When

Gary looked out over a landscape, for instance, his ability to point out features of the landscape (life zones, patterns of tree growth, subtle changes in the topography) that I was directly looking at but hadn't quite taken in reminded me of the ability of the best art historians, who can ask one to study a painting for some time before then proceeding to point out any number of details unapparent to the untutored eye, thus bringing the picture alive in new and unexpected ways.

The dyad and ENTS 110 featured the same kind of direct and indirect learning. The direct learning took place on field trips that taught the students specific topics more vividly than they could have learned them from a book or photograph alone. In ENTS 110, for instance, we took an afternoon field trip investigating what the syllabus called "Three Views of Corn." A subtitle might have been "Thinking About Place in Terms of Scale, Seeds, and Pest Control."

> When Gary looked out over a landscape, for instance, his ability to point out features of the landscape (life zones, patterns of tree growth, subtle changes in the topography) that I was directly looking at but hadn't quite taken in reminded me of the ability of the best art historians ...

We went to Stanton to hear a slick presentation at an agricultural experiment station, owned by the multinational biotech company Novartis, about the advantages—and unsurprisingly little about the pitfalls—of new "genetic pesticides" in the genetic modification of corn seeds. (Novartis' new "BT" corn, designed primarily for the giant farms of corporate agribusiness, was then being released with all the hoopla of a new model car or a new computer operating system.)

Next we visited a medium-sized farm, fairly typical of Rice County, walking through the half-harvested, bestubbled fields of a farmer whose giant air-conditioned combine the students climbed into for a view of the fields beyond the plexiglass windshield. This farmer used the latest GIS technology in his tractor, with signals beamed from satellites orbiting the earth, to determine where fertilizer should be applied in local fields. He used mostly traditional spray-on pesticides and was interested in but still skeptical about the new corn seeds from Novartis.

Finally we ended up at David Hougen-Eitzman's small CSA (community-supported agriculture) organic farm where a shovel was used as often as a tractor, where special heirloom seeds were planted, and where chemical pesticides were avoided in favor of organic forms of insect control (though David admitted that air-borne pesticides from adjoining farms undoubtedly drifted over on occasion to settle on his plants). It was difficult not to see the colorful, less evenly spaced rows of multi-crop vegetables as a refreshing change from the endless, manicured monocultures of corn and soybeans on other farms. But the students also learned that organic produce is expensive and that David, who teaches part-time in the Biology Department at Carleton, could not make a living on the farm alone.

So, three views of corn actually entailed three views of the biology, technology, economics, and even aesthetics of multiple farms. And all these elements were tied to the implications of scale for farming as a business, as a biotech enterprise, and as "a way of life."

The dyad featured similar field trips where direct learning came in exercises about erosion control. The students counted the number of plowed-up corn stalks and other organic debris lying in a given field after a harvest and then compared notes about the subtle differences of granularity, soil chemistry, topography, and wet and dry areas within the same field. They learned to be geological connoisseurs, if you will, about what at first looked like nothing more than empty, plowed fields. Likewise, the students went to a farm implements store and learned the differences between a sub-soiler (a tillage machine), a combine, and a grain wagon.

At a practical level, the course showed the students the basics of farming, something about which most of them were ignorant. We asked them to think about the history of agriculture in this region, from pre-contact to the present. Brad Carlson, the Rice County Agricultural Extension Agent, spoke several times to the students about how farms are regulated by local, state, and national agencies (another example of multiple, overlapping scales in thinking about place). In addition, the students got a first-hand view of small-town Midwestern life by attending Dozinsky Days, a Czech heritage festival, in the town of New Prague, complete with fried cheese curds and antique farm tractors in the parade. The students gained an appreciation of and connection to the Northfield agricultural community, and they actively articulated, dismantled, and then reevaluated their own preconceptions about farming and farmers in their class discussion, their journal entries, and their essays for the course.

While the direct learning in the course was apparent to the students in the dyad, as the page counts on their T-shirts attest, I think they and the students in ENTS 110 would readily admit that much of what they learned in these educational ventures—perhaps the most valuable part of their learning—was between the lines: indirect and more difficult to quantify. They frequently absorbed more than they fully understood. Small details for the dyad students often had a large impact, helping to humanize farmers and allowing students to see them as something more than simply virtuous ideals or uncouth bumpkins.

> "It is one thing to read in a novel or a textbook what it is like to be a farmer," one student in the dyad wrote in his journal. "It is totally different to hear actual farmers tell of their experiences. ... One thing that really struck me was how smart all of these farmers were. I used to think that farming was a simple occupation ..."[4]

Other students were struck by the fact that one couple running a local dairy farm had been able to leave their farm for a weekend only once or twice in the last 20 years. The reality of farming often came alive in off-the-cuff or parenthetical revelations such as these.

Indirect forms of learning also took place in other ways. On one excursion in a prairie meadow in ENTS 110, Gary asked the students to adjust their perspectives by wriggling along on their stomachs, at ground level, in an attempt to approximate a "mouse-eye" view of the world. From a six-foot-tall human perspective—mine—looking down on this experiment, the result was a writhing, squirming army of students fanning out in a grassy meadow, like soldiers training in boot camp (another sight I had not seen on Second Floor Laird). But who is to say how that ground-level view of the grasslands affected their later reading of, for instance, *A Sand County Almanac*? Certain descriptions of grass or small mammals or the nutrient cycle of the prairie in that book later came alive, many reported in their weekly Response Sheets, in a way at least partly attributable to their own brief crawl through a grassy landscape. A student is unlikely to say, on a course evaluation, "I gained a new appreciation for the perspective of a mouse." But that doesn't negate the subtle value of the exercise.

RE-INVENTING THE AMERICAN SCHOLAR

"Life is our dictionary," Ralph Waldo Emerson proclaimed in his 1837 address to Harvard students (later an essay) entitled "The American Scholar."

Years are well spent in country labors; in town—in the insight into trades and manufactures; in frank intercourse with many men and women; in science; in art; to the one end of mastering in all their facts a language, by which to illustrate and embody our perceptions. I learn immediately from any speaker how much he has already lived, through the poverty or the splendor of his speech. Life lies behind us as the quarry from whence we get tiles and copestones for the masonry of to-day. This is the way to learn grammar. Colleges and books only copy the language which the field and the work-yard made. (p. 61-62)

The students in the dyad and in ENTS 110 were, in Emerson's sense, "learning grammar." They were embodying their intelligence; they were adding atmospheric texture and metabolism to their thinking. Their research and reading were taking on a tactile tangibility. Whether in "frank intercourse" with a local farmer or after hiking across the spongy expanse of an alkaline fen near Chanhassen, the students were learning to reanimate what Emerson, in another essay, called "the fossil poetry" of language by connecting it to the physical world.[5] This process happened constantly and almost by osmosis. It was a gradual, perhaps unconscious, absorption of knowledge "which the field and the work-yard made," rather than deliberate learning.

"The American Scholar" offers a distinguished pedigree for interdisciplinary educational initiatives such as the dyad and ENTS 110. Emerson was looking for a distinctive new American intellectual, one capable of turning away from the "courtly muses of Europe" (p. 70) and embracing the bustling, expanding panorama of 19th-century America and "the millions, that around us are rushing into life" (p. 53). Emerson saw literature or "the Mind of the Past" as one of the three crucial elements in the formation of new American minds. The other two were the study of nature and what he termed "Action," that is, "the dignity and necessity of labor to every citizen" (p. 63).

Both the dyad and ENTS 110 incorporated all three of these areas, week by week, as overlapping and mutually reinforcing fields of reference in studying place. With luck, perhaps these classes have already helped create the kind of broad-minded, unintimidated thinkers Emerson was hoping to inspire.

Interdisciplinary ventures of the kind I have been discussing are not easily or quickly created. They require a great deal of preparation and an enormous time commitment when they are up and running. They require time to reflect on what one has been through once the dust of the course has settled. (They may require special administrative support to ensure that teaching credit for labs is given to those unused to having labs attached to their courses.)

They also require faculty to move outside their comfort zone and relinquish authority on a subject in order to learn about it. Flannery O'Connor once wryly noted that her main social function, as an older woman, at her mother's parties was to cover the stain on the couch. There were times, as I told the dyad students with a wink, when my primary role in field sessions would be to hold up a corner of a topographical map so others could see.

> Interdisciplinary ventures of the kind I have been discussing are not easily or quickly created. They require a great deal of preparation and an enormous time commitment when they are up and running. They require time to reflect on what one has been through once the dust of the course has settled...

The learning, particularly indirect learning, in such courses is more fluid and less structured than in more traditional classes, which may be a challenge for students uneasy in the face of variables. Likewise, the fact that faculty learn in these courses shoulder to shoulder with the students may be a challenge for some faculty used to having authoritative expertise on a subject. Some faculty and students are temperamentally suited for these more open-ended, serendipitous, less conclusive classes, and others are not.

For myself, the rewards of these special opportunities for humanists and scientists to collaborate far outweigh the challenges of creating them. These collaborations offer not only the occasion for friendship, faculty development, and collegial exchange, they also offer the rare chance to craft a synthesis of scientific, historical, and aesthetic understandings of nature and place. Faculty need those opportunities as much as students do, perhaps for high-minded reasons but also simply because we are *curious*. John Steinbeck (1951/1996), in describing his remarkable relationship with the legendary marine biologist Ed Ricketts, said the two men

> ... had a game which we playfully called speculative metaphysics. It was a sport consisting of lopping off a piece of observed reality and letting it move up through the speculative process like a tree grow-

ing tall and bushy. We observed with pleasure how the branches of thought grew away from the trunk of external reality. ... Always our thinking was prefaced with, "It might be so!" Often a whole night would draw down to a moment while we pursued the fireflies of our thinking. (pp. 730, 732)

In their "endless discussion and reading and observation and experiment" the two men worked together so closely, Steinbeck said, "that I do not now know in some cases who started which line of speculation since the end thought was the product of both minds. I do not know whose thought it was."

Sometimes the result of this kind of intricate collaboration, with its endless discussion and experiment and speculation, is a course, like ENTS 110 or the dyad, "the product of both minds." Let's hope there is always room for faculty and students to pursue the fireflies of their own thinking and to wonder if "it might be so!" Our chances for good work together may depend on nothing less.

ENDNOTES

[1] Paraphrase of a conversation with Steve Simmons in the fall of 1996, used with his permission.

[2] Quoted with Ed Buchwald's permission.

[3] "The Tables Turned," whose subtitle is "An Evening Scene on the Same Subject," is complemented by a companion poem entitled "Expostulation and Reply" that also includes an exchange about the competing value of books and nature.

[4] The student was Sean Bryan. The excerpt from his journal is included (p. 4) in the final report on the dyad: Kowalewski, M., & Savina, M. (2000). *Agriculture and the American Midwest: Literature and the environment, new agriculture-related courses for first-year students at Carleton College.* Submitted December 11 to the Minnesota Agricultural Educational Leadership Council.

[5] The essay is "The Poet" and Emerson uses a scientific analogy to make his point: "The etymologist finds the deadest word to have been once a brilliant picture. Language is fossil poetry. As the limestone of the continent consists of infinite masses of shells of animalcules, so language is made up of images, or tropes, which now, in their secondary use, have long since ceased to remind us of their poetic origin." (Emerson, 1844/1983, p. 457).

REFERENCES

Crimmel, H. (Ed.). (2003). *Teaching in the field: Working with students in the outdoor classroom.* Salt Lake City, UT: University of Utah Press.

Edmundson, M. (1997, September). On the uses of a liberal education: As lite entertainment for bored college students. *Harper's, 295,* 39-49.

Emerson, Ralph Waldo. (1837/1983). The American scholar. In J. Porte (Ed.), *Ralph Waldo Emerson: Essays and lectures* (pp. 53-71). New York: Library of America.

————. (1844/1983). The poet. In J. Porte (Ed.), *Ralph Waldo Emerson: Essays and lectures* (pp. 445-468). New York: Library of America.

Hollander, J. (1984). With regard to an old notebook. *Raritan, 4* (No. 1), 48-63.

Love, G. A. (2003). *Practical ecocriticism: Literature, biology, and the environment.* Charlottesville, VA: University of Virginia Press.

Snow, C.P. (1959). *The two cultures and the scientific revolution.* New York: Cambridge University Press.

Steinbeck, J. (1951/1996). About Ed Ricketts. In R. DeMott (Ed.), *John Steinbeck: The Grapes of Wrath and other writings, 1936-1941* (pp. 697-749). New York: Library of America.

Wordsworth, W. (1798/1977). Expostulation and reply. The tables turned: An evening scene on the same subject. In J. O. Hayden (Ed.), *William Wordsworth: The poems: Vol. 1* (pp. 355-357). New York: Penguin Books.

Fast-Talking Dames Writing Slowly: A Cross-Disciplinary Screenplay

Carol Donelan, Adriana Estill, and Mija Van Der Wege

> "A girl has the right to talk, doesn't she?"
> — Olivia de Havilland to James Cagney
> in *The Strawberry Blonde* (1941)

In the script that follows, we recreate our experience of a cross-disciplinary writing group using a form that allows for the expression of each of our voices, sometimes interrupting, sometimes overlapping. We take our inspiration from the Hollywood screwball comedies of the 1930s and 1940s, a genre in which, according to Maria DiBattista, "you triumph if you think fast and talk even faster" (DiBattista, 2003, p. 16) and where female characters are especially swift on the uptake. Thinking fast and talking even faster with each other—with an emphasis on confession and support rather than conflict and debate—served to facilitate our individual writing processes. Our most tangible triumph was in our productivity as writers, in getting words down on the page, but the intangible outcomes of our screwball collaboration—self-knowledge, friendship, a renewed appreciation for the giddy energy of language in thought, speech, and writing—may have the most lasting effects.

* * * * *

SETTING. Goodbye Blue Monday coffeehouse in Northfield, Minnesota. Coffee steamer and Putumayo CD heard in background. Three characters, all

CAROL DONELAN, assistant professor of cinema and media studies, earned her B.S. degree at Iowa State University, her M.A. degree at the University of Iowa, and her PhD at the University of Massachusetts, Amherst. She joined the Carleton faculty in 1999. ADRIANA ESTILL, assistant professor of English and American studies, joined the Carleton faculty in 2003. She earned her B.A. degree at Stanford University, and her M.A. and PhD degrees at Cornell University. MIJA VAN DER WEGE, assistant professor of psychology, joined the Carleton faculty in 2002. She earned her B.A. degree at Wellesley College and an M.S. degree and PhD at Stanford University.

women, are seated around a table cluttered with coffee cups, half-eaten muffins, crumpled napkins, paper with handwritten notes, and a tape recorder. They are laughing and chatting animatedly about episodes of *Desperate Housewives* and other secret pleasures stockpiled on their TiVo® machines.

AUTHORS' NOTE. In order to enhance the reality of the *mise-en-scene*, the characters are to be played by real academics rather than Hollywood legends such as Rosalind Russell, Barbara Stanwyck, or Katharine Hepburn. None of the performers should have any acting experience, but neither should they consider themselves academic neophytes. Nothing happens, but, as in *Seinfeld*, that's when things get interesting.

———————————

Carol
So what are our goals for this paper?

Adriana
I think we're trying to do two things. We want to describe the ground rules we set for the group last year, because that's what made it work. At the same time we're making an argument about the uniqueness and value of a group like this.

Mija
And the ground rules could be a model for other potential groups. This book is going to go off to other colleges and new faculty, and this is something that they might want to think about doing.

Carol
Ok, so number one, we need to articulate our ground rules and number two, the uniqueness of our model ...

Mija
—especially the value of it to us as faculty at a small liberal arts college.

Adriana
I do think our model has more value at a small college. I mean, we don't necessarily have peers in our own areas of study, so we need to rely on interdisciplinary colleagues.

Mija (smiling)

Or cross-disciplinary ones!

Adriana

Also, so many of our discussions revolve around our lack of time, and yet there are external and internal pressures to stay alive with research.

Mija

It's certainly more tempting and easier to let research slide, especially with the heavy focus on teaching.

Adriana

And maybe one more point to add is the place of women in liberal arts institutions: The stereotype is that we are more valued here than at big research universities. Maybe we tend not to notice the impact of gender as much at a place like this.

Carol

But then again, gender has certainly figured in our conversations. In fact, we've talked a lot about why our two male colleagues, who initially joined the group, didn't stick with it. So let's also reflect on that in the paper.

SCENE FREEZES. One by one, each character steps into a spotlight and addresses the audience.

Adriana
Assistant Professor of English and American Studies

I tend to see the world through eyes of awe, which propels me off on new projects like a speeding bullet. But as soon as the dew is off the rose, my interest dissipates and I can't get motivated to write anything up. I have a computer file thick with conference essays, mish-mashes of article beginnings, middles, and ends, and numerous "brilliant" ideas, none of which has amounted to much beyond a few hundred megabytes on my hard drive.

Last spring I realized I needed help—a super squad of sorts—that could keep me on track. I needed collaborators who could push me past the initial excitement of research and development to the nitty-gritty of writing and who might convince me that my ideas were worth pursuing. I had just taught a novel—Caramelo by Sandra Cisneros—and I wanted to work through some ideas I had about place, female embodiment, and Latino identities.

So after I saw Carol give a riveting talk on melodrama, I approached her and asked if she'd like to be in a writing group. Is it silly to admit that I was a little afraid of rejection? Thankfully, Carol agreed.

Carol
Assistant Professor of Cinema and Media Studies

When Adriana approached me about creating a writing group, I pounced on the idea. She'd been on campus only a short time, but she seemed to be a highly productive writer. Academics have a sixth sense about this sort of thing. My track record, on the other hand, was not so hot. I'm certainly inclined towards thinking, reading, and writing but had lately spent more time wheeling and dealing—or whatever it is one does to grow a program. My identity as a writer, so carefully cultivated during grad school, was slowly fading from existence. I had two terms of leave coming to me, and I didn't want to waste them. My plan was to develop an essay on Hollywood melodrama. Maybe Adriana was the Ariadne I needed to lead me back to writing.

Then I met Mija. As we talked, a vision began to take shape in the cartoon bubble floating over my head. Adriana and I shared a background in the humanities, but Mija could bring the different perspective of the social scientist to our writing group. I invited her to join us.

Mija
Assistant Professor of Psychology
and Cognitive Studies

I was finishing my second year as a tenure-track faculty member, and I knew I had to write more. I'd presented at a few conferences, and a couple of papers already in the pipeline had come out. But I hadn't produced or submitted any of the new papers that had been gathering dust on my virtual stack, including revising my dissertation on linguistic reference into one or two articles to submit to journals. The day-to-day demands of preparing for lectures, meeting with students, and grading always seemed to pre-empt my time for research and writing. When Carol mentioned a writing support group, I jumped at the chance.

At our first meeting, I was a little nervous. I was concerned that my particular inability to write might stem from internal, idiosyncratic qualities rather than from general issues we could discuss. I had recently received a particularly harsh peer review of an article on conversational turn-taking in instant messaging programs. Since then I frequently worried about missing critical research, saying the wrong thing, or even saying the right thing but in the wrong way. I wondered if my fear of rejection was pushing me into prioritizing other academic duties over writing. I wanted to hear about how other junior faculty wrestled down their own internal demons.

FLASHBACK. Goodbye Blue Monday coffeehouse. One year ago. A hot summer day in June. The first official meeting of the group.

Carol (knowingly)
"The first rule of Fight Club is ..."

Mija (getting it instantly)
"... do not talk about Fight Club!"

Adriana (laughing)

Seriously, let's make sure we have some ground rules for the group.

(earnestly)

First things first: I think we should all submit a timeline for the work we want to accomplish this summer.

Mija

Then, at each meeting, we'll report on what we've accomplished—and provide proof!

Adriana (hesitantly)

Ummm ... does that mean we need to read each other's work—all of it?

Carol

No way. I've got enough reading to do this summer. I think we should come with writing we've done but only expect each other to read two pages, max. Better to talk through problematic sections than to burden each other with additional work.

Mija

And if someone doesn't meet her goal, she has to pay $5. That'll keep us from slacking.

Carol

Hmm. That's an incentive. We can use the money to fund a dinner party at the end of the summer.

RETURN to present. Blue Monday Coffeehouse. FREEZE SCENE. Each member of the group once again steps into a spotlight and addresses the audience.

Adriana

I came prepared to that first meeting with a way too ambitious timeline and a lot of enthusiasm, but I had no idea how the group was going to work. But the first meeting resounded with laughter as we shared our goals, set down some rules, and got to know each other. And this camaraderie, more than anything, has come to define the group for me. I thought it would just keep me on the right track. Instead, it became a home away from home, that proverbial safe space where I could bare my fears, find allies in the process of writing, and laugh at the good, the bad, and the ugly along the way.

Mija

After the first meeting, I left with hope and excitement. I envisioned the group helping me in a number of ways. They could give me feedback on the accessibility of my writing to people outside my field. But more importantly, they could give me writing support— encourage me to write about my ideas, brainstorm strategies for getting more writing done during the lazy summer months as well as the frantic academic year, and hold me immediately accountable for not writing when I should.

Carol

I am always happy to talk about writing rather than to actually write, so I couldn't wait to join the group. I was looking forward to getting to know my collaborators. Plus we were meeting late in the day, when I'm in need of a jolt of caffeine. I did have some initial worries about whether belonging to the group might take up time I should be devoting to writing. How like me to participate in a social activity instead of a solitary activity like writing. Fortunately, rather than detracting from my thinking and writing time the group has kicked me into gear. I feel jazzed by our conversations and not just because of the double-shot latte I allow myself at each meeting.

UNFREEZE SCENE, conversation resumes. The characters have just been discussing the topic of buying cars.

Carol

How do you manage personalities who get you off-track in the group context? Such as myself, for example.

(general laughter)

Mija

It can be problematic. But I think the three of us work fairly well together.

Carol

We've settled into a good pattern

Adriana

—which is kind of surprising; it was so random ...

Mija

—and now we've developed a level of trust and a set of shared experiences that really streamlines our work together.

Adriana

Plus it's easier with a smaller group to develop that level of trust, and we seem more productive.

(beat)

Remember at one point last year two others joined us, but they ended up not sticking with it, for whatever reason ...

Mija

Yeah—we scared all the men away!

(general laughter)

Carol

But that's to be expected—this is supposed to be a screwball comedy, after all. Didn't Katharine Hepburn scare away Cary Grant throughout most of Bringing Up Baby?

Mija (thoughtfully)

No really, where did they go?

Adriana

I'm not sure. Maybe this group evolved into something that wasn't helpful to them right then.

Carol

You know what? Our method might not work for everyone. A little therapy combined with progress checks.

Adriana

Maybe the combination of what we do just works better for women than for men. It is a little telling that we ended up being an all-female group.

Mija

That's supported by language research that Deborah Tannen (1990) has done. She talks about how men and women stereotypically have different conversational styles, which can work at cross-purposes. For example, women like to talk about problems with the goal of soliciting empathy, while men talk about problems with the goal of soliciting solutions. When you have one goal and someone gives you the wrong response, you get frustrated.

Carol

Oh, but I'm all about working at cross-purposes. I like to mix things up.

SPOTLIGHT on Carol, who addresses audience.

Carol

Allow me to hijack the proceedings while Adriana and Mija continue to debate the merits of Tannen's research. Perhaps you'd like to take this opportunity to go buy some popcorn? Don't worry—I'll fill you in on the details. Adriana is suspicious of Tannen's research as being too premised in essentializing notions of gendered behavior, while Mija thinks Tannen's argument is more nuanced than that—that Tannen clearly posits gender as a social construct. They seem to be intent on wanting to identify the gender dynamics in our writing group without invoking stereotypes. A worthy endeavor.

RESUME group conversation.

Adriana

OK, grrrrls, I'm ready to get down to business. What are your goals? What do you want to shoot for this summer? Personally, I'm hoping to be a little bit more productive this summer.

Carol

More productive?? You're going to leave us in the dust!

Adriana

Well, it's my last summer before my tenure review year, so I want to make sure that I'm really productive.

Carol

I was just rooting through my desk and came across my tenure timeline. I've decided that I'm going to post it on my wall. I'm going on the offensive, man!

Mija

So you're both starting the review process this year?

Carol and Adriana

Yeah.

Adriana

I hate the way external factors like reviews color our relationship to our writing. We start seeing our motivation to write not in terms of the good stuff, the carrot, but in terms of this big stick. That's one thing that freaks me out about academia, because I know that stick. I want to try to remove myself from thinking about writing as something that's related to the stick.

Mija

I'm the same way. When I was a grad student, I was just so excited to think about research and to do research and to write about research, but now, I'm always worried about the stick. When it comes to writing now, I'm slow, and I get writer's block because of the stick. For me, it's all about fear of the stick—peer review and tenure review. And it's sad to lose the joy of doing research.

Carol

My trauma is lack of confidence. I think that my ideas fly perfectly well with students, but anybody in the field is going to think they are just too simple. When I'm writing, I hear this voice going through my head, "This is a great idea, I can teach this idea!" but then, "I'm sure I've read this in a journal somewhere, and it was stated more eloquently by someone else who knows more than I do."

Adriana

Yes! And my trauma isn't even that I've read it in a journal, but that I'm sure that someone else has already thought of it and explained it much better than I ever could.

Mija

And isn't that just your greatest fear? To send something in to be published and someone says, "Well, you big idiot, where did you get your degree? Didn't you know that there's this whole literature on ..."

Adriana and Carol (laughing)

Exactly!

Carol

Lit reviews have become more complicated now that many of us are approaching our topics from interdisciplinary perspectives. It's not enough to account for one literature. Now we have to account for two or even three, and it's that much harder.

Adriana

And add to that the bunny-like proliferation of journals, both online and paper ... it's a little frightening.

Mija (amused)

Only Buffy: The Vampire Slayer fans will get that joke. So, maybe this summer we should try to focus on the carrot and remind each other to think about our writing in a positive framework: why we like our research, how cool our ideas are, how we're going to share these great ideas with our colleagues by getting them published. I'm going to try not to dwell on writing as a dreaded time of self-flagellation.

SPOTLIGHT on Mija, who addresses the audience while Adriana and Carol discuss designer brands of hair shirts.

Mija

All this talk of carrots and sticks gets me thinking about my own occasionally asinine relationship to writing. I've been dreading writing because I always, perhaps unnecessarily, anticipate the worst. So, four years after receiving my doctorate, I'm still struggling unhappily with draft after draft of my dissertation. But I remember loving to write as an undergrad, and I don't want my relationship with writing to be dysfunctional. I need to focus on the enjoyment of writing.

RESUME group conversation.

Carol

We can also remind each other of how we see each other. I see you both as role models, as very productive and high energy.

Mija (laughter)

But, I'm not!

Adriana (smiling)

You see, the irony is that probably all of us see each other that way.

Mija

I've never really thought of myself as a role model in terms of writing or research ...

Carol

But you are. You're my role model. See, we're role models for each other. And we might not be aware of that.

Mija

We seem to have trouble seeing ourselves in that light. This reminds me of a chapter I read in the book Arming Athena (Collins, et al, 1998). It discusses how women often have a harder time seeing themselves as scholars, since the prototypical scholar is male. When we're growing up, our social skills are more likely to be praised than our intellectual skills, and we're more likely to be given credit just for trying, even when we don't succeed. A lot of women academics struggle with feelings of self-doubt and low self-confidence. And other scholars exacerbate this by not citing women in publications as frequently as men. This probably isn't anything sinister—just the "old boy network" at work—but it just perpetuates the cycle.

(beat)

The other part of the Arming Athena argument, and I'm not sure I agree with this, is that women want to be more social—

Carol

relational!

Mija

Right, so sitting in the office, trapped alone, writing on the computer, is not as satisfying as being in the classroom—

Adriana

Or going to a conference—because you're in a social environment and you get instant feedback on your ideas.

Carol

For me, writing and research entails going into the void, and I don't thrive in it. So, in fact, next week I'm going to a symposium to mix and mingle.

SPOTLIGHT on Adriana, who addresses the audience while Mija and Carol discuss fantasy locations for future conferences.

Adriana

Wow. I've never ever thought about going to a conference without giving a paper. What an eye-opener, especially since I'm hard at work right now on a conference paper about the representation of Chicago in Cisneros's Caramelo. I love the energy and exchange of conferences: To take a page from Putnam (2000), conferences give me the opportunity to bond and create academic social capital. But all that's getting lost under the pressure of making this paper coherent while also trying to keep my head above water in my classes.

RESUME group conversation.

Mija

That all fits well with one point Arming Athena makes over and over again. Women should collaborate because it provides a social dimension to research.

Carol

Isn't that in keeping with social psychology research on identity formation in little girls? They're supposedly more collaborative in their play ... little girls' toys are designed around networking and collaboration more than competition—

Adriana

—I think boys collaborate too, but it's a different kind of collaboration ... team sports, for example.

Carol

I went to this talk on video games by Brenda Laurel (2002), about how she's designing games to sell to girls that focus on collaboration—

Mija

—and a lot of the games pitched to boys are more competitive.

Adriana

Does the book suggest that women should collaborate because of a stereotype about what women need to succeed ... learning communities, research collaborations, etc., or is it simply a practical kind of suggestion?

Mija

There is the notion of identity ... if women don't have the identity of being a scholar, talking to other women who are also scholars might help them develop that identity—

Adriana

—oh, right, they talk about "impostor syndrome." You know, lots of other marginal groups—not just women—might feel like impostors because they don't fit the definition of a traditional scholar. I know sometimes I think my impostor-y moments have to do just as much with being Latina as with being a woman.

Mija

Yeah, you feel like you're an impostor because you don't have good role models. The prototype or mental image of a scholar isn't female or minority, and you've never done the social learning that helps establish your identity.

Carol

Right, and belonging to this group helps with that.

Mija

Yeah. By collaborating with each other, we develop our self-image as scholars, which in turn builds our respect for women and minorities as scholars, which then changes our prototypical image of a scholar.

Adriana

Exactly. I know that seeing other Latina scholars at conferences always inspires me.

Carol

I need models. It's just how I operate, what I think I need. Have you had good role models in your undergraduate and graduate careers? As scholars, not just as teachers ...

Mija

I went to Wellesley!

Carol

I worked at Mount Holyoke. There are advantages to women's colleges ...

Mija

—but I didn't have good female mentors in graduate school. There were female role models, but they always seemed somehow different or special.

Adriana

Yeah, in undergraduate not at all ... there were strong models of women teaching, but not doing visible scholarship ... and then in graduate school, well, my dissertation chair is a woman, but I have to say that she didn't get close to any of her students, for reasons that are probably smart. She was protecting herself. What that meant is ... I didn't even see her doing her own work. There was a way in which it was very opaque and veiled. I don't think I learned how to be a scholar in graduate school.

Mija and Carol

I didn't either.

Mija

I learned how to be a good experimentalist, to come up with ideas, but a lot of the process was veiled. That was how my advisor worked. He would do his thinking and writing at home and then come to work around 12 or 1 and take care of teaching and advising. It was all very separate.

Adriana

I think I told you guys that I used my own timeline for my essay on the library in Buffy the Vampire Slayer (Estill, 2007) as a guideline for my senior research students. I wanted to model more transparently for them how to be a scholar. I actually talked to them about the essays I'm working on, and I had never done that at University of New Mexico because there was this expectation that you go into the classroom and do your teaching, and then you do your "real work" whenever you get out of the classroom.

SPOTLIGHT on Adriana, who addresses the audience while Mija tries to turn Carol on to watching Buffy.

Adriana

Let's face it, there are limits to how transparent I'm willing to be in the classroom. As a woman, I'm constantly aware that some revelations detract from while others add to my authority and to students' willingness to learn through and with me. Revelation is such a risk. ... But then I think of bell hooks (1989), who reminds us that the personal is political and that the private and the public are inseparable. Maybe if I reveal myself to the students, they'll see more clearly how messy the research and writing process can be and how we're all in the knowledge game together.

RESUME group conversation.

Adriana

And then they asked me about how my essay was going all term. It was a great way to help them see research and writing as a process, not simply a product. Plus I felt buoyed by their interest.

Carol

When I taught the melodrama course, I said to students, 'OK, look, I'm working on this project. Here is the question I'm stuck on. What do you think about this?' and so on.

SPOTLIGHT on Carol, who addresses audience. Mija and Adriana go get refills on their decaf coffees.

Carol

Sure, I've assumed the role of all-seeing, all-knowing oracle in relation to my students. I know how to erase the signs of having labored over difficult material in order to be able to pull a rabbit out of the hat when I'm in the classroom. Ta da! How gratifying for me—a little bit of magic, seamlessly performed. But I think masking our labor as thinkers and researchers really contributes little towards helping our students become better thinkers and researchers.

RESUME group conversation.

Carol
Anyway, students actually seemed to enjoy hearing about my research. They'd ask, "What are you writing about? When will we get to read it?" I was really motivated to produce something for them to read.

Mija
That's interesting. Do you find that bringing your work into the classroom makes research and writing easier?

Adriana
It's funny, but it's easier for me to be vulnerable in the classroom—to be excited about the process of developing the idea rather than worried about the seamlessness of my exposition of it. That's why I like talking out ideas, whether at conferences or with you guys. I can focus on figuring it out right here and now and making it understandable.

Carol
Yes, it is sometimes easier to think things through when you've got an interlocutor. I do better when I'm running at the mouth than when I'm writing.

(general laughter)

Mija
Me too. Especially when I'm talking to someone who's not in my field. Then I'm forced to think more specifically about what words I'm using and how I'm framing the argument.

(beat)
I had a student who had real trouble writing, but she could say things clearly and concisely, so I told her to start carrying a tape recorder with her everywhere she went and just talk to people about her project. She did it, and her project was more readable for it.

Carol
I find I have to slow things down so much when I'm writing that suddenly the idea just loses its energy, its rhythm, its pace.

Adriana
Yeah. Writing stuff down the first time seems onerous and heavy. And then you have to go back to add your voice in, shape it into what you really want it to say.

Mija

Exactly. Even when you have writer's block, it's important to bang out something. You have to be persistent, even in the face of producing crap.

Adriana

Only recently have I really understood how important free writing and multiple drafts are. Now I'm like a new convert, preaching to all of my students, "Free write your ideas! Low-stakes writing! Lots of drafts!"

(beat)

I was talking to one of my composition students about how many rough drafts I go through—she was so surprised! Students think that all professors are born knowing how to write.

SPOTLIGHT on Carol, who addresses the audience while Adriana and Mija crack jokes about students' misconceptions about faculty members.

Carol

I'd like to invoke the advice of experienced writer Anne Lamott here, because it dovetails with what Mija and Adriana are saying. Lamott is the author of Bird by Bird: Some Instructions for Writing and Life (1994). The two single most helpful strategies she uses in her writing process are 1) short assignments and 2) crappy first drafts. She suggests that all we need to do when we sit down to write is to simply write as much as we can see through a one-inch picture frame. That's all! No need to get freaked out about producing an entire essay or book. Start by writing one tiny, tiny paragraph. Her second bit of advice, crappy first drafts, is fairly self-explanatory. Write them. Have the courage to spill it, uncensored.

RESUME group conversation.

Mija

I've actually learned a lot about my own writing from critiquing my students' writing ...

Carol and Adriana

Yeah!

Mija

Although when I sent a draft of a paper to my former advisor, he told me the same things that I tell my students!

(beat)

I didn't actually spend a lot of time on writing in my graduate career, which I regret now. I think one of the reasons I'm such a slow writer is because I didn't spend a lot of time learning how to write when I was a student. And I'm having these growing pains now.

Adriana

You know, a really great book about writing that might even tie into some of the research that you do is Trimble's <u>Writing with Style</u> (1975). It talks a lot about writing for your audience.

Mija

That's great! A lot of my research is about how people try to take other perspectives when speaking. I've been doing some thinking recently about how those processes might translate to writing.

Adriana

Oh, and that's exactly what Trimble gets at! He has this whole section on the difference between the novice and the experienced writer, which basically argues that experienced writers can anticipate the readers' responses; they can put themselves in their audience's shoes. Novice writers can't.

(beat)

Personally, I'm always trying to figure out how to make my writing worthy of academic journals and still have it be readable.

Carol

For my part, I think I have a tendency to want to refuse academic pretension in my use of language, and that has served me well in the classroom. I've been able to engage students with a rhetoric that really allows them to connect and get the ideas. But I don't know if it's working for me in my writing. I've become so intent on refusing a certain voice that I can't adopt it when I need it, to my own detriment.

(beat)

Ok, this is getting into therapy realm, now, and I don't know if we want to go there ...

Mija and Adriana

No, no, that's what we're here for ...

Carol

I'm realizing that I have a certain amount of anxiety about my standing as an academic and a researcher, and my reaction formation to that anxiety about other people seeing my work and seeing my writing and finding it not adequate or what have you is to refuse the pretensions of the whole process, especially the voice. There must be a diagnosis for this.

Mija

Maybe you're anticipating problems. I do the same thing. Maybe you just need to take the leap and send your work out.

Adriana

Continuing the therapy session ... I can relate to your fears, Carol. When I finished my dissertation, my advisors told me it would make a fine book. I spent one summer working through it, but then I decided it was a time sink. I decided it wasn't worth it because it wasn't valuable enough to publish.

Mija

That's exactly what I do. It's that evil inner voice, telling us, "This isn't worth it." "That's a stupid idea." "You're such an impostor."

Adriana

The funny thing is, recently, I picked up a draft that I wrote five years ago. It's not half bad. It's a great candidate for an LPU.

Carol

What's an LPU?

Mija

It's the Least Publishable Unit, the smallest thing that you can get into print.

Carol

I've never heard of that before. I've got a whole file cabinet full of LPU's!

Adriana

So why haven't you ever done anything with them?

Carol

It's like you with your diss, Adriana. I don't think they're worthwhile. Yet it's so weird, because in the classroom I don't think that. I'm confident about my ideas. Of course I'm talking rather than writing.

SPOTLIGHT on Adriana, who addresses the audience while Carol and Mija continue to talk rather than write.

Adriana

That reminds me of an article in that book, <u>Arming Athena</u>, that Mija mentioned earlier. In it, Joan Chrisler cites a study from the '60s that divides faculty into two categories: those who focus on teaching and those who concentrate on scholarship.

(beat)

That study found that women tended to be teachers and men, scholars. There may be something to this divide since Mija, Carol, and I have all agreed we feel more comfortable at the head of the classroom. But of course we hate that! We want—and we fight—to think of ourselves as confident writers and scholars and ... innovators.

Adriana

I know what you mean. In the classroom I'm willing to take risks. It's why I like teaching intro-level courses—you get to learn at the same time that you're teaching!

Mija

Or seminars, because you can explore new ideas and research areas through discussion. At least, that's how I feel about my seminar on language and deception. Incidentally, Adriana, I walked by your office twice a week last spring, but you always seemed to have students around so I never dropped in.

Adriana

I have regular office hours, but I tend to leave my door open always which—

Mija

—invites ...

Adriana

Exactly. I want to be that kind of teacher.

Carol

I've done that too. Of course, I didn't get a thing done in terms of my own research and writing. I think we need to be judicious about how we use our time. Personally, I don't think it's healthy to send a message to students that they can have access to us any time they want. What kind of role modeling is that? I think we should set appropriate boundaries, close the door once in a while, and post the "writing in progress" sign. Or a "gone fishin'" sign. Or whatever. It's about trying to model a balanced life.

Adriana

I don't want to give up on the idea of being an accessible teacher, though. I really enjoy getting to know the students and, in general, it translates into a more productive and generous classroom atmosphere ... don't you think?

Carol

Of course.

Mija

Oh yeah, especially at a place like Carleton. It's necessary, really!

(beat)

You know, this group has really sparked my research, which has, in turn, let me give a lot of students great research opportunities—either through comps or by having them work on my projects. Last term I actually got two experiments run, mostly because I had this small suite of student research assistants helping me out.

Carol

A suite of assistants? Is that the collective noun for research assistants?

Adriana

Part of me thinks that sounds like a lot of work, but the other part thinks, "Oh, you're just so popular!"

Mija

It is exhausting, but in a good way. I get to know the students better, which then helps me out in the classroom.

SPOTLIGHT on Mija, who addresses the audience while Carol and Adriana debate what the collective noun for research assistants is.

Mija

Talking with Adriana and Carol made me realize that the humanities differ from the sciences and social sciences in this. They tell me that humanities research is generally more solitary. In the sciences and social sciences, collaboration is helpful and often necessary. Like in my research, my suite of research assistants collects and codes data, creates materials for the studies, and even designs studies or conducts statistical analyses ... you know, all the tedious work I don't want to do! But this collaborative approach is beneficial for them too: They learn about how science is done by actually doing it.

RESUME group conversation.

Mija

Before I came here, I'd never really thought about how teaching and research could dovetail so well. It's a challenge to do sometimes, but when it works, it's just great! And ironically, this integration turns out to be the student-centered learning that everyone is talking about.

Adriana

It's just that student-centered learning wears me out! I'm serious ... as a woman I need to be more aware of how to convey and use my authority and as a teacher I need to be ultra-prepared for all the directions that the discussion or project might go in.

Mija

I know. And then add in administrative duties and new course preps. I'm still amazed at how many new preps you both have developed in your time here!

Carol

All in the service of growing a program. It's a different kind of productivity than research and writing, but I enjoy it.

Adriana

Yeah, I like the excitement of developing new courses. It's a lot of work, but it's also enthralling. You get to figure out how to best shape students' introduction to a particular body of knowledge. How can there be anything more fun?

Carol

Notice how we're back to talking about teaching and students, once again? We're supposed to be talking about writing.

Mija

Well, it's because Adriana and I don't have time to write!

Adriana

Yep. Since last time we met, a month ago, I've added three pages to my conference paper. It's a vast, amorphous mess ... and I'm giving the talk—tomorrow.

Mija

Who has time to write during the school year? Carol, you're on sabbatical!

Carol

Yes, and I'm reveling in the process of research and of having the time to think and write ... honestly, though, I don't know how anybody gets any serious writing done during the term. I know some people do it and do it very well, but I think it's really hard.

Adriana

There was this article in the Chronicle of Higher Education about leisure, about how in the humanities in particular we need leisure to develop—

Mija

—that's true in the sciences and social sciences too; we might be able to run for longer on a project, but we still need time to frame the ideas.

Adriana

I love teaching, but it's hard to make time during the term's intensity for that necessary mental leisure.

Carol

Didn't President Oden (Robert Oden, the president of Carleton College) mention something about that in one of his talks to the faculty?

Mija

He mentioned the "time famine." The observation was, I think, that even though we work less and have more devices to help us work, we still have less time for leisure—both personal and professional.

SPOTLIGHT on Mija, who addresses the audience while Adriana and Carol waste time by exchanging some juicy campus gossip.

Mija

You know, this time management issue is complicated by the different definitions of productivity. Tenure and promotion criteria can be amorphous, and we all seem to have different ideas about what's expected of us and what we want to accomplish. By comparing notes, we give each other a reality check. It keeps us from setting unrealistic goals.

RESUME group conversation.

Mija

And Carleton has always strongly emphasized teaching, but now it slowly seems to be inching towards research productivity and student research experiences. Sometimes I feel like our generation of faculty is expected to be able to do it all. We're caught a bit between the folks who still want everyone to excel in teaching and service and the folks who want everyone to excel in research.

Carol

The paradigm is shifting. It seems that it was once acceptable to be a strong teacher without a very substantial research record, but in this generation there are probably somewhat different expectations.

Adriana

You can demand excellence in one area, but once you start demanding excellence in two or three areas, you're looking at people burning out—

Mija

—or at the very least, feeling guilty about the sacrifices that they have to make to stay sane!

Adriana

It's a balancing act, figuring out how to make time for research while still being fully involved in the classroom.

Carol

I don't think we're unique in having to juggle responsibilities, but belonging to this group helps me claim the time for research and writing—time that usually gets eaten up by the more pressing, day-to-day demands of teaching and committee work.

Mija

This group has been a kind of controlled experiment. We thought we were doing one thing—

Adriana

—and we set all of these goals—

Carol

—and we actually accomplished a few things, got some writing done, but there were some unexpected outcomes—

Adriana

—like strong peer role models, unexpected teaching benefits, increased self-confidence, a renewed pleasure in writing

Mija

—and we've begun to consider how others see us, which strengthens our image of ourselves as scholars. And this group somehow makes both the internal and external pressures seem more manageable.

SCENE FREEZES. Spotlight on each character in turn as she addresses the audience

Adriana

Towards the end of Caramelo, Lala admits that talk, not truth, is all she has going for her. And so she plays Scheherazade and bestows upon us a long, winding narrative, with uncountable, interlocking stories that eventually loop back to the beginning. But it really all comes down to this: Lala and her transnational family live uncomfortably in-between Chicago and Mexico City, Americanness and Mexicanness. And yet Lala discovers that, through talking and writing her family's stories, she can mediate between opposites and find tentative balances, moments of grace in a conflicted world.

As an untenured Latina scholar, I am also familiar with living uncomfortably in-between. But sometimes at Goodbye Blue Monday, as we talk about our writing and, well, lots of other things, I find myself in a place where talking and writing, research and teaching, and the carrot and the stick hover in a momentary equilibrium. In that space, success and failure as defined by the outside world don't mean much, because I've found a brief but breathtaking balance within. That said, it sure doesn't hurt to occasionally get outside strokes—my paper on the representation of Chicago in Caramelo will be in print soon and, strangely enough, I survived two rounds of suggestions and criticisms and still felt good about my essay!

Mija

After studying discourse for many years, I had forgotten the real value of conversation—the intentional and unintentional interpersonal connections and social sharing of information. Our weekly gabfest not only reminded me about the existence of my ephemeral audience, but also gave me a chance to talk through my ideas, allowing them to coalesce and find structure. What's more, talking let me share in the others' writing processes, as well as in their similar struggles and obstacles. Conversation matters.

As a psycholinguist (yes, that can be parsed a couple of ways), I've found our conversations intriguing. One of our ongoing battles has been learning the perspectives of our scholarly audience. At the same time, ironically, one of our greatest triumphs has been learning the perspectives that we have of each other—as role models and successful academics.

According to theories of language, both of these perspectives should be equally easy or hard to learn, because both involve how others perceive us and what we say. But none of these theories can really account for the complexity and richness of our interactions—the seamless role-swapping between mentor and mentored. Being a good audience for each other—for our writing and conversations—has entailed not just listening to and reading words, but developing community—a sense of mutual trust, an alliance forged from parallel experience, and an investment in each other's victories.

Current models of discourse can explain how shared knowledge affects the way we speak, but not how our social and emotional bonds change our conversations. For me, these bonds, developed through our skirmishes against our evil inner voices, have enabled me to enjoy writing again and to finish and send off a couple of manuscripts.

Carol

You know the film His Girl Friday (1940)? The one with Cary Grant and Rosalind Russell playing journalists? It's a classic screwball comedy, one of the fastest-talking films ever made. Some poor sucker of a film scholar somewhere has actually taken the time to count the words and clock the torrent of language unleashed in that film. Anyway, one of the things I love about this frenetic, noisy film is how much you begin to notice those moments when characters slow down, lower their voices, or even fall silent. Watch and listen—you'll see what I mean. The talking is among the pleasures of the film, but so is the not-talking. What a perfect metaphor for this writing group and the writing process. We've had a lot of fun talking, and we've tried to capture some of it here. But keep in mind that part of our experience has also been in the not-talking, in what's going on in the white spaces around the talking, in those moments when we've fallen silent, are lost in thought, and maybe even writing.

As it turns out, the writing of this "screenplay," even more than the talking upon which it is based, has had the biggest impact on me. Writing these words has somehow also loosened my tongue in my scholarly writing. I've rediscovered the pleasure of writing—the carrot rather than the stick, as Adriana and Mija put it. I'm now looking forward to mixing and mingling at an upcoming conference, and this time I'll be delivering my paper on Hollywood melodrama, the one I set out to write in the first place. Look for me there—you'll recognize me as the fast-writing dame.

SCENE UNFREEZES, conversation resumes. The characters have just been engaged in a conversation about Nico's (Adriana's son) first day of kindergarten.

Adriana (mock seriousness)

I just want to point out that the tape recorder has been running this entire time.

Mija (laughing)

Uh oh! Should we really be recording all this? We'll have to take magnets and run them over the tape after we listen to it!

Carol

Why do you think I keep on constructing these elaborate sentences? ... You can actually hear the commas!

Mija

Oh yes, we should keep all our wonderful Faulknerian sentences!

Adriana

And we can always edit out all the inflammatory stuff, and then destroy the tapes.

Mija

Will there be anything left?

Carol

In a roundabout way, we did get to the topic of writing.

Adriana

We always end up getting to writing.

THE END

REFERENCES

Collins, K. H., Chrisler, J. C., & Quina, K. (Eds.) (1998). *Career strategies for women in academe: Arming Athena*. Thousand Oaks, CA: Sage Publications, Inc.

Chrisler, J. C. (1998). Teacher versus scholar: Role conflict for women? In K.H. Collins, et al. (Eds.) *Career strategies for woman in academe: Arming Athena*. (107-27). Thousand Oaks, CA: Sage Publications, Inc.

Cisneros, S. (2002). *Caramelo*. New York: Vintage Contemporaries.

DiBattista, M. (2003). *Fast-talking dames*. New Haven: Yale University Press.

Estill, A. (2007). Going to hell: The library in *Buffy: The Vampire Slayer*. In J. Buschman & G.J. Leckie (Eds.), *The library as place: History, community, and culture* (pp. 235-250). Westport, CT: Libraries Unlimited.

"feeling stupid." (2005, August 9). Thread on Chronicle Careers. http://chronicle.com.

Hawks, H. (Producer/Director), & Hecht, B., & MacArthur, C. (Writers). (1940). *His girl Friday* [Motion picture]. United States: Columbia Pictures.

Hawks, H. (Producer/Director) & Wilde, H. (Writer). (1938). *Bringing up Baby* [Motion picture]. United States: RKO Radio Pictures.

hooks, b. (1989). *Talking back: Thinking feminist, thinking black*. Boston, MA: South End Press.

Lamott, A. (1994). *Bird by bird: Some instructions on writing and life*. New York: Anchor Books.

Laurel, B. (2002). Talk on gender and videogames. Carleton College. January.

Putnam, R. (2000). *Bowling alone: The collapse and revival of American community*. New York: Simon and Schuster.

Tannen, D. (1990). *You just don't understand: Women and men in conversation*. New York: Quill.

Trimble, J. R. (1975). *Writing with style: Conversations on the art of writing*. Upper Saddle River, NJ: Prentice Hall.

Walsh, R. (Director) & Wallis, H. B. (Producer). (1941). *The strawberry blonde* [Motion picture]. United States: Warner Brothers.

I got a lot out of the program, but I think what I got out most was to see what it's like being in a mathematical community and realizing how much I enjoyed it. It was really great meeting all these people who are totally different from me, but we all still share this common bond of loving math.

Photos by Tom Roster

Serendipity and Inadvertence in the Building of Community

Deanna Haunsperger and Steve Kennedy

We're not sure when it happened. It probably wasn't between the minestrone and the Caesar salad, though it may have been. In fact it must have been there all along, growing stronger, but we didn't notice until it hit us with full force at dinner one night in January 2005 at the Joint Mathematics Meetings in Atlanta, Georgia.

We had planned a reunion of the former participants from the first nine years of the Carleton College Summer Mathematics Program (SMP). Participants in our selective program are young women finishing their first or second years at a U.S. college or university who are interested in, and have shown talent in, mathematics. Our program was designed as an intense mathematical experience to give them the impetus they need, along with the support and encouragement, to go on to advanced degrees in mathematics. It's a four-week summer program, and we encourage the participants to keep in touch with each other via e-mail after they leave. We had had small reunions at the Joint Meetings before—four or five of us gathered after the day's talks for conversation over drinks. That January, though, there were going to be 25 former participants and nine former instructors and teaching assistants at the meeting, so we planned a nice dinner out, not as nine individual SMP class reunions from the nine summer programs we'd run, but as one big group.

When we arrived, most of the SMPers were already there, and the natural thing was happening. They were talking to each other. Women at different points in their careers, from different parts of the country, from colleges and

DEANNA HAUNSPERGER, associate professor of mathematics, joined the Carleton faculty in 1994. She earned her B.A. degree at Simpson College and her M.A. and PhD degrees at Northwestern University. STEVE KENNEDY, professor of mathematics, earned his B.A. degree at Boston University and his M.A. and PhD degrees at Northwestern University. He joined the Carleton faculty in 1994.

from universities, some undergraduates, some graduate students, some professors. What they had in common was a love of mathematics and a summer spent in a rural Midwestern town, but that was enough. We didn't need to do any introductions; in fact, we couldn't have because no one could talk over the roar of conversation. The hubbub washed over us—we heard them talking about choosing graduate schools, choosing advisors, doing research, figuring out how to fit a family into a career, and whether to choose a sauvignon blanc or a nice pinot grigio with the grilled shrimp.

Over the years we've heard from SMP graduates who have attended a conference or visited a graduate school and bumped into an SMP graduate from a different year. They have enjoyed the "small world" phenomenon and dropped us a line to report. We had not fully realized, until this dinner in Atlanta, that over the years what we had actually built was an incipient community ready to interact, ready to support itself, and it just needed a tiny push to get it going full strength.

FEWER WOMEN IN MATHEMATICS

The numbers are familiar to everyone in mathematics: Each year nearly 50% of the bachelor's degrees in mathematics awarded by U.S. colleges and universities go to women. However, only about 30% of the PhDs in mathematics go to women.[1] The rate at which qualified women advance to graduate school and the rate at which they persist in graduate school are both lower than the comparable rates for qualified men.

Why do so few women (relative to men) pursue and achieve advanced degrees in mathematics? Although definitive studies on this problem have not yet been done, anecdotal evidence points to several causes. Often, talented women who are drawn to mathematics find it difficult to believe that they can have effective careers in the field. Few of their professors are women. The male students in the class seem to get more attention from the instructor and, for whatever reason, seem to dominate the classroom discussions with their questions and responses. Most students demonstrate a lack of awareness about women mathematicians. Thus, women studying mathematics often have to deal not only with the difficulties inherent in the subject itself, but with the psychological and emotional problems caused by studying in such an environment.

OUR SUMMER MATHEMATICS PROGRAM

Each summer 18 first- or second-year undergraduate math majors, selected from the 100-120 who apply, come to Carleton for four weeks. During that time they spend 3½ hours a day in a classroom setting learning mathematics they would not normally see as an undergraduate (such as Morse theory, coding theory, game theory, fuzzy logic, low-dimensional dynamics, knots and topology) from outstanding instructors, chosen for their ability to inspire in the classroom and engage the students outside the classroom. Each instructor has her own teaching assistant who is a former SMPer either heading off to graduate school or in the middle of a graduate program. The students do homework, take exams, and make presentations, but not for a grade; they do it for the joy of deeply understanding some interesting mathematics.

The students are, by design, kept very busy: Beyond the classroom instruction, the students attend twice-weekly colloquia on a variety of mathematics subjects to give them a peek into the wider world of mathematics. They also participate in three panel discussions. The first is "Making the Most of Your Mathematics Major" (including information on research experiences for undergraduates, the study abroad programs in mathematics, courses they should be sure to take before applying to graduate school, math meetings they could attend, organizations they should join). The second is "Applying, Surviving, and Succeeding at Graduate School" (including information on teaching assistantships and fellowships, how to choose a graduate program, what happens at graduate school, what exams they'll be expected to take, choosing an advisor, and enjoying their graduate program). The third is "Non-Academic Careers in Mathematics" (with panelists possibly including an actuary, a high school math teacher, a biostatistician from the Mayo Clinic, an operations researcher from Northwest Airlines, an epidemiologist, and others).

On Monday nights they have an optional recreational problem-solving session during which they learn about various national and local problem-solving competitions and have several hours to sit and think about challenging problems. All of these activities are meant to give the students a view of the mathematical community that exists outside their own college and give them some avenues to follow to find where they fit into it.

One of the most important goals of the program has always been to join the women into a cohesive community so that after they leave Northfield they will still look to one another for support and encouragement. Toward that end we wind in, around, and through all the programming social opportunities for the students to grow closer together: two picnics each week, walks around the Twin Cities, an afternoon at the Minnesota Arboretum, game night, hiking at a state park, or canoeing in a local river. Besides keeping tabs on the students' progress through the instructors and teaching assistants, we check in once each week to make sure no one is feeling overwhelmed by the intense nature of the classes.

By the time of the program-ending banquet it is clear to us that deep and abiding bonds have been formed. Facing, and conquering, difficult challenges together is the most effective way we know to form group bonds. That's why we insist that our instructors challenge the participants to the limits of their abilities. The intense and rigorous intellectual experience, combined with the supportive and enveloping social interactions, forge our students into a vibrant sisterhood of mathematics. We are very intentional about this; it is the soul of our program. We were astounded and delighted to discover in Atlanta that in fact our nine distinct communities might well be easily melded into a larger, stronger community. We started immediately after the Atlanta meeting to work on consciously constructing that larger community.

The tenth summer of the program, 2005, saw the inaugural "SMPosium," a three-day event celebrating the successes of SMP graduates who have completed their PhDs. In the summer of 2005, there were nine former participants who had finished their PhDs. Of those, seven were able to attend the symposium, and two (of three) former teaching assistants who had also earned their PhDs attended as well.

On the first day of the program, the visitors were introduced to the participants, and four of them presented 20-minute talks on their research. This was followed by a picnic for all involved for informal interaction. At the picnic, a number of participants approached the directors to say what an "inspiration" it was to have these women who've "made it" visit the program.

On the second day, the other five participants gave 20-minute talks on their research. This was followed by the panel discussion on applying, surviving, and succeeding at graduate school. The questions and answers were lively and upbeat. The panelists gave practical, honest answers to eager, thoughtful questions. These visitors weren't women on a poster designed to inspire, nor were they anecdotal evidence of women successful in mathematics passed down over generations of students; these were flesh-and-blood role models, sitting right in front of them, only a few years older than they were.

That evening was a dinner reception to which all were invited. The last

It has been an extremely busy, frustrating, exciting, empowering, four weeks, and today is the final day. I have learned so much math and so much about math it is truly amazing. The whole secret world of mathematicians is one that I never really knew about, but now want to be a part of. These four weeks

Photo by Tom Roster

I have learned that 2+3 is not 3+2, a circle and a triangle are the same thing, a sphere is a two-dimensional object, and that the more useless the problem, the more mathematicians like it. I have also learned how to draw four-dimensional objects on paper, yet still can barely draw two-dimensional objects. My brain has been turned upside down, and I am excited to know that it will probably never be returned to its original orientation. The friends I have made here are ones I hope to never forget. It is amazing how strongly people can bond so quickly by spending hours discussing math. It is going to be hard to have to leave the people I met here, because I feel some connection to every one of them—Raena Bryant, SMP '05, quoted with permission.

day of the three-day event was reserved for hiking in the Minnesota Arboretum, during which time the participants and guests intermingled and walked and talked and made connections.

The SMPosium was an experiment. We believed that from getting together former participants who have since earned PhDs in a mathematical science only good could come. Come it did. They enjoyed talking with each other, learning of their peers' graduate experiences, hearing about job searches and two-body problems, discussing how marriage and family fit into career. The participants talked with the graduates about undergraduate and graduate institutions, enrichment opportunities, exams, advisors. The conversations flowed easily because they all have similar interests; the graduates blended in easily with the undergraduates.

On the second day, when the graduate panel started, and the nine guests took their seats at the front of the classroom, one participant in the front row looked at the guests, with whom she'd been interacting for several days about math and non-math alike, and an awakening visibly crossed her face. She realized that they're no different than she was, just a few years older. She said to herself, in a voice quite a bit louder than she had intended, "Wait, they *all* have PhDs? This is *so* cool!"

We agree; it is cool. And we are looking forward to our next reunion to bolster the young and celebrate the triumphs—to catch up with our mathematical family.

OUR RESULTS

The young women mathematicians immerse themselves in mathematics, living and working in a supportive community of women scholars (undergraduates, graduates, and faculty) who are passionate about learning and doing mathematics. Our intentions for them are threefold: to excite them about mathematics and mathematical careers, to provide them with some of the tools—psychological, emotional, and mathematical—they will need to succeed in a mathematical career, and to connect them to a network of fellow female mathematicians. We have been successful. Over the years, students have reported on their post-program evaluations being recharged and recommitted to mathematics by our program. They also intimate to us their feelings of isolation at their home institutions and the joy with which they entered into new kinships with sisters in mathematics.

Not only do the students, faculty, teaching assistants, and directors admit in their evaluations at the end of the program to being deeply influenced by what happens during SMP, but also the statistics of what the participants do after graduation from their home institutions support our claim.

As we can see from the table, of the 156 who have finished their undergraduate degrees, 29 (or 19%) of the SMP graduates are in a math-related career, most often programmer, actuary, or high school teacher, and a whopping 96 (or 62%) have or are working toward an advanced degree in a mathematical science. (Overall about 20% of female bachelor's degree holders in mathematics attempt graduate degrees.)[2]

The students return to their home institutions eager to plunge into their studies. They have a clearer idea of what mathematics is and a much clearer map of the mathematical community and a vision of what their place in it could be. Their increased awareness of various topics within mathematics has led many to give talks in their home departments on the mathematics that they learned in the summer program. Most have already participated in research experiences for undergraduates, the Budapest Semester in Mathematics, or other further-enrichment programs. All who have done so acknowledge being much better prepared to succeed at, and benefit from, those programs than they

By the Numbers: Where the SMP Graduates Are as of 2005

	95	96	97	98	99	00	01	03	04	05	TOTALS
PhD	3	2	4	7	2	--	--	--	--	--	18
Terminal Masters	4	6	5	2	3	3	1	--	--	--	24
Graduate School	--	4	3	3	7	10	10	10	8	--	55
Math-Related Career	7	3	4	3	3	2	3	4	--	--	29
Adv. Degree (Non-Math)	2	2	--	1	3	1	3	2	2	--	16
Other	2	1	--	2	--	2	2	2	3	--	14
Undergraduate	--	--	--	--	--	--	--	--	5	19	24
Total	18	18	16	18	18	18	19	18	18	19	180

otherwise would have been. More important than the knowledge and renewed excitement for mathematics, each of the students has gained confidence in her ability to do mathematics.

This confidence building is central to the mission of the program. All of these students, and most of the other one hundred who applied, are intellectually capable of achieving an advanced degree in mathematics. Something other than intellectual capacity prevents many women from pursuing one. Heightened self-confidence and a supportive network of colleagues and mentors are two factors that we hope will prevent young women from dropping out. These students return to their home institutions knowing that women can and should be doing mathematics. They will not only be supported by this knowledge, but they also will carry the message back with them to influence their peers and their teachers.

We have an impact on the lives of the young women who come to our program—we see the increased confidence, enthusiasm, knowledge, and mathematical sophistication. We see the electronic messages they post on the program's list-server to let us and each other know what is happening in their lives—mathematical and otherwise.

It is less clear to us how to measure this effect. We can never know how many would have gone on to productive mathematical careers without us—given the talent level, some certainly would. We won't know for some time how long and how far the momentum we give will sustain them in the face of adversity. We do believe that we are making a difference: At the dinner in Atlanta, many of the former students stopped to tell us about the impact SMP had on their lives as undergraduates and what a profound experience it is now, seeing women at every stage from undergraduate to full professor interacting as one big cohesive community, one big family.

FUTURE PLANS FOR THE SMP

As we plan for the future of this program, in addition to the summer program as we run it now, we are going to be more intentional in nurturing the larger community of mathematical women who are the SMP alumnae. Five years from now, we will have 270 SMP graduates, and we expect to have over 50 SMP women with PhDs and at least another 50 with PhDs in progress. There is a community here now, and we intend to take care of it.

It's unclear to us when SMP started to take off on its own; in the early years we were completely focused on each individual summer's group. We learned how to forge strong bonds within those groups but we never really looked at connecting across the groups. We made small steps: We use SMP alumnae as teaching assistants each year; we occasionally staffed the graduate school panel with an alum or two; and in recent years we've had a colloquium or two by alumnae with PhDs. All this was done as much out of convenience and affection for the alums involved as for any other reason.

But now we look up, and we see a budding community of 80 or 100 new or nascent professional mathematicians, and we see how much they could offer one another and how easy it will be to make that happen. We have inadvertently built something much larger than we initially intended, much stronger than we could have imagined. We're running alongside trying to keep up with this group of young women who will influence mathematics and each other for the next half century or so, and we couldn't be prouder of, or happier about, our serendipitous community.

ENDNOTES

[1] Data was compiled by reviewing the November issues of *Notices*, the magazine of the American Mathematical Society for the past ten years.

[2] Data from *CBMS 2000: Statistical Abstract of Undergraduate Programs in the Mathematical Sciences in the United States*, a report published every five years by the American Mathematical Society.

Addressing Environmental Issues and Feeling Comfy

Gary Wagenbach and Richard Strong

Our course, Ecohouse Design and Construction, evolved from a campus need, student interest, a serendipitous meeting of faculty and staff collaborators, and an attempt to integrate concepts of sustainable and restorative architecture into a liberal arts curriculum. More fundamentally, we have aimed to challenge students by critically examining the environmental consequences of their adopted lifestyles.

According to the Massachusetts Audubon Society's report "Losing Ground" (2003), the average house has become 44% larger since 1970, and the lot it sits on is 47% larger. Many of today's Carleton students (born in the Reagan/Bush I era) seem to define human comfort as having a TV, iPod, SUV, and maybe a large house and yard. Intellectually, they consider themselves environmentally conscious, but talk of alternative energy sources, composting toilets, or alternatives to clothes dryers sends uneasy shivers up their spines. When shown a picture of a house built in 1880 and another of 5,000 sq ft (464.5 m²) house with the majority of its windows facing north sitting on a five-acre plot of lawn grass four miles (6.4 km) from the nearest town

> When shown a picture of a 5,000 sq ft house with the majority of its windows facing north sitting on a five-acre plot four miles from the nearest town, their first response is to consider it as the next iteration of human comfort in housing ...

GARY WAGENBACH is the Winifred and Atherton Bean Professor of Biology, Science, Technology, and Society, and director of environmental and technology studies. He earned his B.S. degree at University of Wisconsin, River Falls, and his M.S. and PhD degrees at University of Wisconsin, Madison. He joined the Carleton faculty in 1969. RICHARD STRONG served as Carleton's director of facilities from 2000 to 2006. He earned his BArch degree at North Dakota State University and masters degrees in urban planning and design at McGill University and Harvard University, respectively.

(Figures 1-2), their first response is to consider the 2005 home as the next iteration of human comfort in housing, an extrapolation of a recent past defined by unmitigated growth. When asked if the newer house has any associated environmental issues that we should be concerned about, they have a sense that this five-acre house and lot is not altogether right with the world but little knowledge of the specific factors that might make this house out of step with the Minnesota environment. What relevance does architectural design have to do, if anything, with this type of student thinking? [1]

Figures 1-2.

"What images come to mind when you view pictures of these two houses in Northfield, built 125 years apart? Can you translate these visual images into comparative language?" We start our class, Ecohouse Design and Construction, with these questions.

< 1880 House

2005 House >

A few years ago a group of Carleton students pushed for constructing campus buildings in a more sustainable fashion. Around the same time, Richard Strong, a green architect with an extensive background in sustainable design, was hired as facilities director. Concurrently the dean of students saw a need to build additional student housing. In 2002, during a junior environmental seminar, Environment and Technology Studies (ENTS) students identified techniques and materials that could be incorporated into a house to enhance energy efficiency and meet a set of sustainability standards.

Building on this work, Richard conceived the idea of developing a full academic course that would recruit students interested in designing comfortable student housing utilizing alternative energy sources. When he sought a faculty member with whom to collaborate, Gary Wagenbach from the Biology Department stepped forward.

The two of us proceeded to develop a syllabus for an "ecohouse" course with a broadened perspective. The idea was to teach students how to design and construct an energy-efficient, low-impact, aesthetically pleasing campus residence for 15 students that would serve to enhance an adjacent local ecosystem[2] as well as serving as a model in the region for "good design." We co-taught three sections of the course, one in each of the academic years 2003-04, 2004-05, and 2005-06.

Gary is a biology professor and Richard is a registered architect—what did our collaboration bring to the course?

Well, first of all, built environments overlap with natural environments. It seems sensible that an architect and a biologist could constitute a functional pair to examine the impact of each on the other.

In addition, our disciplines have in common form, structure, and function. Consider birds and airplanes. Flight is energetically expensive for both birds and aircraft. Flightless birds (such as the New Zealand kiwi) conserve energy for other life functions. Moreover, don't forget the food supply needed to provide energy for bird flight, comparable to jet fuel for airplanes. In a broader sense, an understanding of energy flows, food and waste cycles, and creature comforts in natural and built environments is essential to creating sustainable housing for humans and restorative impacts on surrounding ecosystems.

> With the advent of the fossil fuel era ... occupied structures no longer needed to respond to the natural environmental conditions of the site—because people could overcome extreme conditions by using more and more energy.

Gary and Richard's strong backgrounds in quantitative reasoning and Richard's architectural experience in visual literacy also added dimension to the full experience for the liberal arts students in our course. We were confident that discoveries relevant to student housing would accrue if we taught together.

As we taught the ecohouse course for the first time, we learned that undergraduate students, especially freshman and sophomores, are not experienced in the language of design and sustainability. The environment they grew up in is, in many cases, urban and very different from landscapes without buildings. As a result, student connections to the natural environment are more cerebral and not visceral.

It turns out that these perspectives are not parochial but, rather, are widely shared among many people living in Western countries who are conditioned to viewing human comfort as disconnected from their surroundings. We found we needed to incorporate discussion of what "comfort" means, as well as reflections on living environments, some ethics, and other ideas from the humanities and the natural and social sciences.

One way we framed these ideas was by offering a brief tour of the traditional and innovative roles of architecture in environmental thought.

For the last 10,000 years, architecture has been concerned with the issues of human comfort, beauty, design efficiencies, and solving functional problems. Initially, cultures built structures to create an envelope that moderated local existing climatic conditions to the range of human tolerance. Over thousands of years, these envelopes—perfected through small design changes—resulted in structures that were highly responsive to the climate and the available materials in the surrounding environment as well as beautiful to the eye.

With the advent of the fossil fuel era in Western countries in the 19th century, however, occupied structures no longer needed to respond to the natural environmental conditions of the site—because people could overcome extreme conditions by using more and more energy. As a result, working within the natural environment of the specific place became irrelevant. Instead, solving functional problems, often times with iconic contemporary design, became the norm. The global architectural design aesthetic that resulted produced cities all over the world that looked identical.

After the oil crisis in the 1970s, Minnesota and other U.S. states developed energy codes; Minnesota's became effective in 1978. While these codes required buildings to become more energy efficient, the requirement was only a *minimum* design standard, rather than a higher enforced baseline with strong incentives.

The result has been increasing energy consumption, despite the guidelines. At Carleton, for instance, energy usage, especially electricity, has progressively risen since 1987 in spite of more energy-efficient buildings constructed in the 1990s and the early 21st century. While newer buildings have greater in-

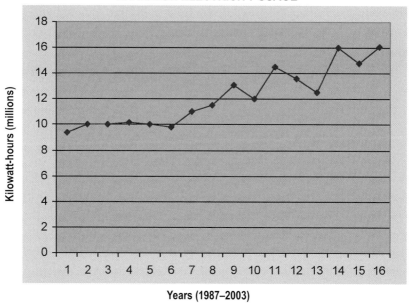

CARLETON ELECTRICITY USAGE

Figure 3. Carleton Total Electrical Energy Use for the Years 1987-2003

sulation value and more efficient motors and lighting systems, all of Carleton's buildings[3] summed consume more net energy than they did ten years ago (Figure 3). Not all of this increased energy consumption results from increased square footage.

During the last 25 years, a group of designers who disagree with the policies and accumulated inertia that fostered the continued heavy use of fossil fuels have redefined "good design" to include reducing natural resource use and connecting building with the natural energy flows of the specific location. These views are represented by the architectural work of Sim Van Der Ryn and Stuart Cowen in *Ecological Design* (1996), the landscape architectural work of John T. Lyle in *Regenerative Design for Sustainable Development* (1994), and closed-loop systems for waste streams in Nancy J. Todd and John Todd's *From Eco-Cities to Living Machine* (1994).

Recently Edward Mazria, founder of Architecture 2030 and an internationally recognized architect, author, and educator, has been playing a major role in urging the architectural communities and decision makers responsible for the built environment to take the lead in reducing energy use, for economic and ethical reasons (global warming). For example, Mazria reports that 76% of the electricity produced in the U.S is used to operate buildings.

The intent in the 1970s and 1980s was to reduce the resources required to build structures, using durable materials and reducing pollution at the same time. Residents of sustainable structures would also be assured of continuous, available, and reliable inexpensive sources of energy, a healthy indoor environment, and lower lifecycle cost.[4]

Within the last ten years, concepts of sustainable design have evolved into "restorative design," which seeks to reduce the ecological footprint of humans, yet attain human comfort and allow occupants to live in abundance. Restorative design is intensely interested in connecting human experience in a built environment with the natural amenities of "place."

This approach also looks for opportunities to benefit existing or restored adjacent ecosystems. As Bart Johnson and Kristina Hill note in *Ecology and Design: Frameworks for Learning* (2002),

> Design is a cultural action that structured ecosystems. We believe that design and planning education must be steeped in knowledge of how humans, as biological social and spiritual beings, inhabit a world filled with myriad other species, a world that is maintained and changing through crucial biophysical processes often invisible to the immediate senses. (p. 12)

In our ecohouse course, we concentrated on restorative design because we thought it was imperative that students take responsibility for the impact that design has on surrounding ecosystems.

EVOLVING METHODS, RESULTS

As we write this, in spring 2006, we are three years into a five-year journey of discovery. We have utilized some of the usual classroom methods, but our students also have worked on hands-on projects in design teams with an emphasis on visual and quantitative thinking, something unusual at a four-year liberal arts college with no architecture or pre-architecture program.

Our intention has been to provide theory and then have students quickly move to designing solutions for the challenges of constructing a student residence with a high standard of sustainability. The course also includes a construction phase that emphasizes real world implications of a given design and the accompanying choice of materials. Throughout, we have sought to provide students with an opportunity to experience elements of an architectural studio course; in our case, we have adapted to a liberal arts setting, confronting environmental issues associated with the built environment.

Students have entered the course from a wide range of majors: all the natural sciences and mathematics, the social sciences (psychology, political science, sociology-anthropology, and economics), history, studio art and art history, Spanish, and Latin American Studies as well as several special majors. One St. Olaf College student joined the class and other Oles have expressed interest. Since the course is taught without prerequisites, freshmen through seniors have enrolled. Teaching assistants with prior experience have helped support this wonderful array of students as we engage the active learning components of the syllabus.

The variety of majors has had a positive effect on the course, encouraging us to identify social issues that might be implicit in sustainable design and, in particular, to develop a broader perspective of sustainable housing in developing countries. Further, we realized, the course has provided a window into selected environmental issues, such as comparative energy budgets for buildings.

We have sought to make the class student-centered and been pleased to see participants take active roles in class activities. For example, during the 2005-06 class the students reorganized their design teams, selected content they wanted to present for their final presentations, and coordinated efforts among the three groups. They took ownership of both process and content.

We thought it would be instructive, early in the term, to look at indigenous housing in the Americas and other locations around the world. Those efforts led to recognition of how important climate, culture, and materials are to enhancing human comfort. Besides searching for examples from countries in both the deeper and more recent past, we centered attention on the tipi of Dakota Indians, one of the indigenous peoples of southern Minnesota. We learned that the tipi provided an example of sophisticated adaptation to the climate, material availability, and culture of the Great Plains. When Dennis Sun Rhodes, a Northern Arapahoe and an architect living and working in the Twin Cities, paid a visit to class with his sister, we learned that, culturally, the proper assembly of a tipi is a special duty of women in a tribe.

During 2004, students constructed and determined R-values[5] for four different wall systems: conventional wood frame construction, rammed earth, cordwood, and strawbale. With valuable assistance and guidance from Warren Ringlien, Carleton's instrument maker, students instrumented the walls, measured, and analyzed the R-values.

A review of the literature on R-values for cordwood and strawbale walls revealed a lack of reliable values. This finding led us to conclude that students made an original contribution of values for those materials configured as a wall.

The insights gained from this project led Richard, aided by student workers, to design and construct a campus warehouse that incorporates a strawbale wall system.

During our 2005 class, we examined natural flows of energy and, specifically, how to design a house that could keep residents within a comfort zone of 65° F to 75° F (18.3° C to 23.9° C) for as long as possible, ideally for the full year. In Minnesota, this is a large challenge indeed, due to extreme seasonal temperature differences, especially those occurring during the academic year (September to June).

Student design teams were urged to recognize that humans, compared with many organisms that utilize natural energy flow, can design buildings that can also utilize natural energy flow to maintain comfort. The key elements in both cases are capturing energy, storing, and then releasing energy. This cycle

Figure 4.

The goal: To design a house that could keep residents within a comfort zone of 65° F to 75° F for as long as possible. The passive solar structure produced by the 2005 lab maintained target temperatures for 10-12 hours during cool days in May.

of energy capture, storage, and release is what many animals, some plants, and humans have to master in order to maintain body temperature within a suitable range. We suggested the student house would have to do the same by design.

The lab for 2005 produced a strictly passive solar design (no supplemental energy supply or control system) consisting of greenhouse window panels incorporated into a south-facing wall. An interior energy storing mass of concrete blocks retained and released enough energy to maintain target comfort temperatures for 10-12 hours during cool days in May.

In addition to the task of trying to maintain human comfort under climatic conditions found in Minnesota, we challenged students to consider the health and welfare of the plants and animals affected by placement of a house on the land. If possible, we told them, it should have a net positive effect, i.e. "restorative design."

How does an attempt to engage in restorative design play out in class? One of the emphases in the ecohouse class during 2004 and 2005 was a site selection exercise. One potential site was on the south-facing slope of a hill adjacent to one of the constructed lakes on campus, an area that has mixed hardwood and Scotch pine.

Learning from Myles Bakke, arboretum manager, during a field tour in May 2005 that this was is a wildlife corridor and thus a point of intersection for habitat used and desired by both wildlife and humans, students initially responded to the overlapping and potentially conflicting uses by concluding that we should not build on the site. Then, in an especially creative response, one design team tried to accommodate the needs of wildlife by having a portion of the house below grade and tucked into the hillside. An added feature was a roof that would allow animals to travel on top of the building. As a result, the exercise became a thoughtful discussion of what it could mean to have a collaborative, restor-

> Student design teams were urged to recognize that humans, compared with many organisms that utilize natural energy flow, can design buildings that can also utilize natural energy flow to maintain comfort. The key elements in both cases are capturing energy, storing, and then releasing energy. This cycle of energy capture, storage, and release is what many animals, some plants, and humans have to master in order to maintain body temperature within a suitable range…

ative, and nurturing relationship with nature. This example also illustrates our charge to students to have a working knowledge of the biota relevant to potential house sites.

RIPPLE EFFECTS

The tendency of humans to (innately) focus on life and life-like processes was defined by E. O. Wilson (1984) as "biophilia" (p. 1). Wilson's pioneering writing on this topic has evoked further critique and the assertion by S. R. Kellert (1993) that

> An ethic of nature conservation and protection is no mere luxury or indulgence. It is the celebration of nature's capacity to enrich and enlarge of life's experience. Biological diversity and the ecological processes that make it possible are the crucibles in which our species' physical, mental, and spiritual being have been forged. (p. 26)

Richard Louv, in *Last Child in the Woods: Saving Our Children from Nature-Deficit Disorder* (2005), argues that connection to nature is essential for the wellbeing of people and especially children. He laments the reduction of natural un-programmed spaces where children can play and imagine. He attributes this deficit to the effects of suburbanization of the landscape and increased attention to liability issues, both of which have removed natural areas from children's worlds.

By contrast, through the ecohouse course and in our other teaching, we are encouraging students and the college to develop a house design and educational program that fosters interactions with the natural world.

Creating an actual Ecohouse at Carleton, a student residence and its surrounding land, could create further opportunities for continued learning, not only for residents but for a larger community. During the academic year, residents could aspire to a zero net footprint (or even better) by managing acquisition of goods, services, and foodstuff; managing energy acquisition, storage, and release (Amory Lovins' style[6]); and managing all aspects of the waste stream. During summers the house could serve as the center for a variety of community outreach programs, including the Prairie and Wood (PAW) summer day camp, which has been in continuous existence since 1975 and is designed and run by Carleton student-counselors as their summer education-related employment.

Ecohouse issues could contribute to other classes, too. They already have, in fact. During spring 2005, Gary taught a topic-oriented class, Biology of Disease, which enrolled mainly non-science majors seeking math-science distribution credits. For the required final projects, one team of students was assigned to write a report to future Ecohouse residents about likely disease-causing infectious agents (a spectrum from food-borne pathogens to people-transferred microorganisms) that they would be well advised to avoid or manage. The assignment provided strong motivation to learn about pathogens! As in many other cases, the fact that students were producing something useful to others elicited excellent work. Their recommendations, in the form of class reports, are now available for use by the future residents of Ecohouse.

With respect to food for residents, Gary soon realized the possibility of linking the Ecohouse design effort to a third course he and a colleague (Tsegaye Nega) teach: ENTS 110, Food and Agriculture. During this class, end-of-term projects involved investigating how Ecohouse residents should feed themselves. The final reports concluded that residents should be able to grow 35% of the food they needed and acquire the rest from markets. The class recommended growing the ancient American Indian "milpa—the three sisters" of corn, beans, and squash. Like the final projects in Biology of Disease, these projects generated a surprisingly high level of motivation and high quality reports.

THE ENERGY TO BUILD, SUSTAIN

Even if we design an ecohouse to have a complementary and nondestructive relationship with local ecosystems, establishing an adequate energy supply remains an extremely challenging issue—both the energy needed for construction and that needed for day-to-day operation.

Lyle in his *Regenerative Design for Sustainable Development* (1994) characterizes 20th-century energy consumption as a set of one-way flows, especially to cities, in which—after being used by urban consumers—energy is deposited in sinks. The net result, from an environmental perspective, is "landscape pathology" (p. 4).

Architect Ed Mazria (2007) notes that

Data from the U.S. Energy Information Administration illustrates that buildings are responsible for almost half (43%) of all energy consumption and GHG (green house gas) emissions annually;

globally the percentage is even greater. Seventy-six percent (76%) of all power plant-generated electricity is used just to operate buildings. Clearly immediate action in the Building Sector is essential if we are to avoid hazardous climate change.

Given projected growth in housing, we won't be able to curb global warming without drastically reducing the proportion of energy we devote to the built environment—not even if we improve efficiency and add more solar and wind energy to the mix. Here is where the challenge begins for the next generation of designers (our students) and for the thousands of students enrolled in 125 accredited schools of architecture (ACSA, 2007)—creating buildings that use little or no fossil fuels.

What if a design for student housing had generous interior spaces and produced much or all of its energy onsite? What if water left the house cleaner than arriving water did? What if it recycled all its waste? What if we did all this while still keeping the human body warm and cooled, spiritually nurtured, aesthetically inspired, and academically supported, fed, and healthy?

During the 2006 ecohouse course, we began an investigation of options for managing black and grey water streams emanating from a 15-person household. Findings to this point include designing a system to utilize rainwater, recycling grey water and urine for application to a garden of trees, and composting fecal matter. Because of concern about pathogens and ordinances that define permitted uses of grey and black water, this sector of design presents new challenges and opportunities. The "living" nature of the waste stream brings microbiology strongly into the syllabus and has required adding a consultant engineer experienced in working with wastewater (David Austin, Northwest Wetlands Engineering).

Within two years the ecohouse class evolved from a more technical "how to" class to one that also asked students to design a restorative place of human comfort. The diversity of backgrounds and majors allowed us to explore the impacts of creating environments for human habitation and provided a conduit for discussion of local, regional, and national environmental issues.

In our students, we have sought to foster a paradigm shift defined by authors previously mentioned and by McDonough's 2002 book *Cradle to Cradle*. His message is that we are personally responsible for designs that are not detrimental to our neighbors or the rest of the world. He suggests that we turn our waste (technical and biological) into nutriment for other systems, whether in recycling inorganic material (technical) or using it as inputs for production of food and fiber (biotic).

We found it challenging to move students in these directions. Students had some difficulty in recognizing issues that seem obvious to us. Their pre-conception about their lifestyles and the conveniences they have come to enjoy blinded them to changes that could bring them more in touch with the environmental cycles of energy, waste, and food around them. They did not readily see the options and the great richness that these cycles might include.

We hope this, at least—that at the end of our course, students understood that in a special-design house embedded in a landscape that invites cool breezes on a hot day they *could* simply open windows. Instead of turning on the air conditioner in the summer, they *could* let nature—aided by thoughtful design—do the work. We all need to consider the implications of the energy devoted to the built environment—you, too.[7]

ENDNOTES

[1] Some suggestions: Design and style? Water? An energy supply? Comfort in winter or summer? Food? Animals or pets? Site selection? Impact on wild life or rare plants? Choice of materials? Expected life span? Embodied energy? Environmental impacts? Location in an ecosystem? Infiltration of air or water? Presence of mold and allergens? A basement? Cost to build? Cost to heat and maintain? Aesthetics? Cultural and social connections? Status symbol?

[2] An ecosystem consists of living organisms, their interactions with each other and the surrounding non-living environment.

[3] From its conception in 1866, the design and placement of buildings has been guided by a traditional perception of a campus set in Arcadian environs. Half of Carleton's buildings were constructed before 1930 and placed on the land in a "City Beautiful" design of avenues, quads and large open spaces. This template still influences the present placement as well as the perception of what a college campus should look like in the 21st century. Most buildings built since the 1960s have followed the typical modern and postmodern style of architectural design.

[4] Cost of total energy required to maintain and operate a building during its lifetime.

[5] R-value: "A measure of the resistance an insulating material offers to energy transfer. Higher R-values indicate more effective insulation." (www.excalibursteel.com/glossary.htm, accessed August 22, 2006)

[6] To do our part in reducing dependence on fossil fuels, we need to design housing that uses minimal or no fossil fuel and captures most or all of the needed energy

from the sun and local sources. It is possible. Amory Lovins has done so, eliminating the heating system for his 1984 house in Snowmass, Colorado, where it is as cold or colder than Minnesota in the winter (Lovins, 2005).

[7] If you are looking for a green architect, try www.usgbc.org/chapters. Learn more about construction techniques at www.eere.energy.gov/RE/solar_passive.html.

REFERENCES

Association of Collegiate Schools of Architecture (ACSA). Architectural education. Retrieved from https://www.acsa-arch.org/students/education.aspx

Ausubel, K., & Harpignies, J. P. (Eds.). (2004). *Nature's operating instructions: The true biotechnologies.* San Francisco: Sierra Club Books.

Crossroads for Planet Earth. [Special issue]. *Scientific American.* September 2005.

Johnson, B. R., & Hill, K. (Eds.). (2002). *Ecology and design: Frameworks for learning.* Washington, D.C.: Island Press.

Kellert, S. R., & Wilson, E. O. (Eds.). (1993). *The biophilia hypothesis.* Washington, D.C.: Island Press.

Louv, R. (2005). *Last child in the woods: Saving our children from nature-deficit disorder.* Chapel Hill, NC: Algonquin Books.

Lovins, A. B. (2005). More profit with less carbon. *Scientific American, 293*(3), 74-83.

Lyle, J. T. (1994). *Regenerative design for sustainable development.* New York: John Wiley & Sons, Inc.

Massachusetts Audubon Society. (2003, November 10). *Losing ground: At what cost?* Lincoln, MA: Breunig, K.

Mazria, E. (1979). *The passive solar energy book.* Emmaus, PA: Rodale Press.

Mazria, E. (2007). Retrieved from http://www.2010imperative.org/webcast.html

McDonough, W., & Braungart, M. (2002). *Cradle to cradle: Remaking the way we make things.* New York: Durabook.

Todd, N. J., & Todd, J. (1994). *From eco-cities to living machine: Principles of ecological design.* Berkeley, CA: North Atlantic Books.

Van Der Ryn, S., & Cowen, S. (1996). *Ecological design.* Washington, D.C.: Island Press.

Wilson, E. O. (1984). *Biophilia: The human bond with other species.* Cambridge, MA: Harvard University Press.

Cognitive Science as a New Liberal Art

Roy Elveton

One of the joys of my career at Carleton has been the many opportunities I have had to not only think about the integration of diverse academic disciplines, but to participate in the creation and implementation of integrated courses and programs involving a variety of disciplines.

My first involvement was a proposal with five faculty colleagues for a program in the "Arts and Sciences" which, in its complete implementation, would have occupied a two-year sequence of courses integrating foreign languages, mathematics, the natural sciences, the humanities, and social sciences. Needless to say, our complete vision never got off the ground. However, we did manage to create a series of courses forming a scaled-down version of the original program that lasted for well over 20 years and involved faculty from the Departments of English, Classics, Mathematics, Philosophy, Physics, and Political Science.[1]

My most recent attempt has involved participating with Kathie Galotti (Department of Psychology) and Susan Singer (Department of Biology) in several incarnations of Carleton's first "triad," Origins and Minds, a linking of courses in biology, psychology, and philosophy focusing on questions surrounding the biology, psychology,

> No master plan preceded these events. The vision we all shared grew apace with our conversations, interactions, and shared perceptions of how we could bring together the disciplines of computer science, linguistics, psychology, philosophy, and, later, biology and the neurosciences.

ROY ELVETON, the Maxine H. and Winston R. Wallin Professor of Philosophy and Cognitive Science, joined the Carleton faculty in 1968. He earned his B.A. degree at St. Olaf College and his PhD degree at Northwestern University.

and evolution of the mind. This project has close connections to the Carleton program in cognitive studies whose history and rationale I will narrate below.

What has emerged for me from these (and other) enriching collaborative experiences is two convictions: first, that the aim of the liberal arts should be to integrate diverse modes of access to the worlds of nature and human affairs and to afford an enhanced grasp of human life, not just to offer a smorgasbord of the latest university specializations; and second, that the humanities and the sciences can meet on common ground. An attempt to coordinate their distinct perspectives does not eliminate their differences and uniqueness. It does, however, imply that a perspective encompassing both and attentive to their differing technical languages and approaches is not only possible but mandatory for today's liberal arts student.

Beginning with Socrates, self-understanding has been a hallmark of Western humanity. Contemporary sciences of the mind, for instance, have themselves become critical of the inadequacies of overly abstract theoretical models of cognition. In these contemporary cognitive sciences, the traditional inquiry into the nature of human language, meaning, reasoning, creativity, perception, and society is vigorously at work and within an increasingly broad and interdisciplinary field of diverse resources, models, methods, and important self-evaluations.

COGNITIVE SCIENCES AT CARLETON

As described in its mission statement in the *Carleton College Academic Catalog* (2005-06), Carleton's program in cognitive studies

> ... examines different approaches to questions concerning the nature of mind; the representation of knowledge; the acquisition, comprehension, and production of language; the development of learning and intelligence; the use of information to draw inferences and make decisions; and the assessment of "goodness of fit" between purportedly similar systems (e.g., the computer and the mind).

> Exploration of some or all of these questions has been and is being undertaken in such disciplines as cognitive psychology, linguistics, philosophy, artificial intelligence, neuroscience, social cognition and others. The concentration in Cognitive Studies therefore represents a formal means of bringing together students and faculty in different disciplines who share common interests. We seek to

enrich the view provided by any one discipline through an exploration of the methodologies of others.

Carleton's exploration of the field now known as the cognitive sciences initially began with a very modest curricular effort: Roger Kirchner's creation, in the early 1980s, of a computer science course in artificial intelligence in Carleton's (then-named) Department of Mathematics. Artificial intelligence (AI) represents the promise made by Alan Turing in 1950 that by the turn of the century, digital computers would be able to respond intelligently to a wide variety of questions in such a manner that their response would be indistinguishable from the responses of flesh and blood human beings. This was indeed the hope of the cognitive revolution that occurred in American universities in the mid-1950s, a revolution that eventually led to the establishment of what is today known as the cognitive sciences.

The computer revolution, so critical for the revolution in cognitive studies, emerged on the Carleton campus on two fronts. Carleton was an early leader in the application of computers to administrative and educational ends, beginning in the mid- to late-1960s, with a DEC computer that not only supported limited administrative applications but was also used by faculty for artistic and curricular purposes. Simultaneously, several members of Carleton's computing support staff began the creation of SPSS (Statistical Package for the Social Sciences), a commercially successful software venture that eventually became independent of Carleton.

The introduction of desktop computers by Apple, IBM, and Texas Instruments in the 1980s aided and accelerated the development of a curriculum in computer science at Carleton. Roger's first course in artificial intelligence used the innovative Scheme language, a language that was both more suited to the fledgling PC, a type of platform much less expensive than the Lisp-based machines[2] current at the time. (When Lisp-based programming became available on desktop computers, Roger's AI courses migrated to this platform).

In adopting Scheme for the classroom, Roger was also adopting the philosophy of the period's most important Scheme textbook, Abelson, Sussman, and Sussman's *Structure and Interpretation of Computer Programs* (1985). According to the authors, to employ Scheme was to adopt a "procedural epistemology," by which they meant that Scheme represented "the study of knowledge from an imperative point of view" (p. xvi.). Writing a series of procedures in Scheme amounted to writing a set of detailed instructions the computer was obligated to follow, hence the word "imperative." The "epistemological" component stems from the AI belief that such computer programs reflected actual processes of human cognition.

Following Roger's introduction of advanced treatments of AI into the Carleton curriculum, I developed a course in the early 1980s for first-year students ("freshman seminars" were ubiquitous at the time) that employed Scheme to introduce non-computer science students to elementary AI programming. Since no Scheme-based texts specifically intended for the beginning humanities student were available, I wrote a short, self-published text, "Scheme and Schemata," translating a few elementary Lisp AI programs into the Scheme language. These materials accompanied standard topics in elementary logic, logic circuits, and Turing machines in order to acquaint even the most formal-language-phobic first-year student with issues fundamental to the emerging field of artificial intelligence and the underlying technology of the digital computer.

These first steps were followed by an unforeseen opportunity that encouraged Roger and me to continue these efforts. Dean of the College Peter Stanley asked a small group of Carleton faculty to reflect upon the role of the humanities in higher education. To that end, a Carleton trustee funded campus visits of several distinguished humanists. In 1983, toward the end of our yearlong meetings, several members of the committee argued that the relationship between the humanities and contemporary technology should also be addressed at Carleton. As a member of the committee, I was asked to draft a position paper on this topic. Later, Peter encouraged me to draft a response to the Alfred P. Sloan Foundation's invitation to Carleton to submit a preliminary proposal prior to the foundation's official announcement of their New Liberal Arts (NLA) program. A year after that, during the first year of my own service as Carleton's dean of the college, Carleton was awarded one of 10 $1 million grants given to a select group of liberal arts colleges to support NLA activities. (Three years later, Carleton received an additional million-dollar grant in the final stages of the Sloan program).

Sloan's rationale for the NLA program was initially stated in a widely distributed essay authored by Stephen White (1981), then the director of special projects at the Alfred P. Sloan Foundation. White argued that "If it is the goal of a liberal education to provide an acquaintance with the culture in which it is embedded, then the nature of liberal education must evolve as the culture itself evolves" (p. 1). White then introduced several assertions, each of which would be subsequently debated and discussed extensively by the foundation and the colleges eventually selected to participate in the NLA program.

First, White stressed that since today's culture was a technological one, the liberal arts student required some acquaintance with technology.

Second, White noted the critical importance of "analytical skills" in today's world. "There are many kinds of analytical skills, but perhaps the most powerful involve the reduction of complex phenomena into hard atomic data and the consequent comprehension of the relationships among those data" (p. 3f). These analytical skills also included "mathematical modeling" and "applied mathematics."

Finally, White linked the computer revolution to the cognitive revolution as a technology intimately connected to the exploration of human cognition. In his essay, he initially introduced the computer as a vehicle for manipulating vast amounts of data, but soon referred to it in a more global sense: "...like writing, it is a technology of thought" (p. 4). The prevalence and importance of the digital computer represented a medium which, like writing, was assumed to mirror human cognitive processes, processes whose analysis promised to shed light on the basic structures responsible for human intelligence, thus making possible the fulfillment of Turing's dream of the functional equivalence of machine intelligence and human intelligence.

The funds Carleton received in the first phase of the NLA program were used for a variety of purposes, including curriculum development and faculty workshops, many of which introduced Carleton faculty to the use of the computer for the first time. However, for the eventual development of the cognitive studies program, the most important use of these funds was to support the further exploration of the field of artificial intelligence in the form of public conferences and convocation speakers. This focus turned out to be distinctive of Carleton's NLA efforts in comparison with our sister institutions and provided an important stimulus for the next phase of the development of our eventual program in cognitive science. The NLA funds offered a unique opportunity to enable a rural liberal arts college to assemble a wide range of university and industry experts to discuss the nature and value of the emerging technology of computer applications and computational models of human cognition.

Carleton's initiation of a program in cognitive studies also reflected a more national rethinking of the liberal arts curriculum. 1985 saw the publication of the Association of American Colleges' *Integrity in the College Curriculum: A Report to the Academic Community*. Responding to what was perceived as a "decline and devaluation" of undergraduate education, the AAC report urged renewed attention to a curriculum structured more rigorously "than simply a major and general distribution requirements and more reliably than student interest" (p. 15). In 1987, Ernest Boyer's *College: The Undergraduate Experience in America*, also voiced concerns about fragmentation and unfulfilled expectations in undergraduate education and included a positive reference to Carleton's Arts and Sciences program mentioned at the beginning of this essay and specifically to one of the courses included in this program, "The Rise of Modern Science" (Boyer, 1987, p. 97). Finally, Robert Zemsky's *Structure and Coherence: Measuring the Undergraduate Curriculum* was published in 1989. Carleton had cooperated closely with Zemsky and his project. Written in large part as an attempt to document the validity of the AAC report and its concern with curricular structure and coherence, *Structure and Coherence* noted "the large numbers of students graduating without broad exposure to the natural sciences and mathematics" (p. 36). It also emphasized the correctness of at least some of the criticism of Bloom (1987) and Hirsch (1987) of the current state of the humanities and the "fragmentation of the learning experience" (Hirsch, 1987, p. 39).

At Carleton, discussions prompted by these reports and by the NLA led to renewed on-campus debate regarding both the teaching of science and mathematics and the humanities, as well as the development and expansion of "concentrations," well-focused, encompassing, and integrative interdisciplinary programs that students could pursue in addition to their majors. The future concentration in cognitive studies would directly reflect such aims.

In 1984, 1986, and 1989, Roger Kirchner organized three Carleton symposia on artificial intelligence.[3] All three symposia included convocation speakers, followed by panel discussions and other events. Attendees included faculty from many Minnesota colleges and universities as well as computer industry representatives. In the spirit of the Sloan NLA program, the participation of Minnesota computer industries was important in assuring us that the issues we were addressing played a role in the real world of technology and were not simply the intellectual playthings of university researchers. It also acquainted us with the challenges faced by attempts to create such a technology, such as the difficulty psychologists, as knowledge engineers, faced in debriefing experts on the knowledge upon which their expertise was based.

The theme of the first Symposium on Artificial Intelligence reflected the growing importance of expert systems technology, one of the more important contributions of artificial intelligence research at the time at the cutting edge of software development and psychology. If human expertise consisted of principles acquired through experience, principles that could be formulated as a complex set of interrelated rules that could be said to make up the content of expert judgment, encoding such rules in a computer program should be at least possible in principle. Digital computers are fanatically adept at the rigorous application of rules. The knowledge of the human expert would no longer be a mystery, for a hallmark of expert systems technology was the ability of the user of such software to have the expert system explain just what rules and inferential processes it had employed in arriving at its expert conclusions, something that human experts were oftentimes unable to do.

> While all three symposia were significant successes for a small, non-urban liberal arts campus, they were accompanied by a lingering question: How could these issues regarding the formal modeling of human cognition and their technological application be made available to our students on a continuing basis?

The theme of expert systems was continued in the Second Symposium on Artificial Intelligence, featuring Victor Yu, a Carleton alumnus from the Pittsburgh School of Medicine. Victor played a significant role in the development of MYCIN, a medical expert system for the diagnosis of blood infections. Containing about 450 rules, the first versions of MYCIN performed as well as some medical experts and considerably better than junior doctors.

The theme of the Third Symposium was connectionism and its challenge to more traditional, symbol-processing models of human intelligence. Connectionism is a powerful theoretical and technological alternative to computer technologies based on the explicit encoding of rules and the manipulation of well-defined symbols at which digital computers are so adept. A connectionist cognitive model is not created by incorporating preconceived rules in a programming language, but by training a network of linked nodes to produce appropriate output on the basis of extensive training, complex learning algorithms, and distinctive network architectures.

While all three symposia were significant successes for a small, non-urban liberal arts campus, they were accompanied by a lingering question: How could these issues regarding the formal modeling of human cognition and their technological application be made available to our students on a continuing basis? Neither Roger's nor my courses touched upon connectionism. Nor did our meager course offerings provide resources for raising one all-important question: What, indeed, was the psychological reality of these amazing computer technologies? What evidence was there that such procedures adequately captured important aspects of human cognition?

Some years later mathematician Reuben Hersch (1997) provided a provocative formulation of this issue:

> What is logic? ... Is it the rules of correct thinking? Everyday experience, and ample study by psychologists, show that most of our thinking does not follow logic. This might mean that most human thinking is wrong. Or it might mean that the scope of logic is too narrow. Computing machines do almost always obey the laws of logic. That's the answer! Logic is the rules of computing machinery! Logic also applies to people when they try to be computing machines. (p. 140)

This is the sort of question we needed to pose. To do so we had to move beyond White's focus on the computer and the "technology of thought." Writing complex programs to enable computers to solve important problems was one issue. The psychological reality of such models was a question requiring greater scope. Additional faculty expertise was required in order to broaden the curricular base upon which the important issues in the field of artificial intelligence could be addressed.

As it turned out, the most important step had already been taken even before our participation in the NLA program prompted us to survey artificial intelligence and expert systems. In 1983 Kathleen Galotti had been appointed to the Carleton Psychology Department as an expert in cognitive psychology and cognitive development. One of Kathie's first courses at Carleton was an introductory psychology course, The Computer as Metaphor for the Mind. Her general expertise in cognitive psychology, her specific research in reasoning, and her knowledge of the field of cognitive science proved indispensable for the development of our future curriculum.

In the mid-1980s, Kathie's, Roger's and my interests to begin to coalesce into thoughts about a possible interdisciplinary concentration in cognitive science. It was Kathie's organizational skills and persuasiveness that led to the formal proposal of a concentration in cognitive studies and its approval in 1988 by Carleton's Educational Policy Committee. This important step gave us an institutional framework for integrating two new members of the faculty and their expertise in linguistics and cognitive science into a formal, interdisciplinary undergraduate program.

Beginning in 1983, Peter Stanley formed an advisory faculty committee to discuss the optimal form for a linguistics program at Carleton. Frank Heny, Jerry Fodor, and Thomas Sebeock all consulted with the committee. The result of our deliberations was the choice of a Chomskian model for our future program. This choice was auspicious for the future of cognitive science at Carleton for the simple reason that Chomsky's view of language made the study of the mind and its internal structure a legitimate object of inquiry and effectively defeated the extreme behaviorism that reigned in psychology into the 1950s. Michael Flynn was selected to fill the new linguistics position, and in 1986 linguistics was newly added to the Carleton curriculum. His appointment was supported by funds from a Mellon Foundation grant to support "fresh combinations," new ventures in the curriculum that responded to advances and rethinking in the central academic disciplines.

A half-time appointment in cognitive science was also created in the Carleton Psychology Department with these same funds in order to complement the growing development in cognitive science. Lloyd Komatsu was appointed to this position at the beginning of January 1985. Lloyd brought computer skills and an expert knowledge of both the psychological and philosophical aspects of the emerging cognitive sciences. His appointment was the first at Carleton to be explicitly linked with the field of cognitive science. Kathie's now widely adopted textbook in cognitive psychology, *Cognitive Psychology In and Out of the Laboratory* (originally published in 1994 and presently in its third edition), and Lloyd's important collection of classic papers in the experimental research on cognition, *Experimenting with the Mind* (1994), were the first important publications in the cognitive sciences produced by Carleton faculty

The narrative so far may give the false impression of careful step-by-step planning to develop and introduce courses, hire appropriate faculty, and pursue timely grant funding. Instead, the history of the Cognitive Studies Program directly reflects the element of serendipity. Initially, Roger's and my courses in AI were islands in the Carleton curriculum. Kathie's appointment was at first just a commendably strong appointment in the Department of Psychology.

Carleton's expression of interest in a possible linguistics program occurred well before some of these other elements. I would like to think that my interest in curricular integration, especially involving a subject in which I had a strong personal interest, helped us to assemble the pieces at hand into a coherent unity. But no master plan preceded these events. The vision we all shared grew apace with our conversations, interactions, and our shared perceptions of how we could bring together the disciplines of computer science, linguistics, psychology, philosophy, and, later, biology and the neurosciences.

When formal approval of the new concentration in cognitive studies was obtained in 1988-89, we proceeded to seek additional external funding in support of our new program. In 1988, my conversations with Sheila Biddle, program officer of the Ford Foundation, led to a Ford Foundation grant to Carleton of $240,000 to support a variety of activities in cognitive science, including library purchases and support for visits to Carleton of distinguished scholars such linguist Noam Chomsky (MIT), psychologist and cognitive scientist John MacNamara (Montreal), linguist and psychologist Stephen Pinker (MIT), and philosopher Daniel Dennett (Tufts).

In 1993 Carleton was one of several liberal arts colleges (including Smith and Wellesley) and several universities (New Hampshire, the University of Michigan, Stanford, and the University of California at San Diego) invited to participate in a workshop, supported by the National Science Foundation, that dealt with the cognitive sciences. The workshop resulted in the creation of a set of guidelines for undergraduate programs in cognitive science.[4]

Perhaps the most distinguished accomplishment of our program in cognitive science took place in the summer of 1995. Kathie Galotti, then the director of the concentration in cognitive studies, had successfully applied to the National Science Foundation for a summer grant to be administered by Carleton to support undergraduate research in cognitive science as part of the NSF's Research Experience for Undergraduates (REU) program. Carleton was the only undergraduate institution to be awarded such

> The narrative so far may give the false impression of careful step-by-step planning to develop and introduce courses, hire appropriate faculty, and pursue timely grant funding. Instead, the history of the Cognitive Studies Program directly reflects the element of serendipity.

a grant in the cognitive sciences. A total of nine undergraduates from across the country, including four Carleton students, participated. Carleton faculty who participated included Kathie Galotti and Susan Singer (principal and co-principal investigators), Sharon Akimoto, Lloyd Komatsu, and me. Susan and Sharon represented an expansion of faculty involved in the cognitive studies program to include a biologist and another psychologist.

Faculty discussion groups, centered around provocative and essential texts, continued to broaden the reach of cognitive studies in the Carleton faculty. For instance, many of the most recent generation of cognitive scientists have shown an increasing interest in Darwinian evolution questions, concentrating on issues such as the evolution of the mind, language, and communication. In 1998 more than 60 faculty responded to a suggestion from Susan Singer for a Carleton faculty discussion group focusing on Daniel Dennett's recently published book, *Darwin's Dangerous Idea*. We invited both Daniel Dennett and Stephen Jay Gould to campus (at separate times: Dennett and Gould had sparred in print over important aspects of the Darwinian theory of evolution, including its relevance for the evolution of the mind).

The strong connections between biology, philosophy, and psychology expounded in Dennett's work inspired Susan to initiate Carleton's first triad, Origins and Minds, in fall 1998. Forty-five first-term, first-year students took a set of common courses for their entire academic program. The first version of this innovative linking of courses was taught by Galotti, Komatsu, Matt Rand (Department of Biology), Singer, and me. Several years later, at Kathie Galotti's suggestion, Stephen Pinker's *The Blank Slate* served as one of the central texts in a second version of the Origins and Minds triad in fall 2004 and also provided a focus for another faculty discussion group.

THE MEANING OF INTEGRATION

What have the collaborative experiences in cognitive studies, outlined in the sections above, meant for me as a teacher and scholar of philosophy? And what of the cognitive sciences today?

An important issue in today's discussions of the nature of the mind is the question of "reductionism." The increasing sophistication of contemporary neuroscience, together with the explanatory powers of the sciences of the mind now harbored in the "cognitive sciences," might appear to justify the humanistic suspicion that science "reduces" human cognition to neurochemistry, anonymous computational processes, and abstractly innate universal grammars—features that are some distance from our actual experience. Evaluating the frequently unheeded self-criticism that transpires within the discipline of cognitive science itself requires some acquaintance with the disciplinary languages within which the criticisms are advanced and debated. It is not enough to merely hope or believe *a priori* that the various "objective" sciences of the mind capture (or fail to capture) the most valuable aspects of human cognition and experience. As teachers and scholars, we also need to know the precise nature of the perceived shortcomings from the perspectives of the explanatory models themselves. In mastering such a perspective, we also gain an increased understanding of what is distinctively human about our cognitive and cultural lives. Such an understanding represents an important means of encouraging the sciences and the humanities to engage each other productively.

However, an understanding of this internal criticism within the cognitive sciences also forces humanists to develop precise accounts of the methods of understanding they wish to contrast with those of the "objective" sciences of mind. To simply assert that human creativity, emotion, and values are mysterious realms unto themselves risks adopting a defensive posture rather than one open to enlightened inquiry. Many insightful humanists have in fact devoted intense energy to identifying just those structures of lived experience, language, culture, and history that the objective sciences of the mind seem to exclude.

The cognitive sciences offer opportunities to integrate humanistic and scientific disciplines in at least two ways. The first I will term "sympathetic integration." I will refer to the second as "integration by critical inclusion."

By sympathetic integration I mean the kind of integration that can occur when one of two fields of research changes direction in such a way that previous opposing standpoints can now be brought together. One important example of this in the cognitive sciences is the cognitive revolution in psychology. Noam Chomsky's view of language as a partially innate conceptual structure directly opposed the hegemony of behaviorism in psychology and its belief that a stimulus-response theory of learning could side-step all reference to innate cognitive content. Chomsky argued that the stimulus-response view of human learning was unable to explain rapid acquisition of a natural language by young children. A byproduct of this shift in psychology's perspective was that a new "psychology of logic" could emerge that was able to entertain the possibility that much of the structure of logic was also innate (as many philosophers from Plato to Hume and Kant had maintained), an innateness which, following Chomsky's lead, was no longer excluded from psychological inquiry.

Although it shares some of its subject matter with mathematics, logic has traditionally been central to the discipline of philosophy. Throughout its history, philosophy has been concerned with the evaluation of arguments and the codification of valid logical inferences. This tradition has been so robust that the notation of modern formal logic was adopted by the first generation of artificial intelligence enthusiasts as an obvious "first" language of "knowledge representation."

How can one represent commonsense reasoning and expert knowledge in a form that would permit computational processes to manipulate such knowledge in a useful way? The answer was that human cognition operated with a universal and innate "language of thought."

The logical form known as *modus ponens* illustrates this claim. If P implies Q, and P is in fact true, then Q necessarily follows. Since such logical forms appear to play a central role in human reasoning, we can anticipate that the computer's facility in manipulating such forms is well on the way to duplicating important essential aspects of human cognition.

A course that I initiated several years ago in our cognitive studies concentration, Logic and Minds, illustrates this relationship. Prolog is a programming language that employs logical formulae such as the one illustrated above as a basis upon which to construct a complete computer programming language. Prolog encodes a variety of computational paradigms basic to "classical" AI: computational processing that manipulates discrete symbols (Ps and Qs) in order to move from an initial problem state (why doesn't my car start?) to a solution (the spark plugs are faulty) on the basis of a set of rules (engine ignition requires fuel, spark, and compression) and given initial conditions (the gas tank is full, compression is fine, but the engine won't start).

Logic and Minds explores this view of the mind as the manipulation of symbols and rules by first introducing elementary logic and then building a flexible computational language on this foundation. One half of this course is devoted to learning the basics of logic and Prolog and to exploring applications of Prolog to a variety of standard examples of human cognitive processing, such as problem-solving, concept development, and the analysis of natural languages. Recent empirical investigations of deductive reasoning by cognitive psychologists are also incorporated into the course.

The integrative aspect of such a course is significant. Contemporary Anglo-American philosophers have written extensively upon the logical analysis of human language and the nature of the concepts embedded in language. Psychologists and linguists have also written extensively about the psychological reality of forms of deductive and inductive reasoning (recall the thought-provoking quotation from Hersch above) and the universal linguistic grammars that may underpin all natural human languages. Computational, linguistic, cultural, and psychological research are all and equally relevant to the evaluation of even the simplest Prolog programs. The result is a sympathetic integration of disciplines across the fields of computer science, linguistics, mathematics, philosophy, psychology, and anthropology in exploring and identifying well-defined cognitive processes.

The sympathetic integration to which I refer does not just take place upon an abstract conceptual level but also upon the level of skill, practical knowledge, and experience that extends beyond the limits of the traditional discipline. For example, many philosophers have dedicated themselves to acquiring skills in understanding and writing computer programs: Jerry Fodor (linguist, psychologist, and philosopher) is one example; Daniel Dennett, Paul Thagaard, and John Haugeland are others. The influence of a great portion of the history of philosophy and contemporary philosophy upon the early stages of the cognitive revolution demonstrates in depth how a single important shift in the direction of research of a single discipline (in this case, the nature and psychology of natural language) can serve as a stimulus for the coordination of areas of inquiry that had been viewed as foreign to each other.

> The influence of a great portion of the history of philosophy and contemporary philosophy upon the early stages of the cognitive revolution demonstrates in depth how a single important shift in the direction of research of a single discipline (in this case, the nature and psychology of natural language) can serve as a stimulus for the coordination of areas of inquiry that had been viewed as foreign to each other.

The fact that Chomsky himself, a vitally important influence in the development of the first symbol-processing models of artificial intelligence, clearly situated his form of linguistic analysis within the broad historical tradition of Cartesian rationalism prefigures a potential integration of a good deal of contemporary philosophy, assuredly an important element in the present-day humanities, and the objective sciences of the mind in the guise of linguistics and psychology.

I will add that my own initial interest in the cognitive sciences prompted me to first learn Fortran programming, then the Pascal and Scheme programming languages, in evening courses at the University of Minnesota (as well as courses in algebra, discrete mathematics, and calculus). I am hardly a talented programmer or mathematician, but meaningful interdisciplinary teaching requires more than simply "reading one's way into" another discipline.

"Sympathetic integration" needs to occur more often in the liberal arts curriculum. Otherwise, where research programs involving different disciplines overlap and complement each other to a significant degree, we miss an important opportunity to allow our students to experience the importance of approaching an important problem with many tools rather than a single instrument.

More important, however, is the matter of disciplinary integration that occurs by means of what I have called "integration by critical inclusion." I will first illustrate this with an example and then explore the importance of this form of integration for the recent history of cognitive science itself.

A classic analysis in the cognitive sciences is David Marr's 1982 treatment of human vision. The question Marr asked is this: How does the human mind arrive at a three-dimensional view of the world on the basis of two two-dimensional (left-eye/right-eye) images? Marr's answer (treated extensively in Carleton's course, Introduction to Cognitive Science) is cogent and complex: Three-dimensional vision is dependent upon complex computational processes and innate cognitive principles. Our perception of three-dimensional space is the result of pre-conscious computations and innate self-evident constraints, such as that a physical object cannot be in two places at the same time.

Marr's analysis is compelling. Yet he presents a highly abstract account of human perception. After all, I perceive the tiger not only as a three-dimensional object, but as a danger, as something to be avoided, as something approaching me on my left, above, crouching on the ledge of rock. It is striking that, although every image and sketch Marr provides in his account is oriented in normal perspective (the top of the object is located the top of the image, the bottom at the image's bottom), he provides no computational rule for such an orientation. Up-down, left-right, ubiquitous features of human perception are paid no heed in his computational theory.

Marr's analysis provides an abstraction from human perception. However, having said this, we must go on to ask: What *is* the nature of our perception of space? What is the meaning of *up, down, right, left, near,* and *distant*? What is the relationship between vision and action?

At this point we must confront Marr's sophisticated computational analysis of human perception with accounts derived from our own lived experience. We must ask what such abstractive accounts of perception omit and at the same time remain sensitive to the functional principles of stereoscopic vision they have identified. Here "integration" means observing what an account leaves unaccounted for, not because it may be entirely false, but because the computational paradigm it expresses is significantly limited with respect to the human experience it purports to explain and describe.

What is increasingly significant about the cognitive sciences is that this sort of critical integration has become integral to the practices of cognitive scientists themselves. What is happening in the cognitive revolution is a growing appreciation of the richness of human experience that effectively challenges different formal models proposed as explanations of this experience. What makes this appreciation "integrative," as opposed to simply being oppositional, is that the cognitive sciences themselves are in the process of constructing new explanatory frameworks that can serve as correctives for earlier theories.

The origin of cognitive science was created by a classically computational account of thought, language, and concepts that soon proved untenable because of technical and theoretical limitations. To their credit, the cognitive sciences have proceeded to elaborate alternative paradigms of human cognition: connectionism (emphasizing non-rule governed skills); robotics (emphasizing a world-organism interaction that foregoes a centrally located mind that processes symbols and manipulates rules); dynamical systems theories (that emphasize the emergence of cognitive behavior from underlying system-specific complexities), and social/cultural/behavioral theories that emphasize the communal nature of cognition. Each of these models effectively point out dimensions of human cognition and experience that competing models are ill-equipped to recognize and explain.

I must here forego a more detailed explication of the robust interaction of these competing models that is important for an additional aspect of the development of the cognitive sciences.[5] Alan Turing appeared to think of the human mind in an atomistic, Cartesian manner. The mind's resources were literally thought of as reposing "within" the individual mind itself, just as we today think of the word processing software operating on our computers as being clearly located "inside" the machine. Today, increasing attention is being paid in the cognitive sciences to the influences of culture, intersubjective communication, and embodied practical relationships of the mind to its environment. On these accounts, the mind is less a cognitive "atom" than it is a "swirl" in a larger, more encompassing field of culture, communication, and mind-world interaction.

The cognitive sciences introduce us to the realms of logic, problem solving, human practice, linguistic and cultural diversity, and intersubjective communication. The curricular space they open allows for the challenging interaction of the "sciences" and the "humanities." It would be pretentious to claim that this arena paves the way for an ultimate synthesis of all disciplines. What it does signify is a way of posing questions that can be strengthened by the availability of rigorous formal models of cognition (one hallmark of the objective sciences) that can be situated within the broader dimensions of the more traditional studies of the mind: anthropology, linguistics, philosophy, and psychology. Today's cognitive science raises questions such as: How is space perceived and experienced? What computational models of spatial experience are available? What is the relationship between thought and language? Do Mayan languages treat space in a significantly different way than European languages? Does cognition stop with processes located in the head, or does cognition involve external "scaffolding" (Clark, 1997) in the form of other minds, culture, and the external environment?

Since my own background in philosophy involves 19th- and 20th-century European philosophy, I can only be pleased by the fact that many cognitive scientists today are as likely to pay attention to continental philosophers, such as French philosopher Maurice Merleau-Ponty and German philosopher Martin Heidegger, as they are to philosophers in a distinctively different tradition, such as English philosopher Bertrand Russell or American philosopher Donald Davidson.

I find it gratifying to have participated in the evolution of an important undergraduate curriculum that integrates diverse disciplines and methodologies in this age of academic specialization and in this age of an educational philosophy stressing addition in place of integration. Above all, I profoundly appreciate the friendships and intellectual sharing with colleagues that have enriched this curricular path of disciplinary diversity and synthesis and to the many students in cognitive studies who have filled my office hours and graced my classroom. This is Carleton and liberal arts education at its very best.

ENDNOTES

[1] Courses taught in this program included The Poetics of the Divine, The Socratic Turn, Reason and Revelation, Origins of Modern Science, The Rise of the Social Sciences, and The Darwinian Revolution.

[2] Lisp is the name of the first widely used computer language for artificial intelligence applications and is an abbreviation for "list-processing."

[3] Carleton's archivist, Eric Hillemann, has been invaluable in refreshing my memory of these events with materials from the college archives. We are fortunate to have recordings of all symposium addresses available in the Carleton Archives.

[4] Our complete report and the full list of participants can be accessed at http://www//helios.hampshire.edu/~nasCCS/nsfreport

[5] For a more detailed account, see my El Destronamiento de la Razón (pp. 55-70) in Roy Elveton (Ed.). (2005). II Congreso Internacional de Filosofia: Educación para la Democracia Participativa: Paradojas en la Lógica de la Globalización. Guatemala City, Guatemala: Universidad Rafael Landívar.

REFERENCES

Abelson, H., Sussman, G. J., & Sussman, J. (1985). *Structure and interpretation of computer programs.* Cambridge, MA: MIT Press.

Association of American Colleges. (1985). *Integrity in the college curriculum: A report to the academic community.* Washington, D.C.

Bloom, H. (1987). *The closing of the American mind: How higher education has failed democracy and impoverished the souls of today's students.* New York: Simon and Schuster.

Boyer, E. L. (1987). *College: The undergraduate experience.* New York: Harper & Row.

Carleton College academic catalog 2005-2006: Cognitive studies concentration (CGST). Retrieved April 16, 2006, from http://apps.carleton.edu/catalog/catalog.php3?dept=CGST&year=2005.

Clark, A. (1997). *Being there: Putting brain, body and mind together again.* Cambridge: MIT Press.

Galotti, K. (2003). *Cognitive psychology in and out of the laboratory* (3rd ed.). Belmont, CA: Wadsworth/Thomson Learning.

Hersch, R. (1997). *What is mathematics really?* Oxford: Oxford University Press.

Hirsch, E. D. (1987). *Cultural literacy: What every American needs to know.* Boston: Houghton Mifflin.

Komatsu, L. K. (1994). *Experimenting with the mind: Readings in cognitive psychology.* Pacific Grove, CA: Brooks/Cole.

Marr, D. (1982). *Vision: A computational investigation into the human representation and processing of visual information.* San Francisco: W.H. Freeman and Company.

White, S. (1981). The new liberal arts. In J. D. Koerner (Ed.), *The new liberal arts. An exchange of views* (pp. 1-12). New York: Alfred P. Sloan Foundation.

Zemsky, R. (1989). *Structure and coherence: Measuring the undergraduate curriculum* Washington, D.C.: Association of American Colleges.

STUDENT-FACULTY RESEARCH COLLABORATIONS

A MODEL FOR COLLABORATIVE UNDERGRADUATE RESEARCH:

Integrating Disciplines and Institutions to Better Understand the Earth's Atmosphere

Deborah S. Gross

T he stereotypical picture of a scientist is of an older male, dressed in a white coat (maybe sporting a pocket protector), sitting at a lab bench observing something in a glass apparatus that is often bubbling menacingly and might be emitting smoke (Finson, 2002). He watches the apparatus and writes something down in a cryptic code in his trusty notebook. He analyses his results alone (and secretively) and goes on to publish them, with much fanfare, resulting in a fundamental change in the way the rest of the scientists in his field see this man's work. This process has the greatest impact if these results scoop those of other scientists working on the same or similar projects.

As a female scientist who works with other scientists on large-scale research projects, where data-sharing is a must, I am constantly amused at the significant distance between myself and this picture. And yet I still consider myself a scientist!

> The most immediate challenge that I am faced with in these collaborations ... has to do with language. Chemists and engineers don't necessarily speak the same language, and neither chemists nor engineers speak the language of computer scientists.

My group's research is both dependent on and centered on collaborations, and we collaborate with researchers outside of Carleton College and within the college. When I say "we," I mean my group at Carleton, which consists of my research students and myself; we too constitute a collaboration.

As my situation is by no means unique and the pervasive stereotype of scientists is so far from the mark, it is valuable to explore the dramatic disconnect between the stereotype and the reality. Especially at undergraduate institu-

DEBORAH S. GROSS, associate professor of chemistry, joined the Carleton faculty in 1998. She earned her B.A. degree at Haverford College and her PhD degree at University of California, Berkeley.

tions, where our goal is to train students to become contributing members of the modern world, we must make a conscious effort to update which picture of that world we give to students. More importantly, we should update their experience of that world and then encourage students to engage with it and really become a part of it.

In the sciences, research experiences, though challenging for a variety of reasons (Csizmar Dalal and Musicant, 2007), provide the best opportunities for students to truly be scientists. Most scientists work with others through membership in a particular research group, either in academia or in industry. As science addresses more interdisciplinary problems, it is becoming increasingly important for these research groups to work with each other as well.

This model of groups working together, either within disciplines or across disciplines, is becoming especially common at research universities. However, it is not the rule at undergraduate institutions such as Carleton, where research opportunities can be somewhat limited by the pace at which research is carried out. At undergraduate institutions, most research groups operate alone or with individual points of contact to larger groups at other institutions, and most interactions with other research groups involve giving or obtaining help with a particular skill or technique, for instance by running a series of analyses on equipment at a larger institution. Rarely do the groups work together as equals to address different aspects of the same research problem.

In contrast to the typical research model at undergraduate institutions, my research group focuses on addressing a large issue with a specialized method: gaining a better understanding of the particulate matter (or aerosols) in the atmosphere, using a powerful measurement technique that few researchers in the world have access to, the Aerosol Time-of-Flight Mass Spectrometer (ATOFMS). I have this equipment in my lab (see Figure 1). Thus, we can offer unique skills and types of data to a study of the atmosphere.

Because the atmosphere is such a complex system to study, few researchers "go it alone" regardless of the instrumentation required—atmospheric chemistry is a highly collaborative field in general. Much of the fundamental understanding of the aerosol particles in the atmosphere (and other factors as well) has come from results obtained from large field studies. These studies are designed to bring together many researchers, using similar, complementary, and disparate methods, to measure the atmosphere at the same place and/or time. Thus, rich data sets are created, and complicated processes are put in place both to analyze one's own data and to participate actively in the sharing

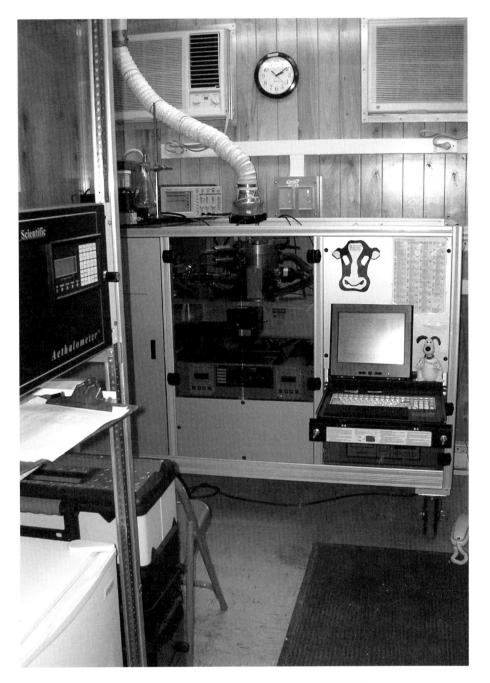

Figure 1. The Aerosol Time-of-Flight Mass Spectrometer (ATOFMS)

The ATOFMS, located at the U. S. Environmental Protection Agency (EPA)-funded Midwest Particulate Matter Supersite in East St. Louis, Illinois, December 2003: The white tube descending from the roof is bringing ambient air into the instrument for measurements.

of one's data so that other groups can use it to further understand their own work. This is a very different model from the one used by the majority of laboratory-based scientists and certainly different from the behavior of the stereotypical scientist, as it includes many groups bringing their own expertise to bear on a large problem and trying to form a unified, larger picture of the system.

In this essay, I will explore the advantages and disadvantages of doing science in such a collaborative way at an undergraduate institution like Carleton. This will include exploration of the benefits and challenges of engaging in these research collaborations, both for the faculty and the undergraduate students involved. After describing what it is that we do, I will address each of these topics and try to consolidate my experience into a series of suggestions for faculty members who are interested in establishing large-scale research collaborations of this type.

TYPES OF COLLABORATIONS

I am trained as a chemist. My research interests in the field of atmospheric chemistry are increasingly interdisciplinary and fall within the larger realm of atmospheric science. Although the name of the field makes it sound more like a narrow subset of chemistry, atmospheric chemistry is in reality a broad field that interacts directly with research carried out by engineers, physicists, meteorologists, climatologists, and others. Atmospheric science, and especially the study of particulate matter in which I am engaged, has until recently been dominated by engineers. When the need for a chemical understanding of the particulates began to emerge, in addition to the already well-developed physical understanding, chemists became increasingly involved.

Over the past few years, my research in atmospheric science has included collaborations with a wide variety of people: 16 Carleton undergraduates, all sophomore, junior, or senior chemistry majors; a Carleton computer science faculty member and the eight computer science undergraduates who have been working with him; two research groups at the University of Minnesota, in the Department of Mechanical Engineering; and two research groups at the University of Wisconsin–Madison, one in the Environmental Chemistry and Technology Program and one in the Department of Computer Sciences. Through my projects with these collaborators, I have also come to interact in scientifically significant ways with a broad array of other researchers in my field, especially those who have hosted field experiments in which my group has participated.

A typical collaborative project starts this way: I have discussions with someone about possible research collaborations, and we meet or communicate regularly for some months to refine the idea and generate a grant proposal. If the proposal receives funding, we then have to discuss more details, figure out where and with whom our experiments will be conducted, determine the solutions to the logistical challenges of moving a lot of air sampling equipment to a new location (including shelter, power, accommodation for instrument operators, etc.), and figure out when the experiments should be carried out. This all takes a significant amount of time and effort, especially the logistical details. Then, of course, we have to carry out the experiments, analyze the results, and find time to meet to discuss them. Finally, the results have to be consolidated for presentation at conferences and publication in the literature. The process repeats for multi-part projects, and can go on for many years.

The students in my research group are largely shielded from the organizational aspects of these projects for a few reasons: Their research horizons are typically too short, as the planning for a project typically occurs at least two years before funding might arrive, and they don't yet have the experience necessary to identify worthwhile research questions in the field. Instead, their role is in actively participating in the planning for each excursion, carrying out the experiments, analyzing the data, and contributing to the discussions of the larger interpretation of the whole datasets.

CHALLENGES OF COLLABORATIONS

The most immediate challenge that I am faced with in these collaborations, beyond the logistical aspects of arranging locations for measurements and finding the time to get together with my collaborators to discuss the projects, has to do with language. Chemists and engineers don't necessarily speak the same language, and neither chemists nor engineers speak the language of computer scientists. This creates challenges as we plan experiments and discuss the next steps and as we create a conceptual framework in which to think about the project as a whole. In our meetings and discussions, we spend a great deal of time asking each other to repeat and elaborate on ideas and plans we mention, to give us multiple perspectives on our collaborators' thought processes. This process helps us to learn how to understand these other languages, even if we cannot yet speak them. In addition, we each have to grapple with how much of the detail of our own piece of the project should be offered to the conversation.

In addition to the language difficulties, there are significant differences in approach taken by each of these types of scientists. When I have a set of data that I want to analyze in a particular way, because I know that this has worked for similar data in the past and should also yield fruitful results in this case, my computer science colleagues look for a generalized rule for how to analyze all data of this type. While my first instinct might be to say, "There is no way to generalize this!" and go off to analyze it myself, this reaction doesn't move a collaboration forward.

As a result, I have found myself spending a great deal of time thinking about how to generalize my approaches to various kinds of data analysis, in order to make them more compatible with the techniques and methods that my collaborators are comfortable with, while at the same time pressing forward the idea that much of what we do in analyzing our own data, which might appear to be based on instinct, is in fact based on years of experience.

> Collaborations with undergraduate research students offer a different linguistic challenge.... I have the opportunity to help them learn the language of research in atmospheric chemistry while also trying to teach them the more general language of scientific research.

Collaborations with undergraduate research students offer a different linguistic challenge. Rather than having to find the overlaps between my atmospheric chemistry language and their "other science" languages, instead I have the opportunity to help them learn the language of research in atmospheric chemistry while also trying to teach them the more general language of scientific research. This is a huge challenge and takes significant time and effort.

Traditional science courses don't prepare students for real research, and most students haven't had the opportunity to take many courses that offer "research-like" experiences before they sign on to a summer research project. It is typically not until students arrive in the research lab that they are confronted with addressing an unanswered portion of a large research question. In undergraduate research, we often measure our students' research experiences in units of summers, as that is the time when they can work in a concentrated manner and really learn the project and its context. Typically, more than half of the summer is spent in vocabulary-building exercises, helping the students to learn how to think and talk about their projects and how to engage with them on the appropriate scientific level. During the remainder of the summer and any subsequent time during the following academic year, the students can use their new-found fluency to contribute to the research conversation.

Another significant challenge associated with the particular types of collaborations that I engage in comes from the fact that my collaborators are at research universities and have laboratories full of graduate students, postdoctoral researchers, and staff scientists working full-time on their pieces of the project. I have only two or three undergraduates working with me at any given time, and we are trying to carry out our portion of the project.

This challenge turns into a terrific benefit for the students who work in my lab (see below), but it also means that summer, the only period in which I can realistically dedicate concentrated time to research, is not the only time that I can be making real progress on it. I have to continually push myself and my research students to maintain productivity, even while teaching and taking courses and doing all of the other activities that make up the very busy academic year at Carleton. I jokingly refer to my research as a bus that's driving fast down a highway. I picture myself hanging on to the back by my fingernails, feet flying, just trying to stay on it. It often feels this overwhelming. To sustain this pace, winter and spring breaks are often periods of frantic work, either collecting data or working to analyze and discuss it, to make up for our limited time during the academic terms.

The effort that my group and I expend to stay caught up is really an effort to prove that we can be valued contributors to these larger projects. We know that our scientific contribution is unique—we have equipment that very few people have and can therefore provide a type of data that is rich with information and not easily added to most studies—but we need to demonstrate that our ability to contribute is not hampered by our lack of specialized personnel or sustained effort throughout the year. This translates into pushing myself hard to keep up and into pushing my research students extremely hard to continue to produce results.

When I first started working at Carleton, I was nervous about pushing the students this hard. I have found, however, something that is no real surprise to my colleagues here: Our students are definitely up to this challenge. I have routinely asked sophomores and juniors to contribute to projects as if they were graduate students, and they routinely succeed at it, with aplomb. The fact that the students are bright, engaged, and extremely capable helps a great deal. The fact that they don't know that what I am asking them to do is somewhat beyond the norm may help as well.

The act of collaborating with other researchers constantly provides me with both a carrot and a stick: It's exciting to be able to participate in the research questions that I am involved in through my collaborations, but I also need to be sure that I am contributing my fair share to the collaborations, to hold up my side of the deal. This can lead to significant pressure, whether self-induced or externally generated, because of the need to get something particular done by a specific deadline.

BENEFITS OF COLLABORATIONS

It takes a great deal of time to carry out significant research at a college like Carleton, where the research workforce is entirely untrained undergraduate students and infrastructure support is minimal. It takes even more time to negotiate the details of joint projects with collaborators at Carleton and the most time to do so with collaborators at other institutions. All of these factors make my research, which progresses slowly enough as it is, go even more slowly.

Given that, I often ask myself "why collaborate?" The answer is always the same and is easy. Without collaborations, and more importantly, without *collaborators*, my research would go nowhere. In my research, we are interested in questions about the composition of the atmosphere that are simply too large to address on our own. Thus, research in my group must include initiating, shaping, and maintaining relationships with faculty and scientists all over the world and the students and postdoctoral researchers who work with them. The extra piece that working at Carleton adds to this process is the full integration of my undergraduate student researchers into this process. My students are full participants in the collaborations—on the same level as graduate students in groups at universities. They are, in fact, doing much of the work, once (and sometimes before) they've learned enough to get started.

An interesting aspect of my collaborations is that they sustain my research financially, as well as scientifically. Without the ability to submit joint proposals (from Carleton and from a research university) to funding agencies, to support equipment purchases and research endeavors, it is unlikely that we would be funded to do what we are doing today.

I am trying to do large-scale research at a small liberal arts college, and it is challenging to get this funded in the atmospheric chemistry realm. Currently, none of my research funding comes from programs earmarked for research with undergraduates. Without the connections that active collaborations and joint proposals demonstrate, it would be virtually impossible to convince funding agencies that our contributions could be meaningful. Comments from reviewers on proposals that I submitted individually, before my collaborations were established, were full of statements such as "no matter how smart and capable Carleton students are, that research just can't be done at an undergraduate institution."

While I can easily argue with statements such as this, with excellent data to back me up, it doesn't mean that funding agencies and reviewers can or will be convinced. However, it is also true that if we were working on our own, with no contacts with other researchers and no joint projects that could grow to be larger than each of our contributions, we wouldn't really deserve funding. We wouldn't be able to address interesting research questions on our own (nobody can!), and our data would be isolated—we would not have other, complementary data with which to compare and expand our understanding.

Finally, research at an undergraduate institution, where there is typically little or no overlap in research areas among the faculty, can be somewhat isolating. By collaborating with others within the college or at research universities, my research group gets connected to a research community that is otherwise hard to find. Connections to faculty at research universities can be tremendously useful in terms of obtaining advice and logistical support—especially with field work, in which my research group is engaged. Also, when we encounter something new that we need help thinking about, we have a ready-made network of people to contact.

I find that connections with faculty at my home institution are equally powerful, providing me with a venue for discussing (rather than just presenting) my thoughts about research questions and topics with someone who is both local and knowledgeable. The community that exists when working with another research group at Carleton goes a long way toward minimizing the isolation that is inherent in research at an undergraduate institution.

STUDENTS' EXPERIENCES OF RESEARCH COLLABORATIONS

All of the issues that I have discussed above motivate me to seek out and sustain research collaborations. However, in my experience, the greatest benefits accrue to the undergraduate students who work on the projects in my lab. They get experience with all of the more obvious skills that students learn when participating in research, such as how to deal with a complex problem, how to work toward an indefinite (and often undefined) answer, how to work as part of a research group with common goals, how to operate and maintain sophisticated scientific equipment, and how to analyze complicated multi-dimensional data.

In addition, however, the students who work in my research group also get to learn how to work and communicate with other scientists who are not doing exactly what they do but whose work is closely related. They have to learn to take tremendous responsibility for their experiments, by working in the field away from their usual support networks. Most importantly, they have to take responsibility for analyzing their data (and sometimes the data of their predecessors at Carleton, due to the time it takes to fully analyze our data), and comparing it to that of others. And, of course, they have to learn to collaborate.

I can best describe the level of responsibility that my students take on within the environment of my research group by describing two exemplary research students, who I will call Laura and Rose. Both students were in the same graduating class of chemistry majors at Carleton.

Laura worked in my research group for three summers, starting after her sophomore year (the third summer was half-time), and Rose worked in the group for the summer after her junior year. During these summers and the intervening academic terms, Laura participated in five multi-week research trips and presented her research at two major conferences. Rose participated in two multi-week research trips and presented her research at one major conference.

Laura's first trip was a summer 2002 study in Atlanta, Georgia, where Laura, another student, and I worked together with a group from the University of Minnesota on two projects. We spent six weeks in Atlanta as part of the Aerosol Nucleation and Real-time Characterization Experiment (ANARChE 2002), a study involving about 25 people from 10 universities and labs, and I was with the group for most of the time. We ran our own instrument and also worked with one jointly owned by the University of Minnesota and Carleton College that we were modifying to obtain different data. This is where Laura really learned to run and troubleshoot the instrument.

Her next trip was to the University of Wisconsin–Madison, where she and I worked with a staff scientist in the Environmental Chemistry and Technology Program to determine the ability of our instrument to detect mercury and other metals within laboratory-generated aerosol particles. The work was exacting and precise. She and I set up the experiments together, and after the first few days I left her to work with the group in Madison on her own.

The following summer, Laura was joined by Rose and a third student. The three of them went, without me, on a six-week-long odyssey through southern Colorado and up into Yellowstone National Park, measuring aerosol particles at three different sites. They were in the company of our collaborators from the University of Wisconsin–Madison and the U.S. Geological Survey (USGS) for the whole trip, but they were completely in charge of our group's measurements. All three students were at the first of the three measurement sites, Laura and Rose went to the second, and only Rose went to Yellowstone, bearing complete responsibility for our two-week measurements there herself.

The following winter, Rose set up our instrument in East St. Louis for three months of measurements. I joined her shortly after it was set up. I found her not only working with our instrument but also designing and carrying out measurements for our USGS collaborators as well, drawing on the experience she had gained in Yellowstone National Park the previous summer. She and I trained staff at this site to run our instrument and came home. Laura went down two weeks later on her own, to check that everything was working as planned and to do some detailed calibration of the instrument.

The following summer, after both Laura and Rose graduated, Laura worked half-time through the summer, including participating in a month of field measurements at a site near Madison, Wisconsin, while Rose was preparing to go off to graduate school. During this study, Laura and I, accompanied by two new students, set up the experiment in Wisconsin. We all spent a few days together getting the new students up to speed. Then we spent the next month taking turns spending three to four days with the instrument, checking that it was working appropriately and analyzing our data. Laura's and Rose's conference presentations stemmed from work done during many of these field experiments.

The work done by these two students sounds like it comes from the résumés of a pair of graduate students. Rose has gone on to do graduate work in chemistry, and Laura is currently employed as a research assistant in a geochemistry lab at a major research university. As their research advisor, I was asked to provide recommendations for both students when they applied for their current positions. It was easy to discuss how their research experiences in my group have prepared them well for future scientific work. Both have gained tremendous experience working independently as well as working as

> The work done by these two students sounds like it comes from the résumés of a pair of graduate students.... They are experienced working as part of a large-scale collaboration, which most students at their stage of education are not.

the local expert on a particular technique within a group of experts focusing on a large-scale question. They are experienced working as part of a large-scale collaboration, which most students at their stage of education are not.

Since Laura and Rose graduated, my research group has expanded the type of collaborations we are engaged in. Rather than working solely with other groups who measure other pieces of the puzzle that is the atmosphere, we have begun a significant collaboration with two groups of computer scientists, one at Carleton College and one at the University of Wisconsin–Madison.

This collaboration began in an interesting manner. My long-time collaborator at the University of Wisconsin–Madison mentioned that he had discussed the complexities of our large atmospheric data sets with a computer scientist there, and they wondered about submitting a proposal to develop new methods to carry it out. I was very interested, and knew of a computer scientist at Carleton—Dave Musicant—who not only had a background in data mining (and had obtained his Ph. D. in the Madison department), but who was rumored to be interested in finding new research collaborations. He was friendly with a visiting professor in the Carleton Chemistry Department, who had mentioned this to me in passing. I called him up and invited him to participate, and our collaborative project has been funded since 2004.

My research students have significant weekly interactions with the computer science group at Carleton, which consists of a faculty member and three research students. This interaction is organized slightly differently from the atmospheric science collaborations that we maintain, in that the goals are different and the type of skills that we each offer are not parallel. This collaboration can best be described as atmospheric scientists enticing the computer scientists to help us solve our complex data analysis problems. This is a research problem for the computer scientists, not just a request for software tools, because our data are complex in ways that require the development of new kinds of algorithms, in addition to the application of developed algorithms in new situations.

This collaboration is much more cross-disciplinary than those I maintain with atmospheric scientists and is characterized by many meetings and discussions. The computer science group and my atmospheric chemistry group get together regularly to report to each other on what we are doing and to discuss our research needs. We get together multiple times per year with our colleagues at the University of Wisconsin–Madison. We atmospheric chemists need to show the computer scientists what it is that we need to do with our

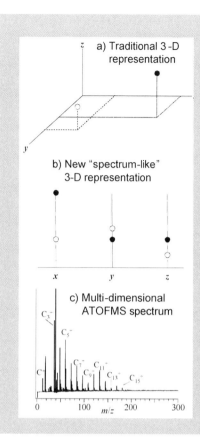

Figure 2.

The traditional way in which multi-dimensional data is visualized, shown in (a) for two three-dimensional data points, as compared to the graphical method the computer scientists developed after working with ATOFMS spectra (b). Each dimension in the data is represented in (b) by a vertical line, and the value of the data point in that dimension is indicated by the height of the point on the vertical axis. For comparison, an example of the data format displayed by the ATOFMS instrument in my research laboratory is shown in (c). This is approximately 300 dimensional data, which would be extremely challenging to represent as a single point as done in part (a). Instead, in the ATOFMS spectrum, each dimension is represented by a value on the x-axis, with the y-value indicating the value associated with each dimension.

data and the processes we have developed to analyze and understand it, so that they can determine appropriate areas in which to concentrate their efforts. The computer scientists then work their particular brand of magic and create usable data analysis tools. These are fed back to my research students to test out. The cycle repeats. These experiences require that each group of students (and the faculty who work with them) learn to think in the language of the other. If we can't explain our data and our analysis process to the computer scientists, they can't work on the problem our data presents. If they can't explain the algorithms they are developing in such a way that we can understand them, then we can't properly evaluate their usefulness.

We typically think we're aware of the situations in which our thinking is heavily influenced by the fact that we are communicating with collaborators who speak a different research language. However, when I look back, I see obvious situations where our significant cross-disciplinary interactions have shaped the way each group of us has approached things within our own discipline. Within the atmospheric chemistry group, this is mostly seen in our efforts to be more systematic in how we approach problems and to come up with more clearly-defined protocols for our analysis techniques.

While this is not required for us to do what we need to do, the usefulness of creating a catalog of our data analysis methods has clearly been shown to us through the conversations we have had with the computer scientists. It has the added benefit of helping create continuity of methods even though the students working in the group change every year.

In a recent meeting of my group and our computer science colleagues at

Deborah's Hints for a Successful Research Collaboration in Science, for Faculty at Primarily Undergraduate Institutions

- **Don't be shy.** If there are people in your field or a related one that you want to work with, call them up! Think about what you can offer and how you would like to interact before you initiate contact.

- **Do be realistic.** Life is busy, and undergraduate students are initially untrained in your field. If you promise to contribute too much to a collaborative project, you'll find it impossible to accomplish, and the experience won't be a useful one. Be sure to ask your students to contribute a reasonable amount. I ask a lot of my students, but I work hard to be sure that what I ask of them is realistic, given their experience level. You can only figure out what is reasonable by seeing how the students do and adjusting what you expect them to contribute based on how they are doing.

- **Do seek joint funding.** Major funding agencies have multiple mechanisms for funding collaborations. You can prepare companion proposals to submit together, or a single proposal can be written to describe the entire joint project. In my case, our projects are not easily separable into "my research question" and "their research question," so we tend to write one proposal that originates from the research university and includes a subcontract to fund my research group. Don't feel restricted to seeking funding from programs earmarked for research at undergraduate institutions.

- **Don't feel like a "poor relation."** The cost of doing research at an undergraduate institution is significantly lower than at a research university—we don't have graduate students to pay! Even though the dollar amount coming to my research group is smaller than that going to other groups working on the same project, I am still a full contributor to the project and therefore should have as much say in it as any other principal investigator.

Carleton, the computer scientists realized that a novel way that they had been visualizing the results from one of their experiments was directly influenced by the time they have spent working with our atmospheric data—in effect, they transformed a difficult-to-display output into a form that looked like a single unit of our data, although there is no similarity between them (see Figure 2). They had not consciously set out to do this but instead found that their approach had been influenced by the time they've spent in our world. We are successfully learning each others' language or somehow creating a hybrid language that lets us work together successfully on a complicated problem.

- **Do remember who benefits.** The reason I do research while at an undergraduate institution is to teach students what it is really like to be a scientist. I am of course interested in the research questions that I am working on, but this is only a secondary motivation. If the collaboration doesn't create opportunities to do your research better and therefore to provide a better experience for your students, then it's not a useful one.

- **Do expand your horizons.** It's less fun to collaborate with people who do what you do—there's less to learn. The terrific benefits of collaborative research emerge when you join forces with someone whose expertise complements your own—then you can tackle broader research questions. Because of the interdisciplinary nature of my research area, I don't collaborate with anyone from my discipline, and my significant collaborators on the atmospheric science side are all in departments that are not even represented at Carleton.

- **Do make connections at home.** It's both wonderful and exhausting to be part of a research community at a university. But unless you are strategically located so that you can meet regularly and really feel a part of the larger research team, it helps to try to recruit other research-active faculty at your home institution to join in the project, as well. This generates a research community on your home campus, one that your students will likely be more directly involved in. I was able to accomplish this through the computer science collaboration.

- **Do find your niche**. It's unlikely that you can do everything while also teaching full time at an undergraduate institution. I have been able to maximize my role in collaborative research by working with fantastic collaborators and also by specializing in a type of measurement that is both of interest to others and rare. This gets me in the door and ensures that I can contribute something important to the project.

CONCLUSIONS

On pp. 118-119, I present a number of suggestions for faculty who are interested in establishing collaborative projects with faculty on and off campus. I urge them to pursue them. Collaborative research offers rich experiences to undergraduate students and faculty alike. By establishing and maintaining collaborative projects with a broad array of researchers, both on and off campus, we can not only access research and resources not available at a typical undergraduate institution but also provide undergraduate research students with an experience that truly represents what they might experience if they proceed in scientific research.

REFERENCES

Csizmar Dalal, A., and Musicant, D. (2007). Engaging students in research: Building community in computer science. In C. Rutz & M. Savina (Eds.), *Building intellectual community through collaboration* (pp. 121-139). Northfield, MN: College City Publications.

Finson, K. D. (2002). Drawing a scientist: What we do and do not know after fifty years of drawings. *School Science and Mathematics, 102*(7), 335-345.

Engaging Students in Research: Building Community in Computer Science

Amy Csizmar Dalal and David R. Musicant

CHALLENGES AND REWARDS: WHY RESEARCH?

Those of us who teach at liberal arts colleges do so because we love to teach. The time and energy we spend on teaching and on service responsibilities cut into what we can devote to research pursuits.

In addition, conducting research at a liberal arts college can be somewhat isolating. In Carleton's small departments, each faculty member is often the sole local expert in a particular subfield. Like country doctors in the Old West, faculty find themselves wearing many different hats and representing wider and wider permutations of their subfields in order to staff the appropriate electives for students.

This diversity is quite good for our students: With only a few faculty members on campus in each department, their having a variety of research interests helps to ensure that students have the opportunity to study as many different ideas as possible. As a result, though, faculty find that we have no one else on campus with research areas professionally close enough to ours to engage in high-level academic conversations or collaboration.

> As teachers, we all live for the times in our students' lives when the wheels start to turn, where the ideas start connecting, and where the subject finally becomes tangible. Research is one way in which these moments can be facilitated.

Larger than faculty time-management and isolation issues looms the is-

AMY CSIZMAR DALAL, assistant professor of computer science, joined the Carleton faculty in 2003. She earned her B.S. degree at the University of Notre Dame and M.S. and PhD degrees at Northwestern University. DAVID R. MUSICANT, associate professor of computer science, earned his B.S. degrees at Michigan State University and M.A., M.S. and PhD degrees at the University of Wisconsin, Madison. He has been a member of the Carleton faculty since 2000.

sue of having personnel available for research projects. Our students are smart, enthusiastic, and eager to learn, but they are not as highly trained or highly specialized as graduate students. The students in this potential pool of researchers have not had the luxury of taking advanced courses related to any one research area. The intensity of our 10-week terms limits both the time and the energy that students can devote to any particular research project with us. Unlike the graduate school "apprentice" model, where graduate students sign on to work with an adviser for years, our students are liberated "free agents" who work on a project for one or more terms or perhaps over a summer.

Despite the complexities and challenges in doing research in such an environment, we have found that having students work with us on our research is a remarkably positive experience and that the payoff is quite high. The collaboration benefits both parties—faculty and students. The end results, though possibly vastly different from what we came to expect from our PhD experiences, are unmistakable, and they can be life-changing for both the students and the faculty members.

Within the Computer Science Department at Carleton, we have been dealing with a number of the challenges mentioned above and have worked hard to overcome them. We are excited about the community-building ideas that we incorporate in our research programs and have found significant success in making undergraduate research a strong and positive experience for our students.

Before we discuss the benefits of doing research with undergraduates, we should define what it means to "do" research as a computer scientist.

Computer science, especially when it is considered as one of the liberal arts, is perhaps best described as the study of formal processes for solving problems. These processes for solving problems, known as algorithms, are somewhat like recipes for baking a cake or directions for navigating on road trips. Computers are wonderful at carrying out algorithms for us, and so they act as a remarkable testing and implementation environment for the algorithms that we create.

While programming computers is interesting, engaging, and fun, programming only describes one aspect of computer science. Computer science research involves not only the design and implementation of algorithms, but also the application of these algorithms to a whole host of real-world problems.

For example, Amy's research interests are in computer networking, specifically regarding streaming media. Have you ever had the experience of watching a video stream on the Internet and seeing it deteriorate? Amy is interested in understanding better how we can automatically determine when a stream is about to deteriorate so that preemptive measures can be taken to improve the situation.

Dave's research interests are in the fields of data mining and machine learning, which address how to automatically find ways to simplify, summarize, and find patterns within large sets of data. Dave is currently collaborating with chemistry professor Deborah Gross in tracking down patterns in atmospheric data (Gross, 2007). Similarly, Dave and Amy are currently collaborating to better understand the relationship between video streaming data and how people rate the quality of such streams.

When we include students in our research work, they are the obvious beneficiaries of such collaborations. Doing research integrates students more fully into the fabric of our disciplines. It helps to create a particular type of community among the students, where students study and have fun together.

When students choose a major, furthermore, they often look at the interactions between students and faculty members. Undergraduate research within a department helps to build bonds between those students who participate in it and provides an example—a community of "student scholars"—for younger students to observe. When undergraduate research occurs regularly and successfully, it can have a powerful effect on recruiting majors. Prospective majors see that the major provides opportunities for close interaction with faculty and other students in a professional capacity outside the classroom. Here, we follow the example of the Chemistry Department at Carleton, which has done an excellent job in weaving student research into the fabric of the major (Gross, 2007).

Research also facilitates those "a-ha!" moments, where a student finally makes the connections among the concepts learned in various classes over the course of his or her time at Carleton or is able to connect a real-world phenomenon to a specific theoretical concept.

> **Amy:** For me, one of the coolest moments is when I show a student how to use a software package called a "sniffer" to view data in real time as it flows across a computer network. Even students who have taken a computer networking course with me, who understand, in theory, how computer networks operate, are completely awestruck by the sight of real, live data going back and forth from one computer to another. For many students, it's an epiphany.

As teachers, we all live for the times in our students' lives when the wheels start to turn, where the ideas start connecting, and where the subject finally becomes tangible. Research is one way in which these moments can be facilitated. Because students are forced to work with whatever existing frame of reference they bring to the project, they need to make connections between what they already know and what they observe. This in turn, we hope, provides them with a more connected view of the field as a whole.

Research gives students a greater perspective on the field itself and on what they can *do* as computer scientists. Often, it allows students to meet people outside their major department and outside the college who are actually working as computer scientists.

For instance, Dave's atmospheric chemistry project involves faculty and students in Carleton's Chemistry Department, as well as colleagues from the University of Wisconsin–Madison (Gross, 2007). Students get the experience of working indirectly with other researchers in the field who they may or may not ever meet. This lets students participate as part of a larger project than the one they immediately see before them, as well as learn from a larger set of researchers than just their advisers and fellow students.

> One benefit to the faculty member of working with undergraduates is that it helps combat faculty isolation. Over time, students become our peers: They learn enough to have deep and meaningful conversations with faculty about their research material.

Students also gain perspective by attending research conferences, where they witness computer science in action and hear about cutting-edge work being done in the field. Sometimes students present their work, communicating their ideas and receiving feedback from colleagues. But even just attending a conference allows students to take part in a community of people working on projects similar to their own, something which can provide a significant confidence boost.

Dave: The Grace Hopper Celebration of Women in Computing is a conference aimed at celebrating the role that women play in computing fields. It provides many significant opportunities for our students, most notably showing them a large community of women computer scientists that they don't necessarily see immediately around them. The content of the Grace Hopper conference is both technical and societal: Some of the talks are by women in computer science presenting their cutting edge research work, whereas other talks relate to important societal issues involving women in computing.

Our students get really fired up by the technical talks. The 2004 Grace Hopper Conference provided a significant "adrenaline shot" to one student in particular, a young woman who had been doing research with us and thus was primed to understand and appreciate some of the talks she saw. At the 2002 conference, two female majors presented a poster on research work that they had done at Carleton. Both have since gone on to graduate school. We believe that this project and the opportunity to present their work played a role in helping them make that choice.

How faculty members benefit from this collaboration is not as obvious. After all, getting students up to speed and keeping them motivated, as we will see later on in this essay, can be very time-consuming, and undergraduates are rarely able to produce the same kind of sophisticated results as graduate students. But undergraduate research does have a net positive impact on the final research product.

One benefit to the faculty member of working with undergraduates is that it helps to combat faculty isolation. Over time, students become our peers: They learn enough to have deep and meaningful conversations with faculty about their research material. Working with students (and thus thinking about research problems creatively) also leads to interesting and unexpected collaborations among faculty members. For instance, an idea for obtaining Hughes' (Howard Hughes Medical Institute) summer funding for two students led to a collaboration between Dave and Amy. Similarly, funding from a program designed to encourage research among female undergraduates led to a collaboration between Dave and computer science professor Jeff Ondich. These collaborations allow us to learn more about different subfields within our disciplines and get us thinking about our own fields in new and exciting ways.

More importantly, though, undergraduate research changes how faculty members view our own research. It forces us to think more carefully about research problems, boil down the big questions into smaller questions more quickly, and resolve detailed issues at a faster pace than before. Doing this can give us a different perspective on a research problem, solidify our own thinking about the problem and its possible solutions, and illuminate how solving the problem will change the field for the better.

Breaking down the big questions for students in order to try to find appropriately scaled projects for them also helps clarify the paths to solutions. Focusing on the smaller tasks helps faculty to better define a do-able research agenda. In the act of motivating students, we become stronger and more vocal advocates for our own work, understanding and conveying better why it's important and crucial. This makes our own writing and arguments stronger.

Collaborating with students affects faculty in smaller ways as well: It helps us gain more control over our time, carve out time for research, and reframe our work in smaller, more easily addressable pieces.

> **Amy:** One of the traps I often get caught in is the trap of only publishing the "big" stuff. My tendency is to not feel ready to publish until I have some Big Important Insight to share with the world. It's been difficult for me to embrace the concept of the Least Publishable Unit (breaking down big ideas into many individually publishable items).
>
> Working with students has caused me to reevaluate my approach toward publishing. When students work with me, I try my best to get their work published. When the work represents just 10 weeks of looking at a problem, this can be quite a challenge. So I'm forced to be creative: With what previous unpublished work can I combine this, to get it accepted into a competitive conference? What work-in-progress conferences would be a good venue for this work? Could I structure next term's project to tie up the loose ends of this term's project and thus get a stronger paper out of the deal?
>
> I am often pleasantly surprised by what the students produce in such a short time. Recently, a paper that I had co-authored with an undergraduate, based on a term and a half of work, was accepted to a competitive conference. It turned out that this "small" project yielded an appropriately sized research nugget. As a bonus, the work was very well received at the conference.

In the next section, we talk a bit more about the mechanics of doing research with undergraduates—how to reap the benefits described here.

MODELS AND STRATEGIES FOR SUCCESS

Once we decide to collaborate with students, the focus turns to logistics: the mechanisms that need to be in place to make student/faculty research collaborations successful in a liberal arts setting. What follows is a collection of best practices gleaned from our combined nine years of working with undergraduate researchers in computer science at Carleton. We don't claim to have all of the answers—rather, we continue to learn and refine our best practices as we collaborate with more and more students. But we do know that, in order to succeed in collaborating with undergraduates, we need to pay attention to the following areas: selecting appropriate research problems, project management, compensation, mentoring, and student self-esteem.

Identifying Appropriate Research Problems

Collaborating with undergraduate researchers begins with identifying appropriate research problems. We want to work on problems that inspire us and motivate us and that we have the skills to work on. At the same time, the problems must be accessible to undergraduates. Finding research problems that fit both criteria is challenging.

A logical starting point is the research area in which we did our dissertations. We have already made significant progress there, and we have at least some fledgling experience in these areas. We then need to find a specific problem within that area that is accessible to our students. Unfortunately, the area of research

> [Undergraduate research] ... forces us to think more carefully about research problems, boil down the big questions into smaller questions more quickly, and resolve detailed issues at a faster pace than before. Doing this can give us a different perspective ...

that we studied in graduate school may simply not have many such problems within it. This means, as new faculty, that we may find ourselves reinventing our research areas soon after we arrive just so that liberal arts undergraduates are better able to participate.

> **Dave:** My graduate school research area requires significant specific mathematical background that few if any Carleton students learn. In fact, in graduate school I was recruited by my adviser in part because I had already taken an intro-level graduate course on

this material. What did this mean for me as a new research adviser at Carleton? How could I find a computer science major to work with me on my research when not even the math majors at Carleton typically learned the material needed to understand my work?

For my first summer at Carleton I was lucky enough to hire "Alan," one of our brightest computer science majors. Alan was a particularly good choice for this position because he had taken more math than most of our majors. Still, I had to teach him all of the specific math that was needed for the project. I also did all of the *creative* mathematical work for the project. Nevertheless, Alan did a phenomenal job critiquing my work. He also wrote computer software that implemented the technique that I developed.

The project was a smashing success. Alan's software worked well, and to this day it continues to be downloaded by colleagues across the world. I was dissatisfied with a number of aspects of the work, however. Alan had been unable to contribute to the actual development of new ideas. Though he helped me present the work at a conference, the subject matter at the conference was way over his head.

While I managed to make the project work, it seemed to me that there had to be a better way. And so rather than trying to mold future students to match me, I began to try to change my work to meet them somewhere in the middle.

The story of Alan illustrates the tension between finding tasks that students can already do—such as writing software—and finding tasks that are compelling, research-wise, to us.

If we're lucky, the student will have taken a course that's at least peripherally related to the work they will do. If we're *really* lucky, we'll have taught a course directly related to our research and be able to recruit research students from this course. In practice, however, this is difficult to pull off in a department such as ours, where particular electives are taught every other year. In addition, just because students have seen material before does not mean that they will easily make connections between course material and research. Students often remark that they thought they understood the course material, but that doing research in that same area challenged both their assumptions and their understanding of what is "correct."

How can students with limited understanding of an area contribute meaningfully to research in that area? In the more common case, when we don't have the luxury of background, the challenge is to connect the theoretical ideas in the project to theoretical ideas with which the student is already familiar. From there, it is up to the students to assimilate this knowledge into their existing bases of knowledge. One trick that has worked well for both of us on a variety of projects is to start the students out on a data analysis task. Data analysis involves skills that the students already possess: writing small programs to organize the data, performing basic statistical analysis on the data, and plotting the results. As the students examine the data, they begin to see patterns and ask questions: How was this generated? Why is this anomaly here? We can then use these questions as a springboard to introduce the relevant theory.

Project Management

Faculty members starting out in research collaborations with undergraduates bring a lot of fears to the table. Some of these are more philosophical in nature: fears that the project is not important enough or that the faculty member is not emotionally equipped to supervise a student's research. But many of the fears stem from logistics or how to successfully manage a research program using unseasoned researchers.

One of the main challenges in managing a research project with undergraduates is getting them up to speed on the project. We need to introduce them to the relevant background information, make sure they understand it, and still leave enough time for them to make progress on the problem, as Alan's story demonstrated.

Here, the careful choice of personnel goes a long way toward easing this process. One technique that works quite well for long term projects is for the faculty member to stagger participation of students on the research project. In Dave's atmospheric chemistry project, for example, he requires that students sign up for a two-year stint and staggers participation so that there are always a junior and a senior on the project. The senior student plays a strong role in educating the junior student. This impromptu mentoring serves two purposes: It takes some of the load off of the faculty member and builds community among the students. In shorter-term projects, a similar strategy—hiring an older student and a younger student—achieves similar results. Often, the students can help each other get unstuck.

Another advantage to having students work in pairs or teams is that it helps them manage time better. One of the challenges for students in doing research when compared to class work is that there are no clear deadlines or motivation to work at a particular pace. When students need to prioritize all the important things that they need to accomplish, they typically do the immediately pressing ones first. Research has a tendency to be the first thing to be put aside when other pressures arise. Multiple students act as checks on each other: "If my research partner is working, I need to be working, too!"

> One of the challenges for students in doing research when compared to class work is that there are no clear deadlines or motivation to work at a particular pace.

That's not to say that single-student projects cannot succeed. They can, as long as the faculty member fills the roles that a peer in the above scenario would fill. For instance, the faculty member needs to do a bit more hand-holding in the beginning and watch for signs throughout that a student is stuck on a problem. In the absence of peer pressure to work, the faculty member must find other ways to motivate—often, by reiterating the importance of the project to the field and/or to the larger research question. Much of the success, however, lies in picking the right student for the job, one who is exceptionally self-motivated and inquisitive.

Regardless of whether our students are working alone or in teams, at some point we have to direct their productivity.

In the summer, when students work for us full-time, this is less of an issue. We have the luxury of meeting with them daily or at least several times a week, which allows us to catch problems early. All of our summer students also work in a communal computer lab, which facilitates the sharing of ideas within and across projects.

During the school year, directing the students' efforts is a bit trickier. Frequent meetings are a must. Twice weekly, for a half an hour each time, has worked well in our experience, particularly since students tend to procrastinate until the night before they meet with us. Having to meet with an adviser and explain what's been done since the previous meeting is a strong motivator. Explicitly specifying research goals and assigning specific, small tasks can also keep students on track and help them work more efficiently toward the larger project goals.

Unfortunately, there is no magic number in terms of how many students, or projects, a faculty adviser can handle. It depends on the complexity of the project and on the abilities and personalities of the students and the faculty member. In our case in computer science, research in general is varied enough and research with undergraduates is new enough that there are few departmental guidelines or expectations in this area. Here, we've relied on trial and error to figure out what works for us. As mentioned earlier, Dave prefers to supervise multiple students over multiple terms. Amy, on the other hand, has found success more consistently while working with one to two students on smaller projects for shorter periods of time.

Compensation and Rewards

As researchers, faculty are intrinsically motivated by the value or perceived future value of our work. Students, however, do not always possess, or recognize that they possess, this intrinsic motivation. We thus have to come up with other ways to both motivate them to maximize their achievements and reward them for their accomplishments.

Compensating students for the work that they do for us can have an effect on the amount of effort that they put in. Grant money is sometimes available to us to pay students for the work that they do during summers. Unlike other departments at Carleton, we even occasionally have money to pay students during the academic year. More often, though, academic credit through an independent research course is all that we have to offer the students.

When granting academic credit for research, we have to handle the murky issue of how to evaluate the student's contribution to the project.

> **Dave:** During the summer before I came to Carleton, I learned from the CEO of a small software company that his product (I'll call it "SuperMiner") was lacking capabilities that my research area directly addressed. Moreover, he heavily promoted the fact that SuperMiner was "hot pluggable," meaning that anyone could program additional capabilities and just wire it right up. This sounded like a marvelous opportunity for a student project. The project would be self-contained, the goal was clear (add a certain piece

of technology to this product), the skills needed were in reach of a junior or a senior, and it related to my research area. The CEO expressed enthusiasm for the idea and sent me a free copy of SuperMiner.

During my first year, I hired a junior ("Ellen") to work on the project. We started off enthusiastically with a literature search. According to the SuperMiner documentation, any plug-in that we created needed to be written according to a particular industry standard. Ellen spent weeks trying to track down the details of this standard, and eventually both she and I concluded that these details were in fact not documented anywhere. This frustrated Ellen, understandably. I therefore suggested that we try another approach to the problem. Could we reverse-engineer SuperMiner itself to try to figure out how a plug-in might be built? After another week or two, Ellen reported back to me that no sample plug-ins came with SuperMiner and there were no obvious places where a new plug-in would go. Ellen and I ultimately called up the CEO and discussed the problems that we were having. He contacted one of his software developers and learned (to his surprise as well as ours) that such plug-ins were, in fact, not at all possible! This had taken most of the term at this point, and by now Ellen was so fed up that she was uninterested in trying other directions. We limped along until the end of the term and let the project die a quiet death.

Here's a quiz for the reader: On an A-F scale, what was the appropriate grade to assign Ellen? For that matter, what grade would be appropriate for me, the adviser, were I to receive one?

Research doesn't always proceed as we'd hope. A research idea that ultimately doesn't work shouldn't reflect poorly on the student. Should we assign a grade based on effort only? Clearly not, as this isn't the standard that we use in our other courses. In the end, the only grading scheme for research that seems to make sense from an evaluative perspective is Carleton's three-tiered pass/fail system (S/Cr/NC, or "Satisfactory/Credit/No Credit"). Essentially every student who signs up to do research does enough work that assigning a grade of "Satisfactory" (S) seems reasonable.

How do we ensure that the student does not just put in enough effort to gain the S but that he or she works in earnest toward the project goals?

Using some of the motivational techniques outlined in the previous section—reiterating the importance of the work, relying on peer pressure—can help. Other motivational techniques include ensuring that the student's work becomes part of (or the whole of) a published paper; having the student present his or her work, either orally or as a poster; or having the student produce something concrete, such a piece of software. Finally, letters of recommendation can serve as motivation as well. As collaborators on research projects, we are in the unique position of being able to comment not just on a student's research potential, but on his or her actual performance on a research project. For students planning on going to graduate school, such commentary is vitally useful.

Mentoring

As we collaborate with undergraduate researchers, we also become their mentors. Mentoring undergraduate researchers effectively is a skill we were most likely not taught in graduate school. The only precedent we have is the mentoring we received from our research advisers. While there are no doubt lessons that can be gleaned from this mentoring relationship (some of them positive, we hope), mentoring undergraduates is an entirely different beast than mentoring graduate students.

Part of the challenge of mentoring is in picturing ourselves as research mentors in the first place, as this next story illustrates:

> **Amy:** As I waited in my office for the student to arrive for our scheduled meeting, I fought conflicting feelings of exhilaration and dread. On the one hand, I was excited by the prospect of working with this student, of starting a project that had been brewing in the back of my mind for several years, and of launching a new endeavor. But the worries came out in droves: Did I really know what I was doing? Was this project really worth the time and energy? What if we failed? What if I was the reason we failed?
>
> Yes, my first foray into the world of student research was nerve-wracking. Six months earlier, I had been a junior researcher in a large corporate research lab. I had full direction over my own project, but there was always a senior person to go to for advice, for technical assistance, and for commiseration.
>
> Fast forward to the present scenario: I was now a very junior professor, struggling my way through my first year on the tenure

track. Yet, in this context, *I* was now the senior researcher, the person to whom my student would come for advice, for technical assistance, and for commiseration.

It was a terrifying thought.

Luckily (for me and for the student), the collaboration worked out very well. I am happy to report that most of the time exhilaration won out over dread and doubt. And the collaboration with this student led to other successful collaborations with this student, which in turn led to (mostly) successful collaborations with other students.

As junior professors, we are asked to make a fairly large transition from graduate school or post-graduate work to the faculty world. After years of being a peon in someone else's lab and taking directions from senior people, we are expected to become the senior person in our own research fiefdom overnight. Adding students to the mix moves this already difficult transition into hyper-speed. We are asked not only to become the senior person and direct our own work but also to direct the work of the most unseasoned of researchers.

In some sense, though, working with student researchers can help speed along this transition. Nothing forces us to confront the "impostor syndrome"[1] head-on more than having to confidently present our work or project proposal to a group of undergraduates. Nothing forces us to know our stuff more completely than having to explain a complicated research concept to a student who at best has taken a handful of courses in the field. Nothing forces us to confront the logistics of project design head-on more than trying to design a project to suit the skills of our research students, one that blends the appropriate amount of cutting-edge work with the background knowledge that the students are bringing to the project.

> [Our students]...see that research doesn't happen in a vacuum and that progress is made by being slow and steady and not in flashes of brilliance.

One way in which we mentor undergraduates is by modeling the research behavior that we expect from our students. Working alongside us, they can see us struggle with difficult problems, think out loud, try different approaches, and reach dead ends. They begin to learn what researchers do, how they spend their time, and how they make progress. Most importantly, they see that research doesn't happen in a vacuum and that progress is made by being slow and steady and not in flashes of brilliance.

The role of peer mentoring should not be ignored here either. As mentioned before, peer mentoring can be a valuable tool in ensuring that students stay the course and in bringing students up to speed. Younger students get the experience of discovering that not all knowledge has to come directly from the faculty adviser, and older students get the experience of passing on their knowledge, strengthening their own understanding of the concepts in the process.

Student Self-Esteem

One of the most important things to watch out for while mentoring undergraduate researchers is how to help them deal with the inevitable research setbacks. While Ramage, Bean, and Johnson (2003) point out that, pedagogically, students should be exposed to "ill-structured problems" (p. 25), in our experience undergraduates are more comfortable with questions that have one right answer or at least a finite set of right answers. They operate best when questions are well-defined and well-phrased. The world of the undergraduate, at least in an academic sense, is one of neatness and order. So it is a shock to most when they are confronted with the messy, unordered world of research, when they learn that not every question has an easily attainable answer. They are unsure what to think when they find out that even the best-planned projects can fail because, it turns out, we were trying to answer the wrong question or the answer we got was not at all what we expected. Unmanaged, the shock and frustration that a student feels when research goes awry can lead to a disinterest in research and a feeling of isolation.

> **Amy:** One student—I'll call him "Joe"—unfortunately learned this lesson many times over. I often assigned Joe riskier projects because I thought that he had the intellectual capacity to struggle with less well-defined problems. What he lacked, and what I didn't anticipate, was the emotional maturity to deal with the frustrations of research.
>
> In one case, Joe spent an entire term struggling to add some functionality to an existing piece of open-source software only to discover at the end of the term that what we thought would entail a minor change would in fact require a major overhaul of the existing software. Joe faced similar struggles the very next term while

trying to port a piece of software from Windows to the Macintosh: As it turned out, doing so required rewriting the software from scratch, which was not possible in the allotted time.

To me, Joe's "failures" were windfalls. I identified something from each project that could be salvaged to produce a nice, neat, short-term result. More importantly, Joe's missteps unearthed some truly valuable insights into the larger questions inherent in my work. This in turn led to some natural paths of exploration for the next student(s) that would work on this project. Understandably, though, he was extraordinarily frustrated at the end of each term and in some cases started to question his own ability to do real computer science.

How did I deal with this situation? Having Joe write about his experience not only allowed him to salvage something concrete from his research experiences, but it also gave him valuable practice in the art of technical writing.

Dealing with the emotional side was trickier. Joe's frustration was real, expected, and palpable; this may have even been the first time he had faced failure in an academic sense. I spent a lot of time talking about the messiness of research. I also brought up the wrong turns I've taken in my own work, how some of them worked out serendipitously, but how most were just that—mistakes, wrong turns, dead ends. I talked about how important it is to figure out what we learned from the experience and move on. But mostly, I reiterated the value of Joe's work to the project as a whole and how his mistakes would provide springboards into future work on the project.

How can we help students deal with the inevitable frustration? Is the answer to protect them from wrong paths as much as possible, or is it more important to expose them to the mistakes as well as the triumphs? How much do we let them struggle with a problem before we step in and assist? This is one place where a practical method—meeting often with students—can help mitigate or lessen the problem. Frequent meetings with students make us more aware of what and how the student is doing. They help the professor to catch potential problems in the making and head them off at the pass. Ellen's struggle with the SuperMiner software is a prime example of this strategy.

Of course, even the most vigilant professor will fail to catch some of the train wrecks before they happen—and then, it is important to deal with the student's ego appropriately. The adviser can point out that research by its very nature doesn't always work out as one hopes and that such failures ultimately lead to significantly better insight into the problem at hand.

Coming up with something concrete that the student can contribute to a failed project can help mitigate some of the student's feelings about failure. Having the student write up his or her work, as Amy did with Joe in the previous story, is one great way to accomplish this. (Such an effort has an important additional positive side effect: Since technical writing is largely ignored on our curriculum, this is a marvelous opportunity for students to gain that kind of writing experience.) Writing about failed work can allow students to succeed by having something to show for their efforts.

THE TRANSFORMATION(S)

Collaborating on research projects benefits both faculty and undergraduates. In the "Challenges and Rewards: Why Research?" section, we explained the benefits that research brings to both students and faculty. In the "Models and Strategies for Success" section, we demonstrated practical aspects of carrying out research projects with undergraduates. In conclusion, we would like to highlight some of the ways that doing research with undergraduates transforms all those who participate.

From the students' perspective, research can create a community where none currently exists. Research with students allows for lots of interaction between students and faculty. While it is true that those students who choose to visit us in office hours get something of the same experience, research puts students and faculty on more equal footing. This undoubtedly helps form a community bond among the research team, including the faculty member.

Research can also transform the attitude students bring to their work and the confidence they have in their own abilities. Solving problems that do not have an obvious or known solution—or, more importantly, where even the faculty member does not know the solution ahead of time—provides a tremendous confidence boost to students. Working in an area where they lack the appropriate background forces them to make connections between what they know and what they observe and can appropriately broaden their ideas about a field and their understanding of the field as a whole.

Furthermore, the sense of ownership that students gain by working on research problems can significantly enhance their motivation to learn appropriate background knowledge on their own. Even failure teaches the students how to recover from a setback and how to learn from the experience. Experience on an unsolved problem can result in a renewed interest in academics: Course material could contain the right tool for solving the next big problem. In some cases, doing research is just the impetus a student needs to propel him or her from so-so status to academic superstar.

The transformations to students are perhaps more obvious, but how are faculty transformed? Doing research with students transforms our own attitude toward our work, sometimes in non-obvious ways. Working toward smaller goals, for instance, can bring unprecedented clarity to our own work. Managing the progress of others keeps us honest about our own progress and can often kick-start us into completing work that we might otherwise be tempted to let slide. Dealing with student failure reminds us that valuable insights can be gained even from the most egregious mistakes—and can help us be more tolerant and forgiving of our own setbacks.

One specific benefit to faculty occurs when we have our students write up their work—our own writing benefits as a result. We typically read student writing with the critical eye of a reviewer, looking not only for correct voice and grammar but also to detect the logical holes: What would a reviewer say about this claim? Did we explain this algorithm thoroughly enough or test appropriately for the exceptional cases? Often, these logical holes are easier to spot when the writing is not originating from us. Catching the flaws and ambiguities in our research early on saves us time in the long run (by preventing us from going down unfruitful paths) and helps us strengthen our own arguments about the value of our research.

Collaborating with undergraduates on research problems can also help ease the transition into being a tenure-track faculty member. The instant confidence we must exude about our work in order to "sell" it to students teaches us to value our own work and contributions to the field more highly. We can more easily envision ourselves as senior researchers and project leads because we are forced into this role early on. This helps us combat the ever-present impostor syndrome, the bane of the new faculty member.

Finally, the departmental community that research fosters among students can also improve the relationships among faculty. Working so closely with students integrates us more fully into the fabric of our departments, particularly as new faculty: We get to know the students, but we also establish rapport with the rest of the faculty as we ask for advice and share ideas. Collaborating with students can open us up to ideas for collaborating with faculty in our own disciplines or other disciplines. An offhand remark from one of Amy's former research students about a concept he learned in a psychology course led Amy to seek advice from a colleague in the Psychology Department about designing a survey to collect feedback from users on video stream quality. A comment from Dave at a faculty retreat led to a conversation with colleagues about their research, which eventually led to the collaboration between Dave and Deborah. Serendipitous encounters such as these broaden and enrich our own work. Extending our networks beyond our departments broadens our social networks, helps us grow our support networks, and opens us up to new and fresh ideas for our own disciplines. This in turn integrates us more fully into the fabric of the college as a whole.

ENDNOTE

[1] Impostor syndrome: the feeling that one doesn't really "belong" as a researcher or faculty member. This is often exacerbated among members of underrepresented groups.

REFERENCES

Gross, D. (2007). A model for collaborative undergraduate research: Integrating disciplines and institutions to better understand the earth's atmosphere. In C. Rutz & M. Savina (Eds.), *Building intellectual community through collaboration* (pp. 105-120). Northfield, MN: College City Publications.

Ramage, J., Bean, J., & Johnson, J. (2003). *The Allyn & Bacon guide to writing* (3rd ed.). New York: Longman.

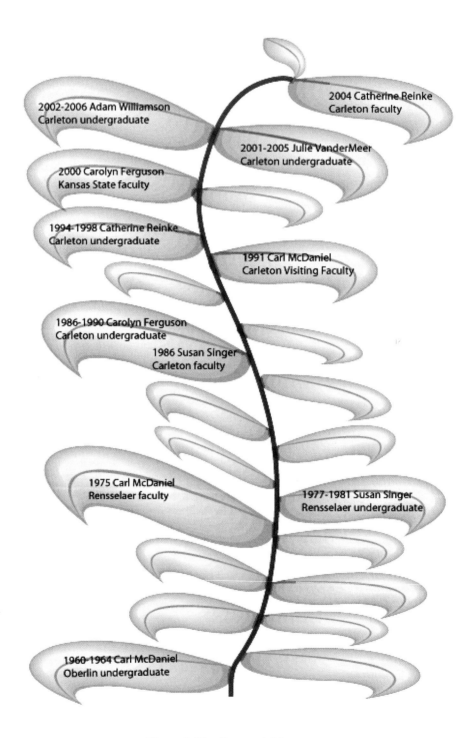

Figure 1. The Research Lineage

From Observers to Participants: Joining the Scientific Community

Catherine A. Reinke and Susan R. Singer
In collaboration with Carl McDaniel, Carolyn J. Ferguson, Julia Vandermeer, and Adam Williamson

How one becomes a scientist can be a bit opaque, given the persistent stereotypes of scientists and varied perceptions of science in our society. We believe that undergraduate experiences are critical in the transformation of a scientific observer to an active participant in the scientific community. In this essay, we have integrated the voices of our mentors and students to explore 47 years of undergraduate research experiences and their role in shaping our scientific community. The perspective is multigenerational with professional lineage as a common thread. In considering our collective experiences, we see undergraduate involvement in research as a rich source of community development, one that has both touched our lives and influenced our teaching.

The stories of those who have contributed to this essay are linked by a research lineage dating back to 1963 (Figure 1). Carl McDaniel began his undergraduate research career in Tom Scott's lab at Oberlin in 1963, and Susan Singer joined Carl's lab at Rensselaer Polytechnic Institute in 1978. Susan and Carolyn Ferguson arrived at Carleton

> In this essay, we have integrated the voices of our mentors and students to explore 45 years of undergraduate research experiences and their role in shaping our scientific community.... In considering our collective experiences, we see undergraduate involvement in research as a rich source of community development, one that has both touched our lives and influenced our teaching.

SUSAN SINGER, the Laurence McKinley Gould Professor of the Natural Sciences, earned her B.S., M.S., and PhD degrees at Rensselaer Polytechnic Institute. She joined the Carleton faculty in 1986. CATHERINE A. REINKE, assistant professor of biology, earned her B.A. degree at Carleton College and her PhD at the University of Chicago. She was a member of the Carleton faculty in 2004–05.

the same year, as faculty member and student, respectively, and Carolyn began her research in Susan's lab in 1988. Carolyn has been mentoring students as a faculty member at Kansas State for the past seven years. Carl, Susan, and Carolyn all entered the world of research as students under the mentorship of newly minted faculty members. Catherine Reinke joined a more established version of Susan's lab in 1995 and now speaks with the voice of a new faculty member at Carleton. Both Susan and Catherine have mentored Julie Vandermeer and Adam Williamson, contemporary students. We hope that our collected stories will offer a glimpse of the nature of collaboration in the scientific community and the importance of bringing undergraduates into the world of research.

Development (def.): a relatively slow process of progressive change. (Gilbert, 2003, p. 4).

Together, our voices describe different developmental stages in our lives as biologists, stages that occurred during revolutionary changes in the scientific community. Carl's venture into science began just as the genetic code was cracked. During Susan's early years, a few genes were being sequenced. The study of development and genetics were merged just before Carolyn's undergraduate years, and the exploration of the evolution of development became a central focus of inquiry as Catherine began her undergraduate studies. Adam and Julie have recently entered the scientific community, during an unprecedented age of large-scale, collaborative projects, including the sequencing of the human genome. In both process and theory, the biological world has exploded in the past 47 years. Yet, as we explored our development as biologists, we uncovered a common thread of experience across decades.

DEVELOPING INTELLECTUAL AUTONOMY

Intellectual autonomy is the ability to trust your reasoning abilities and continually challenge your assumptions and interpretations. A sufficient, discipline-based knowledge, curiosity, and self-confidence are necessary prerequisites. Serendipity played a role in each of our forays into biology that led to undergraduate research experiences. While facing insecurities, we began to participate in science; our changing perceptions led us to assume roles as scientific mentors.

Unexpected Beginnings

None of us imagined ourselves becoming research scientists. We each had an experience that sparked our interest in doing research; those experiences were a beginning.

Catherine: My interest in learning and teaching biology extends back to a single high school English class. One afternoon, Dr. Goodman began by writing three words on the chalkboard: "Perception precedes observation." During our discussion that day, pushing those three words around in my head made me think hard about what I thought I knew, what I really knew, and how I knew any of it in the first place. Those questions were a starting point. Perception without observation seemed dangerous, prone to error. And yet, perception had power in the absence of observation. What did we really know, and how did we know that it was true? Observation took on a new importance for me—I would believe it when I could see it. As I look back, I see that this was the beginning of my life as a researcher.

Carolyn: I landed in Susan's lab by sheer luck. At the time I was pre-med and also entertaining thoughts of a teaching career. I really had little idea what research was about but thought spending some time in a lab would give me some good experience. My experience was eye opening! I found that I loved the *doing* of science (much more, in fact, than the learning and teaching!), and I experienced the thrill of discovery.

Susan: Along with 999 other first-year students at Rensselaer Polytechnic Institute, almost all planning to be engineers, I marched through a first term of physics, chemistry, calculus, computer science, and a fifth course of my choice in the humanities or social sciences. Spring semester, I had an additional course choice and wandered into Genetics and Evolution, a mid-level course. That singular choice would find me still studying genetics and evolution almost 30 years later.

After almost going to Genetics and Evolution office hours half a dozen times, I mustered up enough courage to cross the threshold of Dr. Wilson's office and choke out, "I'm going to be an engineer, but I like biology a lot more." Somewhere in the ensuing conversation I answered yes to a question about liking plants. I soon found myself being introduced to Dr. Carl McDaniel. By fall of my sophomore year I was working in Carl's lab on herbicide transport in cultured cells, actually understanding Michaelis Menton kinetics, and screening for herbicide-tolerant mutants.

Carl: I don't recall why I wanted to do research but, perhaps, it was to have "my place." I was accepted by Tom Scott, a new faculty member, to do a project employing the facility that Oberlin had built for Scott to measure auxin activity by the *Avena* curvature assay.

Clearly, we didn't know much about what we were getting ourselves into.

Research Anxieties

The beginning of a career in research, like most beginnings, reveals little about the road ahead. While it makes perfect sense to an active researcher, as students it took time for us to appreciate that the path of discovery was uncharted territory. The majority of our experience in the classroom was aimed toward arriving at the right answer—in research, there was no back of the book.

Susan: What was intimidating and exciting was the freedom to engage my mind. Designing my experiments and conducting literature searches seemed incredibly open-ended. Wasn't someone supposed to tell me what to do next? In reality, I had a huge amount of support, every step along the way. I just didn't believe deep down that I could actually do real science.

Carl: I was certainly inadequate intellectually and in the skills and talents required for scientific research, but I worked hard. I was overwhelmed by the difficulty of understanding enough to do meaningful biological research.

Catherine: High school provided my first formal research experience, determining optimal fertilization treatments to improve wetland restoration efforts. Doing research sounded glamorous to me. Glamorous, however, was probably not the best way to describe spending the summer alone in a swamp. By the end of the summer, I felt ambivalent about my results and even more skeptical about drawing any conclusions. Had I really done it right? I'd been making my observations without a real scientist in sight.

At this point we were on our way, but we didn't really know where we were going.

Making a Real Start: Changing Perceptions

New research students are often told that they will not accomplish anything during their first year in the lab. Upon hearing this, most students are incredulous. The idea of spending an entire year accomplishing absolutely nothing doesn't resonate with a track record of academic success. And then it happens. Experiments are at-

tempted. Results are uninterpretable. Frustration mounts. Throughout this process, techniques are mastered, and the student's perception changes. During our first days in the lab, though we may have been accomplishing absolutely nothing, we were learning how to do research.

Susan: At some point I said, "I don't have anything to do in lab today." Carl's puzzled look made me gag on my words. Slowly it occurred to me that not only should I take a bit more responsibility for my own thinking but also that I could. As I became more and more immersed in the research, it became my research.

Julie: I came across a simple change to a protocol that saved some time. It made work a bit easier, and I wanted to share it with the lab. Suggesting even such a trivial change and taking responsibility for it was probably the point at which I realized that I was starting to actually contribute to what was going on in lab, rather than only following instructions from other people.

Carl: At Oberlin, a thesis student had to defend his/her thesis to a committee of a few faculty. I have images and emotions of the event but no details except the conclusion—I was probably not PhD material. In the faculty's opinion, I would do well as a high school science teacher. When I talked it over with a classmate who knew me well, he said, "You are too intellectually curious and would soon be bored."

Catherine: Having survived Carleton's daunting introductory course Biology of Animals, I wanted to learn more. Susan's lab was a fascinating new world where students, technicians, and post-docs were all working to understand the genetic basis of flowering. In the lab, my understanding of genetics and molecular biology changed completely. Classical genetics wasn't just used to predict eye color; classical genetics was something that happened in the greenhouse. Flowers on one plant were deconstructed, and pollen from another plant was introduced to make a new hybrid. Recombinant DNA was not just pictured in my textbook; there were bacteria that contained plant genes in the refrigerator! In the lab, everything that I knew about biology became real to me in a completely new way. It started to become clear that all of the information that I had learned up to this point actually came from research and that I could contribute.

Becoming undergraduate researchers changed our perception of science from something mysterious and beyond our grasp to something that we could understand and do.

Evolving Responsibilities

As scientists, we enjoy the simultaneous roles of students, teachers, researchers, and mentors. The balance and degree of expertise changes, but becoming a scientist is an iterative process that occurs progressively over the course of a career. Our undergraduate research experiences provided us with our first opportunity to transition from observer to participant, to experience the parallel nature of our many roles.

Adam: Courses and laboratory research complement one another throughout the undergraduate experience. The projects I've worked through in lab have been applied directly to biology classes at Carleton. In Plant Development, students sequenced relatives of pea genes in partridge pea, a native prairie plant. I contributed to the lab protocols and TA'ed the lab, where I could help students work through research issues that I had encountered myself.

Julie: For the first year that I was in the lab, I was the new person who was unsure of what I had to offer beyond a pair of hands to follow protocols. By the second summer, I was the "old" student in the lab and was shocked to find that the students who had just joined the lab would ask me questions. I found that sometimes I knew the answers.

Susan: Most of my students now work in pairs on their research. Students mentor each other and can keep a project moving during a busy term by sharing the workload (experimental organisms don't have any respect for mid-terms and major papers). Research has its ups and downs and can be a lonely endeavor when one first starts. Having a research colleague helps. Modern biology has become a collaborative endeavor. I hope that's a lasting lesson my students take from their experience in lab.

Carolyn: Research involves the student in the activity of science—the fun part—rather than simply the study of the results. As a mentor, I am continually reminded of the process and excitement of science. A high school student who spent a day "job shadowing" me told me, "You have the coolest job ever!" These reminders are very motivating.

In mentoring undergraduates, the most important thing to me is that they experience that sense of doing science that I experienced as an undergraduate. I want them to truly grasp that, for all they are faced with learning in their science classes, there is a whole world out there for us to discover and they are a part of the active process of discovery. Whether they continue in a research field or not, these students gain a critical appreciation for the process of science.

Catherine: When I began teaching Carleton students, I was a little surprised by how much they thought I knew, and yet how skeptical they were of their own knowledge. I came to realize that their attitudes were rooted in the fact that science is often thought of as a collection of facts known by scientists and memorized (and then forgotten) by middle-schoolers. What was lacking in my students was an understanding of the way that scientists do science. Armed with this realization, I decided to begin my teaching at this point: teaching my students about the real world of research.

I assigned my students primary literature articles to read, despite the fact that this task is often overwhelming even to new graduate students. An article might generate only a single piece of new information, but that information is almost always hard-won, gained slowly, at the expense of research hours that spill over into years. I wanted to introduce my students to this research experience, so our plan was to talk about how we knew what we knew—to explore the origin of the information in the textbook.

Our first discussion that Friday took up most of the following week. As the term progressed, we all got better at the discussions, which became filled with student-generated questions *and* answers. As the course went on, the students felt as if they'd learned the material but also that they'd learned how to do something.

Because our discipline changes so rapidly, we constantly need to learn new information. As perpetual students, we never feel as if we know it all; we are always teaching from the point of what we know today. With that in mind, we try to inspire our students to contribute whatever they have to offer at each stage in their learning.

SCIENCE AS A COLLABORATIVE ENDEAVOR

A collaborative approach is becoming essential as the scientific community answers new kinds of questions. For example, at its completion, the Human Genome Project was a multi-researcher, multi-institution, international accomplishment. In research labs, students often begin with some skepticism about the importance of their individual work. Over time, we learned that every advance requires a series of small contributions.

Susan: Carl's commitment to mid-morning lab tea left a lasting impression. In retrospect, it was such a simple way to build community in the lab. Swapping simple how-to ideas to deeper discussions about concepts and theories helped me see that my tiny bit of work actually fit into a broader project that the USDA (United States Department of Agriculture) actually thought was worth funding.

As a faculty member, I love spending time in the lab. A room full of equipment and reagents is not the draw; it's the people and the intellectual vibrancy of our small community that make lab a home for me. During the best terms and most summers, weekly lab meetings are part of the rhythm of the research lab. The difference in sense of community is palpable when we have regular meetings.

Catherine: In Susan's lab, my work was only a small part of the way that I was learning. Our group met together every week and brainstormed about specific questions that people were trying to answer and the technical challenges that they encountered along the way. During those meetings, I saw that research was collaborative and progress came from the fact that each lab member brought his or her individual knowledge to the table. In our lab meetings, my observations were no longer just a data set; they were part of our collective knowledge. In lab meetings, I saw myself as something more than just the data collector.

Within the microcosm of the lab, we first saw how our individual efforts fit into the bigger picture.

Being Challenged

Being smart is not enough. The development of an intellectual community depends on each member discovering his or her own role. Ideally, mentors encourage students toward what is possible. Memories of being stretched as students are crystal clear to us, even decades later.

Carl: I believe being an average Obie (Oberlin student) has been an asset to me in nurturing undergraduates to achieve within the context of who they are. I've tried to discern what students wanted to do so they would own their projects and do what it took to complete them. In the laboratory I believed in guiding students to the possible. If they worked hard, they should have something to show for it.

Susan: Carl had lots of suggestions for what I should be doing—writing my senior thesis, writing a research paper, giving a research talk to his postdoctoral advisor's lab group at Yale, applying to graduate school, and applying for an

NSF (National Science Foundation) graduate fellowship. I would procrastinate and Carl would nudge. In the end I actually tackled this list.

Catherine: In Susan's lab, it was my job to observe the effects of introducing an *Arabidopsis* gene into mutant pea plants. The tricky part was that no one in the lab actually knew how to get an *Arabidopsis* gene into a pea plant; Susan told me that it was my job to come up with a protocol. I tried to develop an original approach to a real problem. I made a small amount of progress: more importantly, I felt like I was really doing research.

I started to make actual progress after Susan gave me the opportunity to interact with other researchers at a professional meeting at Michigan State. Susan gave a talk at the meeting, which was also attended by Jan Grant, a researcher from New Zealand who had some ideas about how to get genes into pea plants. I managed to sit next to Jan at lunch and talk to her about my project. I left that meeting with a copy of her new, unpublished protocol and a plan. Looking back, I see how easy it would have been for Susan to talk to Jan herself.

At some point along the way, most of us suspected that our mentors were crazy to leave us alone in the lab unsupervised. Collectively, we have experienced a variety of nudging styles; in the end, this encouragement led us to do more than we thought we could do.

Joining the Larger Intellectual Community:
Why We Take Our Students Out into the World

Our students begin their development in the classroom and the lab, where they first hear the language of our discipline. Ideally, they gain fluency through active engagement with us and with each other. Their skills, and our efforts, are put to the test out in the larger scientific community.

Catherine: Analyzing primary literature is just another classroom technique. I still wondered whether my students were "getting it"—whether they saw the real excitement of the scientific process. While teaching genetics, I brought my students to a day of seminars and discussions sponsored by the University of Minnesota. At this meeting, researchers, genetic counselors, doctors, and public health workers were exploring the emerging intersections of their work. My students were noticeably excited when talks would include information that they'd encountered in class, and many of them asked questions. It was immediately obvious to me that the conference made an impression. On the ride home students took turns describing conversations that they'd had and asking questions about graduate school and research. I gave them postcards to return over the summer to let me know about genetics encounters beyond the classroom. The steady arrival of postcards in my box demonstrated that their learning did indeed continue after the final exam.

Susan: When possible I try to get my students to meetings. The validation of their work by my colleagues is something I cannot replicate alone. I want them to see that their work is legitimate science, and whenever possible my students co-author papers as well as posters and talks. Seeing scientific meetings through student eyes infuses me with a fresh dose of enthusiasm for my own work. At a meeting in Vienna this summer, I watched two of my students sort out the excitement of hearing about work yet to be published with the intimidation of joining conversations with people known previously only as authors on papers. Navigating professional meetings is a bit like learning the nuances of getting around in a foreign country, where nothing can quite substitute for experiential learning.

Catherine: Near the end of my time in Susan's lab, I assembled my research into a presentation for a regional meeting of the American Society of Plant Physiologists to be held at the University of Wisconsin. When I gave my talk, I was amazed at how many people seemed interested and asked me questions. Suddenly, in a room full of scientists, my work was real science. At the next coffee break, several graduate students congratulated me on my talk, told me about their projects, and asked me about my future plans. As a first-generation college student, I have to say that that was the first day I began to think seriously about getting a PhD and pursuing a research career.

In classes and labs, our students explore their interests, often with little idea of how those interests might relate to life after college. By bringing our students directly into our intellectual communities, we can offer them a glimpse of where their budding interests and passions could lead.

THE RESONANCE OF AUTONOMY AND COLLABORATION

Community interactions build intellectual autonomy. And, intellectual autonomy allows one to more deeply engage in collaboration.

Community can be defined in many ways, as seen in the examples we have presented. Classrooms, research labs, and professional meetings create communities that exist at an instant in time but extend and intersect temporally. These communities can be supportive, but we have all also experienced daunting moments. Perhaps we had insufficient intellectual autonomy at times, or perhaps the community failed to seize the opportunity to mentor a newcomer or colleague.

The journey from introductory college biology to undergraduate research, in our collective experiences, is a bridge from observer to participant. It is a period for personal as well as professional growth. Carl puts it this way:

> I believe my responsibility in undergraduate research is to provide a congenial place where the craft of science can be viewed and attempted and each individual is able to achieve and grow not only as a potential scientist but also as a person.

Not all entering college students are immune to the broader cultural perception of scientists working in isolation in white lab coats thinking brilliant thoughts. While our undergraduate years launched our careers as biologists, the more important outcome was the shift in perception from science as other to science as an accessible path to understanding the material world. One of the challenges of the undergraduate years is to move from inaccurate perceptions of science into the world of doing science and into the community of scientists that do this work. For us, this journey has yielded lifelong friendships that have enriched our personal and professional lives.

REFERENCE

Gilbert, S.F. (2003). *Developmental biology* (7th ed.). Sunderland, MA: Sinauer Associates.

Maastricht, Netherlands

Natural Experiments in Collaborative, Off-Campus Student Research in Comparative Politics

Alfred P. Montero

A s one well-known journalist has recently declared: "The World is Flat!" (Friedman, 2005). Globalization has placed intercultural knowledge, including the mastery of foreign languages and familiarity with foreign travel, at the top of most colleges' expectations of what students will learn in four years. In the social sciences, and particularly comparative politics, international study abroad programs offer a rich opportunity for students to pursue the development of their intercultural skill set and their application of what they have learned in their campus-based classrooms. Yet few scholars have (re)evaluated the design of these programs to assess how students learn. This chapter does just that for two iterations of an off-campus program based in Maastricht, the Netherlands, that I directed for Carleton College in the springs of 2002 and 2005.

The Maastricht Program focuses instruction on the political economy of the European Union and subnational regions of Western Europe. It was comparative in its methodological approach, encouraging students to use empirical comparisons of cases across space and time to test hypotheses available in the political science literature or hypotheses of their own construction. The program in 2002 employed strictly qualitative tools consistent with the training of Carleton students at that time.

> Just as a laboratory enables a biologist or chemist to make empirical observations, so international travel, speaking with contacts abroad, and acquiring documents and statistics enable students of comparative politics to produce original research.

ALFRED P. MONTERO, associate professor of political science and director of political economy, earned his B.A. degree at University of Miami and his M.A., M.Phil, and PhD at Columbia University. He joined the Carleton faculty in 1998.

After the integration of a quantitative literacy component into the Political Science Department's second-year methods course shortly afterwards, these analytical tools were added to the 2005 program.

The opportunities afforded by off-campus instruction of this type provide students with a laboratory of what could be termed *natural experiments*. Students of comparative politics are only able to engage in empirical research themselves if they gather data and assemble findings in the field. Just as a laboratory enables a biologist or chemist to make empirical observations, so international travel, speaking with contacts abroad, and acquiring documents and statistics enable students of comparative politics to produce original research. Of course, the term natural experiment has a dual meaning in this chapter: (1) students' comparisons of regions and time periods in the study of European political economy and (2) my own comparison of two iterations of the Maastricht Program. My purpose here is to discuss the second dimension to provide a global assessment of how well the design of the Maastricht Program achieved its pedagogical goals.

Given all that can go wrong in preparing collaborative fieldwork of this type under strict time constraints, it is not surprising that sustained inter-student cooperation composes the heart and the most harrowing aspect of the pedagogical mission of the Maastricht Program. The intention of this design is to train students to work out the differences and inefficiencies that are inevitable in small group work and to take advantage of the creative possibilities that can only be generated by small groups. These are precisely the kinds of skills most in demand in a variety of fields, particularly the nontraditional (high-tech) professions that are the prime movers in the flattening of the global economy (Florida, 2002). Given few opportunities for sustained collaborative fieldwork in comparative politics in campus-based classrooms, off-campus programs afford the best opportunity to develop these skills. Group work also facilitates the completion of a large amount of fieldwork in a relatively short period of time.

The Maastricht Program provided many of the characteristics of a natural experiment. Students did not engage in original field research during any of the previous iterations of this program, so my design simply took advantage of the placement of 20 or more Carleton students in Europe. Since I also knew that I would direct the program twice using the same design, I could isolate the effects of the design on two cohorts separated by three years. I did not expect the opinions of the students from the first program to affect those of the second. The separation of three years meant that all of the 2002 cohort members were graduated by June 2004, a full year before the 2005 program. Given the small number of sophomores on the 2002 program (three), the vast majority of the 2002 program membership (21 total) was graduated two full years before the second cohort of 26 students went on the program. These students left no discernible record of their experience, save for the research reports and photos published on the program Web page. Therefore, my design for 2005 could reasonably shape expectations independently of the 2002 experience.

The main learning goals of both iterations of the Maastricht Program were the following:

- Develop data gathering and analysis skills
- Acquire the abilities to work collaboratively with colleagues on a common project under intense pressure
- Deepen understanding of the state-of-the-art in the analysis of political economy of the European Union and subnational regions
- Develop substantial knowledge of particular subnational regions, their political culture, economic and political histories, and major actors (e.g., political parties, leaders, businesses, and social movements)

Each of these goals reflects a major dimension of the fieldwork experience in comparative politics. Although trained scholars usually have deep knowledge of the cases under study and competence in the language before they venture to the field, the undergraduates in the Maastricht Program did not have these advantages.

The purpose of this chapter is to compare two iterations of the Maastricht Program to examine how design affected the ability of undergraduate students to develop the skills of field methods. Yet it should be emphasized that this is an inherently messy process. The actual application of comparative methods in the field requires developing skills not specifically taught in the classroom. The Maastricht students learned much about comparative politics by encountering the inevitable challenges of fieldwork—e.g., the inability to gain access to data, the nonresponsiveness of some contacts, bureaucratic and scheduling conflicts, and not being able to acquire timely transport to a research location. Cultural misunderstandings and logistical hassles composed a large part of the learning process.

A TALE OF TWO PROGRAMS: MAASTRICHT 2002 AND 2005

The structure of both iterations of the Maastricht Program was essentially the same. Figure 1 illustrates the program schedule. Weeks 1-5 were dedicated to classroom study of the politics of the European Union and preparation for a comparison of selected subnational regions. During this first half, the students were divided into four research teams. Each team was designated a single subnational region as part of the "Europe of Regions" seminar that is taught alongside a seminar on the European Union (EU). Since the study of EU regional policy—designed to elevate the economic development of less well-off regions—is a major component of subnational political economy, these two seminars are complementary.

More important, the student groups arrive at a research question during this time. Typical questions address the causes of high-tech development, why regions with a long history of heavy industry restructure successfully while others do not, or how some regional political parties use nationalist demands to develop their regions while others do not. After settling on a central question, the groups develop a hypothesis to explain the analytical puzzle they have chosen. It is also at this time that they decide on which subnational regions to compare, since the logic of selecting cases must be related to the puzzle and hypothesis they have chosen. In both iterations of this program I selected the first region for each group prior, but left the choice of a second region to the research teams.

Once agreed on their strategy, the groups conduct preliminary library and Internet-based research at the European Institute of Public Administration (EIPA) in Maastricht. They also make calls to contacts in their designated region to prepare speakers and events for a visit of the entire program during Weeks 6, 7, or 8 of the program. Typical examples of contacts and speakers include economists who provide overviews of the economic development of a region, political party leaders who assess the political history of the area, directors of public agencies with expertise in the promotion of foreign investment, venture capitalists who assess current economic and technological trends, and union representatives who focus discussion on labor politics.

The choice of a second region to compare with the designated case determines where students will go during the "research week" in which they are free to travel to the region of their choice without the members of other groups. Each group must engage contacts and prepare their access to data in the field weeks beforehand. This makes the middle weeks (Weeks 5-7) particu-

Figure 1. Overview of the Maastricht Program

Weeks 1-7	**Weeks 6-8**	**Weeks 9-10**
——————————>	——————————>	——————————>
Maastricht-based work	**Work in two regions**	**Maastricht-based presentation and write-up**
Program Activities: Complete course work (European Union seminar; Europe of Regions); text-based discussion. Classroom discussion of group projects.	*Program Activities:* Travel to designated regions to hear speakers and engage in activities planned by the groups.	
Group Work (Planning): Develop central analytical question, a hypothesis, and a case selection logic.	*Group Work (Planning):* Prepare independent research visits of secondary regions by members of the group.	
Group Work (Research): Complete preliminary work at EIPA library on research project. Communicate with contacts (e.g., academics, government personnel, political party officials, union offices, etc.) in regions under study. Set up program visit for weeks 6, 7 or 8.	*Group Work (Research):* Engage contacts and acquire data in the field. (Some members might continue library research in Maastricht).	

larly stressful since meetings with contacts fall through, the logistics of transport may conspire against students' ambitions, and data might otherwise not be available for lack of the proper credentials or time to gain access to specialized libraries or survey agencies. These are all essential challenges that emerge as part of the fieldwork experience.

And while the groups' academic presentation during Weeks 9-10 is the focus of their activities, their experiences during the preceding research weeks very much shape what they can and cannot say regarding their findings. With these limitations in mind, the groups return to Maastricht during these final weeks and prepare PowerPoint presentations of their project to the class and a final written research report.

Beyond the basic pedagogical goals and the core challenge of preparing students for collaborative research in small groups, the two iterations of the Maastricht Program had several differences designed into them. First, the 2002 students created their own groups. I formed the groups in 2005. In the self-selected groups in 2002, students knew the capabilities of their peers and tended to form initially more trusting relationships. These ties would become strained during the research segment of the program, but the initial expectation was that these groups would hold together more easily than groups created by the professor.

Surprisingly, self-selection produced the unintended consequence of encouraging greater competitiveness among the groups. Designating the groups and creating more of a challenge to their internal coherence in 2005 was done in the hope that these competitive energies would become diluted. In this way, the coherence of the groups became a variable of the program design for comparing the two cohorts.

Second, the aforementioned difference in quantitative skill sets between the 2002 and 2005 cohorts allowed me to integrate an additional expectation of statistical analysis into the latter program. I provided a space for it in the European Union seminar by having a different configuration of four teams of 6-7 students collect EU data on the structural funds given to designated regions in support of economic change.

After gathering this information (itself a challenge!) at the EIPA library, each group was asked to analyze it using one of the major statistical packages (i.e., SPSS, STATA). Each team then prepared a PowerPoint presentation during Week 5 on the unifying question of whether EU structural monies have helped Europe's subnational regions over time. Having applied their quantitative skills in this way, the participants in the 2005 program were uniquely equipped to integrate these methods in the "Europe of Regions" segment of the program. So another point of comparison between the two cohorts is an assessment of whether more extensive methodological training prior to the program facilitated the work of the groups.

A third major difference between the two cohorts involved the availability of research support. The 2005 program had the full-time support of an alumnus assistant from the 2002 program who had not only a competence in the subject area but also language skills in French and Spanish that were a boon to students wishing to study regions in France and Spain. (Two of the four 2005 teams focused on Spain; none on France.) The alumnus assistant also provided logistical support, setting up bus, train, and housing accommodations for each team and thus freeing up their time for other tasks. The social science librarian at Carleton provided constant support for the data-gathering work of each team, supplying materials in a timely manner via e-mail and on the library electronic reserves service upon request. By contrast, the 2002 cohort had none of these accommodations.

Although the first program had the benefit of e-mail communication and a cell phone provided to each team, the 2005 teams made more use of these resources. Some of the students in the second program even brought their own cell phones. Wireless Internet access added to the greater connectivity of the second program, whereas the first relied on access to Internet cafes while on the road. Most impressive was the fact that Internet telephony was already widely available in Europe by the time the 2005 program occurred. The Internet program Skype became a popular and widely used means for the students to communicate with one another, with contacts, and with the U.S. during the 2005 iteration.

Apart from these three major differences, which registered in the findings I discuss below, both programs had the same level of institutional support. The program provided housing, train travel (15-day nonconsecutive Eurail passes), and per diem. Students covered hostel costs and any additional travel out of personal funds. Although the 2002 program enjoyed a superior dollar-euro exchange rate, the 2005 students still traveled as extensively, if not more so, than their predecessors. Like the 2002 cohort, the 2005 group used budget airlines (e.g., Ryan Air) for the longest hauls across Western Europe and to Ireland and the United Kingdom.

Below I compare how the two groups achieved the pedagogical goals of the Maastricht Program. I place particular emphasis on the collaborative research, the data analysis and gathering components, since these are the most likely dimensions to be affected by the design of the program. I used personal interviews in addition to group interviews, assessments of written work, and the group oral presentations as my diagnostic tools for evaluating the students' performance. Yet it was the personal interviews conducted at the end of each program that supplied the richest data for assessing the effects of the program's design. With the guarantee of confidentiality, each student was asked to comment on the work of his/her colleagues and how well the design of the program supported the collective effort. As one can expect of Carleton students in particular, none held back their ideas. Each spoke with a candor and frankness that provided ample qualitative data for the analysis I present in the following pages.

BUILDING AN INTELLECTUAL COMMUNITY
IN THE RESEARCH PROCESS

None of the students in either the 2002 or 2005 Maastricht Programs had much experience with collaborative research in the field prior to traveling to Europe. Each had to navigate the complex personal and scholarly challenges of working with a group of colleagues on a common project. Different personality types and group tendencies quickly emerged as markers of each team and even inter-group dynamics. These factors directly affected how successful any one group would be in achieving its research goals. The program's design, particularly in the differences concerning the formation of the groups and in the expectations outlined at the beginning of the program, played a critical role in how group dynamics functioned.

For the purposes of protecting the identity of the students involved, I have designated each group a letter. I will refrain from discussing the particular locations of study so as to guarantee their anonymity. Since my purpose is to examine general patterns of learning, the particular empirical aspects of the research are of secondary importance. And so I will compare eight groups of students: Teams A-02, B-02, C-02, D-02, A-05, B-05, C-05, D-05.

These teams encompass an extraordinary geographical range of paired comparisons, which are listed on Table 1 in alphabetical order. As the table suggests, language competence played a key role in this selection. The designated regions included those in which either English is widely spoken (e.g., Malmö) or members of the research team already had fluency in the language. Half of the selected second regions were primarily English-speaking. Of the non-English second regions, the two Italian selections in 2002 stand out, since none of the students in that cohort spoke Italian. Each team "managed" with a mixture of Spanish, English, and French.

As I note below, the particularly inter-group competitive culture of the 2002 cohort caused certain teams to challenge one another with increasingly more difficult accomplishments. While this was not entirely the cause of the selection of two regions in which none of the students had language competence, my interviews with group members confirmed that competition played a role in the selection. (Given the relatively flexible manner in which Italians handle almost everything in life, the students were wise to choose that country to struggle with language).

Table 1. Paired Comparisons for the Europe of Regions Seminar, 2002 and 2005 Maastricht Programs
(The designated region is listed first)

Bilbao, the Basque Country—Northern Ireland, the U.K. (2005)
Catalonia, Spain—Bavaria, Germany (2002)
Malmö, Sweden—Dublin, Ireland (2005)
Nancy (Lorraine), France—Piedmont, Italy (2002)
North Rhein Westphalia, Germany (the Ruhr)—Scotland, the U.K. (2005)
Toulouse, France—Limerick, Ireland (2002)
Valencia, Spain—Catalonia, Spain (2005)
Valencia, Spain—Tuscany, Italy (2002)

Table 2 summarizes my findings in the comparison of the 2002 and 2005 Maastricht Program groups. I used a combination of qualitative data in my assessment of the groups: individual interviews with students at the end of the program, my notes of meetings in which I attended group activities, my observation of group organization of presentations during visits conducted by the entire program, and the final, formal oral presentation by each group during the 10th week. I summarize this disparate data into several 1-5 scales, with each of the eight groups scored according to their relative coherence and performance.

"Coherence" is based on two indicators: (1) communication—how well the members of the group listened and came to agreement on tasks, and (2) organization—how well tasks were assigned and completed. These categories include decisions concerning cases of study, research materials, and logistics such as transportation and division of group resources. As the anecdotal illustrations below will illustrate, groups that failed to come to agreements on basic decisions or who reflected a high level of confusion regarding which members were responsible for which research tasks scored low on this dimension.

"Performance" indicators measure the extent of data gathering and the quality of the final oral presentation. I would include cooperation among group members in the preparing of the final written report, but my individual interviews occurred before this step, so I do not have a reliable measure of group performance for this activity. This dimension was, as the data in Table 2 show, a result of coherence levels.

Table 2. Coherence and Performance Indicators, 2002 and 2005
(5=excellent, 4=very good, 3=good, 2=average, 1=poor)

Group	Communication	Organization	Data Gathering	Presentation
A-05	5	5	5	5
C-05	5	5	5	5
B-02	5	5	4	5
D-05	3	4	4	4
C-02	3	4	4	4
A-02	3	3	3	3
D-02	2	3	2	3
B-05	2	2	3	2

Source: Based on final assessments completed
by professor at the end of each program.

Below, I provide a global assessment of the groups based on these aggregate indicators. But I also wish to give the reader a sense of the more particular (and sometimes unique!) struggles, little victories, agonizing defeats, and contradictory interpersonal forces that were the proximate causes of group performance. For the sake of organizing the discussion, I address the role of the three main factors that I believe explain the differences across groups on Table 2—(1) the selection matrix of each cohort, (2) the timing and sequencing of group collaboration, and (3) the previous training in methods of each cohort. The first and the third of these factors emanate from designed differences between the two iterations of the Maastricht Program. The second, while also affected by design, is also the product of the particular organizational strategies and research topics pursued by the groups.

SELF-SELECTION VERSUS PROFESSORIAL SELECTION
The most notable finding in comparing the two cohorts on group dynamics is that allowing students to form their own groups does not guarantee internal coherence any more than having the director create the groups arbitrarily. Three of the four most coherent groups (A-05, C-05, D-05, and B-02) were in the 2005 cohort. They reported fewer instances of internal conflict, they tended to agree earlier than the others on which secondary regions to research, and they had the fewest problems handling the logistics of travel and communication. Regarding final presentations, these groups, plus a relatively more

conflictual set from 2002 (C-02), offered the sharpest and most internally consistent presentations of research at the end of the program. It was also not the case that these more coherent groups had the fewest number of "Type A" personalities. My view is that they included a variety of personality types and different kinds of learners.

Having the professor form the 2005 groups and allowing the 2002 students to self-select their groups did have an effect on the inter-group dimension. While the program design does not require inter-group cooperation, it did not encourage in any way inter-group competition. Nevertheless, the 2002 cohort developed intensive competitiveness during the field research periods of Weeks 6-8. As the aforementioned case of the two groups struggling with Italian suggests, inter-group competition led to a ratcheting up of research tasks. Although this was not in itself wholly negative as it reinforced motivation, it did lead to some unproductive inter-group dynamics, including the unwillingness of groups to share data gathered on similar cases. Personality differences might have played a role in these instances, but I believe that the fact that this competitiveness pervaded all four groups, each with very different personality types, suggests a systemic cause. The relative absence of inter-group competition in the 2005 cohort points to the difference in selection technique as a likely culprit. Since the director composed the groups in 2005, the priority of making these "unnatural" groups work as coherent bodies diverted student energies that might have otherwise gone to inter-group competition.

THE STRATEGIC VALUE OF EARLY AGREEMENT

Early agreement on the focus of study—the selection of the second region, the main hypothesis to be tested, and the key literature to be read—was an essential element in determining which groups would evolve as the more coherent in each cohort. The director encouraged early contact in all cases through program-sponsored lunches with the groups, but not all groups made use of this period during the first two weeks of the program to develop a record of successful collaboration. Settling the most nettlesome research issues early allowed some groups to communicate beyond the points most likely to create fundamental conflicts.

By contrast, groups that could not settle on the secondary region nor on the reasons for selection tended to wrestle with those old disagreements, in some cases through the denouement of the program. Moving beyond these discussions, and having a track record of agreement, the members of the more coherent groups could develop a reservoir of mutual trust and use it longer than was the case in the less coherent groups.

A typical example of one of the most coherent groups was a team that decided to conduct a study of partisan politics and nationalism in two regions located in the same country. This team wished to understand why nationalism could motivate dominant parties in one subnational region and not in another, especially when both regions shared the same culture and language. Despite the initial wishes of some members during Week 1 of the program to "shoot for the moon" and try a cross-national comparison with far-flung East European states, this team decided early on to control for the effects of national differences by working within the same European country. This accord, and the early decision to focus on partisan politics and nationalism, allowed this group to identify the relevant literature more easily during the first few weeks when library research in Maastricht was available to them.

One of the 2002 groups demonstrated the opposite tendency. Although this group decided early to assess the causes of high-tech investment on particular regions in two different European countries, the group's members disagreed on the main analytical puzzle. Having agreed on which regions they wished to travel to, they inverted the normal research process and thereby struggled to "find" a hypothesis and an analytical puzzle to underwrite their fieldwork.

In 2005, a similar problem occurred for one group that decided to study why unions and regional governments agree on reconverting old industries in steel and mining areas in some regions and not in others. But agreement on which regions to compare came as late as the fifth week; this was far too late to generate a track record of cooperation or even deepen their knowledge of the relevant literature in the countries to be studied. Disagreement on regional selection continued during the fieldwork portion, dividing those who were enthusiastic about the selection from those who continued to (more quietly now) nay-say the choice.

Timing and communication played vital roles in producing agreements that nurtured the research process. It is also evident that individual leaders played a role in some cases, but this factor must be qualified. Individual leaders played key roles in either accentuating the extant coherence of their group or in getting a wayward bunch back on track, but this phenomenon did not explain the success of the most coherent groups.

Individual leadership, I believe, played a key role only in two instances (A-02 and C-02) and for different reasons. Of the eight groups under study, only one was truly shaped by a single powerful personality (A-02), but the sometimes excessive nature of this person's leadership had to be reined in by other members, thus illustrating the inherent dangers of relying on strong leaders for group coherence. One or two members who were fundamentally in agreement on what the group should do played a key role in shaping C-02, so single leaders are not always necessary or sufficient to group coherence.

Leadership might also be expressed in other terms, such as the ability to mediate conflicts. In the case of D-05, one student played this role. All of the other members claimed that this person held the group together by diffusing disagreements and not allowing them to escalate. This student employed masterful

> Leadership might also be expressed in other terms, such as the ability to mediate conflicts. In the case of D-05, one student played this role. All of the other members claimed that this person held the group together by diffusing disagreements and not allowing them to escalate.

techniques for enhancing communication among a strong set of personalities by setting up the order of speakers at meetings, requiring that no meeting begin until full attendance was achieved, and making sure that no meeting end unless all were satisfied that their voices were heard. This student also facilitated the logistics of the group by acting as a clearinghouse of information—the student did not assign tasks as a leader would, but rather made sure everyone understood how tasks were distributed.

The relative weakness of the "strong leader" factor and the evident importance of early agreement in the development of mutual trust highlight the importance of sequencing the research process so that students have ample opportunities during the first five weeks to settle potentially conflictual matters. The assignment of weekly reports and the use of e-mail or online chat to report progress to the professor can focus groups on completing preliminary research tasks. With a five-week track record of achievements, each group will be more likely to enjoy a common reservoir of trust prior to the high-pressure research period. Group coherence, therefore, is built in small steps and not through grand accords or overbearing individual leaders.

THE ROLE OF PRIOR METHODS TRAINING

Differences in group coherence clearly played a role in determining performance. The data on Table 2 demonstrates that the coherence indicators were correlated with the performance indicators. The 2005 groups had a higher aggregate performance score (33) than the 2002 groups (28). Therefore it is useful to ask if systemic differences between the 2002 and 2005 cohorts played a role in differing performance. Beyond differences in selection technique, there were two additional differences of note. First, the 2005 cohort had the benefit of more training in research methods prior to coming on the program. Second, these students also had the research support of an alumnus of the 2002 program, a social science librarian, and greater access to technology while on the program.

The more extensive methodological preparation of the 2005 cohort proved important in enhancing communication, organization, and data gathering. Students in these groups were able to speak with one another in a lingua franca of causal relations, variables, and confidence measures. Having completed a statistical study of EU structural funding during the fifth week, these methods of comparative social science were at the core of group discussions concerning case selection, hypothesis creation and testing, and data gathering. As one student reported in her personal interview,

> The fact that everyone in our group had taken methods and were already aware of how to form and test a hypothesis saved us a lot of time, allowing us to move onto other more controversial questions before the group (Exit Interviews, 2005).

The exceptions in this experience were the three sophomores in this cohort, who reported that their lack of training in methods made them initially hesitant to participate. But as they "learned by doing," they each became more vital members of their respective research teams. In the end, each reported a renewed enthusiasm to follow-up their involvement in the Maastricht Program with intensive study of methods and additional research seminars.

The fact that the 2002 groups were much less trained in qualitative or quantitative comparative techniques introduced some notable inefficiencies into their research process. Only the four seniors who had completed the senior-year research design course and the thesis requirement ("Comps" in Carleton parlance) were able to direct their groups in methodological construction. But this proved draining on some who reported becoming the de facto coordinators and intellectual leaders of their respective groups, whether they wanted to claim the position or not.

The availability of a methodological lingua franca undoubtedly contributed to the ability of the 2005 groups to organize a common research strategy early during the program. It also enhanced communication of ideas to the entire class during the research presentation as presenters could assume that audience members were all equally trained to understand the logic of case selection, hypothesis testing, and comparative assessments.

The one inefficiency I detected that was linked to methods training involved the fruitless search for quantitative indicators for fundamentally qualitative variables. Two 2005 groups spent time in this way with little result. In one case a group attempted to acquire survey data from a Spanish statistical agency for three weeks with little result. Although this group ultimately gave up and pursued a qualitative comparison, frustration emanating from the failure to acquire the survey data left a lasting impression very much in keeping with the pedagogical goals of the program. As one math major with a special talent for quantitative analysis admitted at the end of the program:

> I felt powerless without the data. Not getting the data we wanted and the daily disappointments with contacts who would not respond made me appreciate all the more the difficulty of fieldwork and how the comparative method is really practiced (Exit Interviews, 2005).

The more extensive research support provided to the 2005 group also played a role in the superior performance of this cohort, but I believe this factor was less positive than the systemic effect of common methods training.

First, although the 2005 groups had more easy (wireless) access to the Internet and to Internet telephony, I received more complaints about the technology than was evident in 2002. Access was sometimes interrupted for hours or days, and students struggled with slow connections at times that produced inefficiencies in the research.

Second, student management of available technology was no better in 2005 than in 2002. Incidences involving the failure of cell phones or their irresponsible use were greater in 2005 than in 2002. Only one student in 2002 succeeded in locking his cell phone through improperly punching in the wrong pin codes. Yet the director had to attend to as many as seven of these instances in 2005. By far the most egregious case involved a student who used the group's phone to contact the personal, Colorado-based cell, of another group member. Both were in the same city—London—and the costs of using international lines to dial across town depleted the group's balance of cell phone minutes within a two-day period! This serves as a reminder that the availability of technology does not guarantee that it will be employed in the most efficient or useful manner.

It might even be argued that the 2005 cohort's greater reliance on technology produced more frustrations in coordinating research than was the case in 2002. The relative ease of access to electronic sources with their attendant limitations on the availability of the most recent or oldest articles created "blind spots" in the research that had to be filled with more traditional library work. This produced a somewhat disjointed division of labor in

> [This division of labor] undermined the goal of a common learning experience...

which certain group members did the "drudgery" of library work while others did electronic research and still others used technology to communicate with and manage group contacts. While this division of labor was undoubtedly efficient in most cases, it undermined the goal of a common learning experience in which each student would exercise the same skills on the same project. The division of labor also worked against the director's hope that collaborative work would diffuse skills across students so that those students with less of a background or more recent exposure to data analysis would learn from the performance of their more experienced colleagues. Instead, the division of tasks was based on students' extant skill set.

The division of labor factor might also explain why two or three of the 2005 groups decided to divide their forces during the field research period while none of the 2002 groups did. Although this seemed efficient, it became the basis of some sustained internal conflicts. Students who traveled less and committed themselves to the heavy use of library resources at EIPA in Maastricht felt that their efforts were devalued by other group members who traveled more extensively and followed up on contacts in the field. These cases were few, too few to appreciably hurt the relative coherence of these groups. But the unintended consequences of an efficient division of labor should be noted nonetheless. Evidently, even when the division of tasks is well organized, the execution of research on an agreed basis may produce a counterintuitive negative effect on group cohesion!

ASSESSING THE RESEARCH EXPERIENCE

The design of the Maastricht Program in 2002 and 2005 enhanced the students' achievement of several learning goals. The small group format made the most of the efficiencies of collaborative research while it provided an opportunity for students to engage in the kinds of collegial work they will experience in their professional lives. The relative adeptness of the groups was based on the particular attributes of individual members, but also the sequencing of the research process. Groups that developed a track record early on during the program had an easier time assigning tasks and implementing their research designs. The chief lesson for future designs of the program is that the director should provide common reporting tasks on a weekly basis from the beginning of the program to encourage the building of mutual trust within all groups.

The differences in selection technique and the availability of common methodological training were the key systemic differences between the 2005 and 2002 cohorts that had direct effects on coherence and performance. The professor-selected cohort of 2005 avoided the inter-group competition that became a distraction in 2002. Even more important was the 2005 cohort's common methodological training. As undergraduate departments of political science make required methods courses a more central part of their curricula, a process facilitated by the availability of user-friendly statistical packages, more students will have the ability to speak in the lingua franca of quantitative and qualitative hypothesis-testing. This will allow directors to deepen students' analytical skills by exposing them to the inherent difficulties of applying these skills in the field, in other countries and other cultures.

It should be pointed out that the learning process in this case was inherently messy. Even when students were properly prepared to employ straightforward empirical tests of their own hypotheses, problems acquiring data and setting up contacts in the field produced frustrating lessons in the real limits of comparative fieldwork. Perhaps no lesson is more important. Evidence for this is the fact that the students in their exit interviews preferred generally to use the time to reflect on what they learned from their frustrations in setting up their studies rather than from their reported findings. In reflecting on their comments, it is not an exaggeration to claim that each student encountered and learned several vital life lessons concerning how to work with their colleagues under pressure and with uncertain research conditions.

My focus in this chapter has been on the effects of program design on learning. Of course, it should be admitted that no matter how well designed any off-campus program might be, students' individual attributes and attitudes will play a decisive role in the outcome. Program directors can only hope that the way the program is assembled will orient students efficiently and effectively toward the achievement of the main pedagogical goals.

The comparison of the Maastricht Program in 2002 and 2005 also offers a variety of insights into how the program might be redesigned for its next iteration in 2008. My preliminary plans call for the students to work in research teams on a *common project* that will integrate fieldwork in the regions under a common hypothesis and debate in the literature on European political economy. Given the findings in this study, I will select the student groups and provide a larger number of reporting tasks during the research process. My role will undoubtedly be more hands-on as I become the common point around which the groups will coordinate their empirical applications of fieldwork to the core hypothesis. Since I anticipate that methods and the course European Political Economy will be prerequisites for the program, the research will benefit from a cohort of students with more equal training. One can only hope that this new design will take advantage of the extraordinary abilities of Carleton students and that it will enhance their ability to study the mysteries of the flat world.

REFERENCES

Bowman, K. S., & Jennings, A. (2005, January). *Pura vida*: Using study abroad to engage undergraduate students in comparative politics research. *PS: Political Science, 38*, 77-81.

Engle, J. (1995, March 17). Critical attention for study abroad. *Chronicle of Higher Education*, A56.

Exit Interviews (2005). Maastricht Program, Carleton College.

Florida, R. (2002). *The rise of the creative class*. New York: Basic Books.

Friedman, T. L. (2005). *The world is flat: A brief history of the twenty-first century*. New York: Farrar, Straus and Giroux.

Hopkins, J. R. (1999). Studying abroad as a form of experiential education. *Liberal Education, 85*, 36-42.

Paas, M. (2004). Experiential learning abroad. In S. Singer & C. Rutz (Eds.), *Reflections on learning as teachers* (pp. 176-185). Northfield, MN: College City Publications.

COLLABORATION AS INCLUSION AND SUPPORT

REFLECTIONS ON COLLABORATIVE TEACHING AND LEARNING:

Establishing a Cross-Cultural Studies Program

Clifford Clark

I did not plan to spend much of my teaching career working with other faculty to develop new courses. I was a historian, and historians are well known for being loners—working independently for years on their books and articles, submitting them to other scholars only after the first drafts are written or the manuscript is submitted for publication. But, in fact, over the past four decades, I have developed and taught new courses with 15 faculty members from nine different departments. Most recently, I helped develop a new cross-cultural studies program that has connected me to faculty in the Anthropology, French, German, Japanese, and Religion Departments. This essay provides me with an opportunity to reflect on this experience with collaborative teaching. It is an examination of what the terms "interdisciplinarity," "multidisciplinarity," and "collaborative teaching and learning" have meant to me. It is a commentary on the parallels that I see in the experience of being an academic outsider: in the one case trying to understand an academic discipline that is foreign to me and, in the other, as a scholar studying another society who is trying to comprehend a culture whose language and values are different from my own.

Before I go any farther, I should explain how I define the terms "inter-

> "Multidisciplinarity" stresses not only the utility of the additive value of two or more disciplines but also the importance of having the practitioners of each discipline gain the self-awareness that comes from seeing the advantages and disadvantages in the methodology of a discipline different from their own.

CLIFFORD CLARK, professor of history and M.A. and A.D. Hulings Professor of American Studies, has been a member of the Carleton faculty since 1970. He earned his B.A. degree at Yale University and his M.A. and PhD degrees at Harvard University.

disciplinarity," "multidisciplinarity," and "collaborative teaching." I find the arguments used by Julie Thompson Klein (1990), in her book, *Interdisciplinarity: History, Theory, and Practice,* to be helpful. Klein suggests that a discipline might be defined as "a stable epistemic community and agreement upon what constitutes excellence within a field" (p. 107).[1] She further insists that an interdisciplinary field "constitutes a unique form of specialization" that enables "a selective integration within a spectrum of disciplines" (p. 116). While she recognizes that the boundaries in any field are to some extent porous and are not necessarily coterminous with the courses in any department, she does stress the commitment made by self-labeled interdisciplinary programs to integrate methodologies and establish clear approaches to analyzing materials. Simon Bronner of Pennsylvania State University (2005a, p. 8, and 2005b, p. 1) calls this integration "conceptual" because it "is a new configuration built out of the attention to themes, areas, and problems for inquiry."

In contrast to the emphasis on "conceptual integration" that is inherent in Klein's definition of "interdisciplinarity," I use the term "multidisciplinarity" to mean using the distinctive methodologies and theories of different disciplines to reshape the ways in which questions are asked and problems are viewed. My view of "multidisciplinarity" stresses not only the utility of the additive value of two or more disciplines but also the importance of having the practitioners of each discipline gain the self-awareness that comes from seeing the advantages and disadvantages in the methodology of a discipline different from their own. Although this kind of multidisciplinarity can reshape the original discipline itself, as happened in the 1950s to biology when physicists like Leo Szilard moved into the field and brought with them a search for underlying principles, a mindset that paved the way for the discovery of DNA (Fleming, 1968, 152-158), multidisciplinarity appears most often to be an effective combination of different theories and methodological techniques. Collaborative teaching, in my view, takes advantage of these disciplinary similarities and differences to begin a discussion that looks for new ways analyze a set of sources and teach a particular class.

> Most of my early experiences developing new courses with other colleagues essentially pooled contributions from different disciplines to provide new angles of vision on a common question.

My own introduction to collaborative and interdisciplinary teaching and learning began by accident in 1967 when I joined the American Studies Program at Amherst College. As a junior faculty member, I worked with colleagues from the History and English Departments to hammer out a new introductory American studies course each year. That process opened my eyes, far more than my undergraduate or graduate education had, to the different ways in which different disciplines framed their questions, mined their sources, and developed their interpretations. Indeed, in the 1970s and early 1980s, American studies programs nationally were fascinated with questions both about how to integrate disciplines and how to use them to understand problems of cultural identity, diversity, and nationalism (Fleming, 1968, 152ff.).

I joined the Carleton faculty in 1970. Two years later I accepted the offer of the directorship of the American Studies Program because it had the reputation of supporting collaborative teaching. I had had too much fun working with other colleagues at Amherst to pass up the opportunity to continue to do so. I had learned too much from them, not only about their disciplines and their teaching methods but also about my own field. Teaching with colleagues from different departments was like going back to graduate school. It energized me, added fresh insights into my own discipline, and expanded my circle of friends. It also confirmed my earlier decision to teach at a small college rather than at a departmentally segregated large university.

Most of my early experiences developing new courses with other colleagues essentially pooled contributions from different disciplines to provide new angles of vision on a common question. In a 1967 course on immigration, for example, that focused on the question of what motivated immigrants to come to the United States, I brought in Oscar Handlin's theory of immigrant assimilation while a sociologist colleague suggested the immigration models of Milton Gordon and an English Department colleague suggested Abraham Cahan's novel, *The Rise of David Levinsky.*[2] Later, in a course called American Music, I contributed background material that set the context for racial conflict in the 1890s while Steve Kelly in the Music Department demonstrated how ragtime composers such as Scott Joplin picked up the themes, melodies, and musical structures from marching band music. Joplin changed the tempos and pioneered a popular new dance music with his "Maple Leaf Rag" and other compositions.

The advantage of these early collaborations was that the courses that we created had richer, more varied sources, a diversity of disciplinary approaches, and a more complex and nuanced context in which to explore questions such as, What is American about American music? or Has there been a common immigrant experience? I particularly enjoyed teaching them both because they added new insights into sources that I was already using and because they forced me to become a student myself. But they were not "interdisciplinary" in the sense that I had mastered music theory or music composition. While the courses gave me a glimpse of the power of such disciplinary techniques, I did not have to master the techniques myself. Instead I relied on the expert from the Music Department. When I later taught some of the same material in a different course, I took insights about musical structure from Kelly's approach but did not duplicate the detail in his line of analysis.

While most of the courses that I have team-taught relied on this collaborative model, two stand out that were different. One course, American Architecture in Context, which I taught in 1978 with Lauren Soth in the Art and Art History Department, took an explicitly confrontational approach. As the syllabus stated:

> Social historians and art historians approach works of art differently. The former are more interested in their evidential value as cultural artifacts; the latter more in their intrinsic value as aesthetic objects. *American Architecture in Context* aims to provide students with a confrontation between these approaches as applied to specific episodes in American architectural history. (Clark & Soth, 1978)

Each class turned into a battle over which approach yielded more insights, that of the art historian or the cultural historian. Was the American public's fascination with neo-classical architectural forms in the 1770s when houses often resembled miniature Greek or Roman temples the product of a generation obsessed with reinforcing the republican political ideals associated with earlier Greek city states? Or did they simply evolve from fascination with classical forms popularized by Christopher Wren, Robert Adam, and other English architects?

Teaching this class was in many ways more difficult than my other attempts at collaboration. Every class meeting turned into a debate. I was forced not simply to state my argument, but I had to defend it, shore it up with evidence, and search for reasons why it was more persuasive than that of the traditional art historical approach. In some ways, the give and take of this class benefited me more than the other collaborative courses that I had taught. Energized by the debate, I began teaching courses in what turned out to be the emerging field of material culture studies.

I had become fascinated by a question that seemed to lie at the boundary between architectural history and social history: What impact did the houses in which people lived have upon their sense of family? It seemed to me that architectural historians studied houses as if no one ever lived there. Symptomatic of this problem was the fact that the photographs of houses in most architectural history books never contained any people. Similarly, social historians of the family discussed family life and gender relationships without ever mentioning how the layout of homes might influence patterns of social interaction and reveal unstated assumptions about privacy, entertaining, and the relationships between adults and children. Intrigued by what appeared to be the interdisciplinary nature of these questions, I continued to work on them and nearly a decade later, I published a book, *The American Family Home, 1800-1960*, which explored the connections between house forms and styles and images of the ideal American family (Clark, 1986).

> Teaching this class was in many ways more difficult than my other attempts at collaboration. Every class meeting turned into a debate. I was forced not simply to state my argument, but I had to defend it, shore it up with evidence, and search for reasons why it was more persuasive than that of the traditional art historical approach. In some ways, the give and take of this class benefited me more than the other collaborative courses that I had taught.

The other course that challenged my assumptions was The History of American Economic Thought, which I taught with Martha Paas of the Economics Department. This course focused on the models drawn from science that were used by the discipline's founders in the 1890s: a biological model used by Thorstein Veblen and others to track the evolution of economic institutions and a model drawn from physics that used mathematics to explain economic behavior. While we agreed on much of the course and explored the reasons why mathematical modeling had come to dominate much of the modern discipline of economics, we ended up in disagreement in our evaluation of the student essays. Paas stressed the importance of student mastery of and ability to replicate the arguments that we read, while I emphasized the importance of critiquing these arguments.

Our disagreement on grading highlighted the different disciplinary approaches taken in the sciences and social sciences from that in the humanities. While I did concede that it was important for students to master and be able to replicate the arguments of a particular author, I wanted students, perhaps naïvely, to evaluate and question the premises on which the arguments rested.

> Our disagreement on grading highlighted the different disciplinary approaches taken in the sciences and social sciences from that in the humanities.... I wanted students, perhaps naïvely, to evaluate and question the premises on which the arguments rested.

We ended up with a compromise by talking out our differences and reassessing the particular papers in question. The course was thus a reminder that collaboration assumes agreement about writing standards and grading, but disciplinary differences need to be taken into consideration.

So this was my experience with team-teaching and with working in interdisciplinary programs when I accepted the dean of the college's request to chair a college committee in 1998 to look into the possibility of increasing the number of international students on campus and help develop a new program in cross-cultural studies that would appeal to them and to American students interested in global and comparative studies. Let me turn now to this project and examine in more detail the ways in which it built on and extended my earlier commitment to collaborative teaching and interdisciplinary studies.

CROSS-CULTURAL STUDIES AT CARLETON

The initial project, which was supported by a planning grant from the Starr Foundation, called for establishing a "concentration in cross-cultural studies." I led 30 faculty members, with eight consultants, in weekly meetings for the entire 1997-98 academic year, including week-long seminars in the fall and spring. Out of these deliberations, we created a proposal for a new concentration (a group of courses similar to a minor at other institutions) that was designed "to create a forum where faculty from the different area studies programs on campus (American studies, Asian studies, French and Francophone studies, etc.) can address common issues and problems in a comparative, collaborative framework" (Clark, 1998).

An important part of our proposal to the faculty was its emphasis on the interweaving of the experiential and intellectual dimensions of learning. We intended to pay close and careful attention to the counseling and support system necessary to help foreign students adjust to the rigorous intellectual and intense social demands of Carleton. All students in the program, both foreign and American, through off-campus programs in both the U.S. and other nations, could have the experience of living in a foreign country and working in an internship.

Initially, because of our funding from the Starr Foundation, we focused on bringing Asian students to Carleton. They would represent our initial "foreign" students. But, even the term "Asian" was problematic. Was a Japanese student, born and raised in Argentina, an Asian student? As we were about to find out as well, American students, who had lived much of their lives abroad, were attracted to this program. Irrespective of how we defined "foreign" students, courses were designed to incorporate and build on the experience of international students in America and on the experience of American students living in Asia or other parts of the world. In that manner, learning would extend beyond the formal curriculum itself, nurture genuine and profound international understanding, and help prepare students to live thoughtfully and effectively in a society other than their own.

The debate within the faculty over the approval of the new program revealed the ways in which cooperation sometimes can be stymied by departmental boundaries. One professor in political science and international affairs thought that no program was needed. His department already covered international affairs. When he attended our meetings, his main objective seemed to be to derail the entire project. Although the group spent a fair amount of time discussing the issues with him, in the end he dropped out. Not particularly interested in the collaborative aspects of the program (that is, collaboration with faculty outside of his department), he also objected to the use of the concept of "culture" which he thought was too vague and amorphous.

Our opponent also argued that traditional disciplines were built on a clear theoretical basis and that they possessed a distinctive methodology. One positive effect of his insistence on the importance of theory and methodology was to force us to look more closely at both those subjects. We soon concluded that within most disciplines considerable debate raged over both topics. As another of our colleagues pointed out, political science itself was internally divided between political theorists, political analysts, and international relations specialists. Theory and method were hotly debated among all three sub-fields.

In part in response to this debate, one of our group, Sudarshan Seneviratne, a visiting professor from Peradeniya University in Sri Lanka, suggested that we had an opportunity to make this a "truly international program" that moved beyond particular disciplines by focusing our efforts on "social, political, economic, cultural, and environmental issues" (Seneviratne, n.d.). Such an approach had an important secondary value as well. Like the transnational student who occupies the borderland between two societies, speaking both languages and moving from one to the other, much as a Mexican-American might cross the border between Texas and Mexico, the multidisciplinary scholar has the potential to occupy a similar borderland, comprehending both what is valuable about his or her own discipline and also seeing its shortcomings from another disciplinary perspective. The advantage of a problem-focused, multidisciplinary approach was that it invited disciplinary collaboration and moved beyond the debates over theory and method that sometimes preoccupied a particular field of study.

Seneviratne's suggestion presaged the direction that the American studies movement itself would take five years later when Bronner suggested in the March 2005 *American Studies Newsletter* that "the driving question for the field in this development shifted from asking how to integrate disciplines ... to identify problems or issues (e.g., cultural identity, cultural diversity, nationalism, transnationalism) that American studies distinctively addresses ..." (Bronner, 2005a, p. 8). In a similar fashion, the faculty participants in our seminars stressed the examination both of particular problems such as environmental pollution or the nature of labor flows in transnational markets and also of processes such as adaptation to new cultures or the experience of being an outsider or of being discriminated against, which cut across different societies and regions.

In our faculty discussions about multidisciplinarity, we came to the conclusion that although it was important to recognize the differences among disciplines, it was equally important to recognize that disciplinary boundaries have themselves changed considerably in the past two decades. In the sciences at Carleton, biochemistry has emerged as an expanding new field that explores the chemical reactions within cells. Our thought was that a similar cooperation could exist among different disciplines in the humanities and social sciences. Indeed, given the importance of language in understanding culture, new linkages have formed among historians, sociologists, and anthropologists and the literary scholars and language specialists.

The proposal for establishing a new concentration in cross-cultural studies was debated and passed by the faculty in the fall of 1998. Our practical concern then became the development of the new cross-cultural studies courses. In the fall of 1999, I headed up a group of faculty who met to develop a new introductory course to be taught the following year. Thanks to the acquisition of major support from the Starr Foundation, the National Endowment for the Humanities, and the Rockefeller Brothers Fund, a group of colleagues from the History, Sociology and Anthropology, Religion, Japanese, French, and Economics Departments met regularly during the year to hammer out a new freshman seminar, Growing Up Cross-Culturally.

> Designed to help incoming international students build upon their own expertise as members of their own societies and to ease their entry into American academic life, [Growing Up Cross-Culturally] focused on four important transitions in society: entrance into schooling (kindergarten), adolescence, courtship and marriage, and coming to terms with the end of life.

Designed to help incoming international students build upon their own expertise as members of their own societies and to ease their entry into American academic life, it focused on four important transitions in society: entrance into schooling (kindergarten), adolescence, courtship and marriage, and coming to terms with the end of life. The course included trips to a Northfield kindergarten class, a high school football game, and a local nursing home.

During the six years in which this course has been taught, the mix of faculty has changed. While historians and anthropologists shaped much of the initial course offerings, more recently faculty from the French and German Departments have emphasized film analysis and fiction. A good example was the suggestion of Christine Lac of the French Department that we compare the American and French versions of the movie, *Three Men and a Baby*. The scene where the men double park and then are confronted by the police is handled very differently in each film. In the American version, the cop is physically large and astride a horse. He represents the law and, implicitly, the threat of violence if the men should question his authority. In the French version, the policeman is on foot and displays a more mocking sense of authority. He is annoyed but is more sympathetic to the attempt of the inept males to deal with the child. Thus, by bringing in faculty from other disciplines, the course highlights cultural differences that indirectly shape the changes in the stage of life.

Our recent discussion, in preparation of the upcoming iteration of the course, focused on the end stage of life. It exemplifies the ways in which multiple disciplines, when they work together, contribute to a more complex understanding of a subject. In this segment of the course we use an article from the *New York Times* on the growth and changes of the American hospice system in the past two decades. In "Will We Ever Arrive at the Good Death?" the author, Robin Marantz Henig (2005), argues that Americans have a reluctance to think about death and dying or to even use those terms. Hospice has become a way of helping people come to terms with the terminal stage of friends or loved ones. The problem is that the American faith in technology and medical innovations makes it difficult for most people to accept or even allow the sick person to die with dignity. To complement this sociological article, we assign Sarah Lamb's *White Saris and Sweet Mangoes* (2000), an anthropological study that focuses on how people in the Hindu tradition in India use their religious traditions as a way of letting go of "maya," their spirit, as they prepare to accept the approach of death. Each article complements the other by looking at the larger issue of how societies ritualize the spiritual and psychological struggles to come to terms with the final moments of life.

THE BENEFITS OF COLLABORATION

Has the course worked well? What are the larger benefits and drawbacks of this kind of collaboration? Returning to my original questions, why do I keep participating in these kinds of courses? What has been the larger benefit for me of collaborative teaching? I began this essay by noting that historians are generally the classic loners in terms of their scholarship. A similar comment might be made about teaching. For most faculty members, they are the only instructors in their classes. They have little chance to observe their colleagues, to gain insights into different ways to approach teaching their subject matter. Working collaboratively with another faculty member has, at the very least, the great benefit of providing feedback and alternate role models for what makes good teaching. It has also introduced me to a wide variety of new materials to use in the classroom. As far as I am concerned, if that were the only benefit of collaborative teaching, it would by itself more than justify the value of the practice. By virtue of having working closely with so many other faculty colleagues, I know that my own teaching skills have improved immensely.

But the other value for me has been to expand my knowledge and understanding of other disciplines and their modes of analysis. From art history and film studies I have gained new skills in the analysis of visual materials, and I now use them in a variety of different ways. From my colleagues in the English Department I have developed a fondness for using short stories as historical sources. From my friends in the Music Department I have gotten some basic tools for analyzing music in my classes. From economics, I have developed an interest in the analysis of labor markets, industrial change, and technological improvements. I have particularly benefited from working with my colleagues in sociology and anthropology on topics such as work, immigration, transnationalism, and the history of childhood.

So, in the end, what would I conclude about the value of interdisciplinarity, multidisciplinarity, and collaborative teaching?

> Multidisciplinarity and collaborative teaching provide, in addition to the breadth of perspective and feedback on teaching already mentioned, an additional layer of expertise. Introducing students to the idea that professional expertise is always helpful counterbalances the tendency of teachers in almost all disciplines to think that their own approach is the best and most effective way to understand their subject.

If true interdisciplinarity means the combination of disciplines into a unified system of analysis, then my experience is that such a fusion rarely takes place. At some point, the differences in the questions asked, assumptions made, and the value placed on methodology come to the surface. Complete integration rarely happens.

Nevertheless, I have become a great believer in multidisciplinarity and collaborative teaching because they provide, in addition to the breadth of perspective and feedback on teaching already mentioned, an additional layer of expertise. Although it is possible to master a second discipline, few of us have the time to do it. Rather than becoming completely transnational in our outlook, with the necessary mastery of the language and culture of another discipline, we are more like tourists, observing the highlights and gaining an introduction to new materials. In the company of another colleague, however, we are tourists with an expert guide who knows the foreign landscape.

So, there is a distinct advantage in having a second authority in class. It allows the class to pursue lines of analysis and ideas that would otherwise re-main closed off. By introducing students to the idea that professional expertise is always helpful, it counterbalances the tendency of teachers in almost all dis-ciplines to think that their own approach is the best and most effective way to understand their subject. Collaborative teaching invariably brings fresh insights to the questions being explored and suggests new ways of analysis. For me it has had the wonderful effect of provoking my curiosity in exploring new ways to study the past.

ENDNOTES

[1] Julie Klein is astute in pointing out the difficulties in these kinds of definitions.

[2] See Handlin (1951), Gordon (1964), and Cahan (1917).

REFERENCES

Bronner, S. J. (2005a, March). American studies and humanities: The challenge to university administration, *American Studies Association Newsletter, 28:1,* 1-2.

Bronner, S.J. (2005b March). Beyond disciplinarity: The new goals of the American studies movement. *American Studies Association Newsletter, 28:1,* 8-9.

Cahan, A. (1917). *The rise of David Levinsky.* New York: Harper and Brothers.

Clark, C., Jr. & Soth, L. (1978). Syllabus: American architecture in context, author's collection.

Clark, C., Jr. (1986). *The American family home, 1800-1960.* Chapel Hill, NC: University of North Carolina Press.

Clark, C., Jr. (with C. Clark, K. Sparling, J. Fisher, R. Jackson, S. Carpenter, B. McKinsey, and others). (1998), Proposal for a concentration in cross-cultural studies. Unpublished typescript, September 23, 1998, author's collection.

Fleming, D. (1968). Émigré physicists and the biological revolution. *Perspectives in American History, II* , 152-158.

Gordon, M. (1964). *Assimilation in American life.* New York: Oxford University Press.

Handlin, O. (1951). *The uprooted.* New York: Grosset & Dunlap.

Henig, R. M. (2005, August 7). Will we ever arrive at the good death? *New York Times Magazine,* pp. 26-35, 40, 68.

Klein, J. (1990). *Interdisciplinarity: History, theory, and practice.* Detroit, MI: Wayne State University Press.

Lamb, S. (2000). *White saris and sweet mangoes: Aging, gender, and body in North India.* Berkeley, CA: University of California Press.

Seneviratne, S. (c1998). E-mail to James Fisher. No date. Copy in the author's possession.

Back to the Books:
Literary Study and Special Collections

Kristi Wermager and Susan Jaret McKinstry

Collaboration is a risk and an adventure, a teaching and learning opportunity for all of the participants. This particular collaboration between an English professor and a library curator began with a shared enthusiasm for rare books and developed into an interdisciplinary model of the collaborative process. As always, collaboration begins with a question or a need that sends the participants on a journey out of their offices, a journey that challenges the traditional parameters of their own fields as each enters into new intellectual territory. So how did our journey begin?

THE PROFESSOR:

One of the delights of literary study creates a teaching dilemma. Literature can seem ahistorical, universal, simply "human," and hence not bound to a particular time and place: "A rose by any other name would smell as sweet" can sound like a human truth rather than a Renaissance phrase. Unlike most academic subjects, literature's object of study is also a cultural commodity and a source of personal and social pleasure. The distinction between popular and academic texts is thin and shifting; literature classes can study J. K. Rowling's Harry Potter books as well as Kahlid Hosseini's *The Kite Runner* or Azar Nafisi's *Reading Lolita in Tehran*. These books demonstrate the dilemma. They are absolutely placed in time and space (real and imagined—certainly narrated—places like Hogwarts, Afghanistan and Iran) even as they tell timeless human stories about personal and social achievement.

KRISTI WERMAGER, bibliographer and curator of special collections in Carleton's Gould Library, joined the staff at Carleton in 1980. She earned her B.A. and her M.A. degrees at the University of Minnesota. SUSAN JARET MCKINSTRY, the Helen F. Lewis Professor of English, earned her B.A. and M.A. degrees at Miami University (Ohio) and her PhD degree at the University of Michigan. She has been a member of the faculty since 1982.

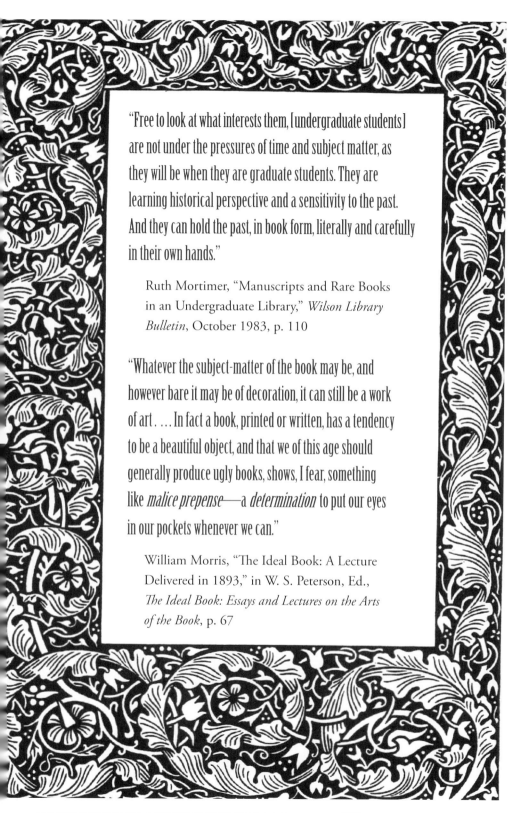

"Free to look at what interests them, [undergraduate students] are not under the pressures of time and subject matter, as they will be when they are graduate students. They are learning historical perspective and a sensitivity to the past. And they can hold the past, in book form, literally and carefully in their own hands."

Ruth Mortimer, "Manuscripts and Rare Books in an Undergraduate Library," *Wilson Library Bulletin*, October 1983, p. 110

"Whatever the subject-matter of the book may be, and however bare it may be of decoration, it can still be a work of art. ... In fact a book, printed or written, has a tendency to be a beautiful object, and that we of this age should generally produce ugly books, shows, I fear, something like *malice prepense*—a *determination* to put our eyes in our pockets whenever we can."

William Morris, "The Ideal Book: A Lecture Delivered in 1893," in W. S. Peterson, Ed., *The Ideal Book: Essays and Lectures on the Arts of the Book*, p. 67

Literature's humanism was institutionalized by the "New Criticism" of the 1930s, with its emphasis on the literary text as a timeless aesthetic object, a "well-wrought urn" interpreted by readers through "close reading" of the details of literary language. This method remained the central method of literary analysis for decades, because focusing on literary language alone gave teachers and students ready access to "primary" materials—in any edition, Shakespeare was still Shakespeare, and his irony and poetry, his insight into human ambition and public flaws, could be read over 400 years with little alteration. Multiple, readily available paperback editions of most texts and a burgeoning used book market on the Internet have made nearly every book ever written available at the click of a mouse and the wave of a credit card. And now, many literary texts are themselves available online, often with links to critical commentary and historical notes, making textuality even more focused on words themselves rather than on books.

Two events made me decide to change my teaching and bring the book back into the classroom.

First, a serendipitous methodological shift in literary study to New Historicism and Cultural Criticism emphasizes literature's role in cultural and social history. New Web-based texts provide extensive links to historical documents and political, aesthetic, and social issues, and the developing Internet resources for literary study connect the roles of history and literature. For example, George Landow's "Victorian Web" and Jerome McGann's "Rossetti Archive" provide computer access to primary resources that had previously been available only in select, distant libraries to certified scholars.

But something was still missing for me. The book is, in my own work, more than a collection of words. It is a material object with beauty and history.

The second event, then, grew out of my interest in the relations between the literary word and the visual object, which had led to research in film adaptations, photography, and painting. Simultaneously, I had discovered that useful and beautiful Victorian books could be found quite easily on the proliferating Internet used book sites. I began to collect Victorian texts that I regularly showed to my students in the British literature survey course so they understood that classic literature was not initially anthologized in huge, ugly books with tissue-thin paper or in throw-away paperbacks but was treasured in small, lovely editions whose paper, print and binding were works of art. I wanted to share that sense of the book with my students, but I also wanted to teach them something that I felt was essential about literature and was being lost. Rather than being humanistic, free-floating collections of words, books should be studied as archaeological and aesthetic material objects with an enormous teaching potential. I wanted to put the book, as material object, as social product, back in the class.

This was tricky. Teaching a course on the art of Jane Austen, I continually tried to make students recognize the historical issues raised by her novels: in the ubiquitous marriage plot, certainly, and the heroines' comic dramas, but more tellingly in the fact that the novels exist at all. Rather than just human connection—the adolescent search for love—I wanted to invoke historical distance and questions. What confluence of events allowed for Jane Austen the writer—and for the development of the novel, the novel by women, and the comic novel? Telling the students about 18th-century codes of conduct still seemed like a backdrop to literature rather than integral to its analysis. How could I move the students from the idea of history as background information, and how could I get them to engage with the material texts in a meaningful way? I wanted to share the beauty of books as objects with my students; I wanted to help them understand what "primary" texts could mean in literature classes in both aesthetic and archaeological terms. And, most importantly, I wanted to answer the question: What does the book as an object contribute to literary study?

Of course I went to the library for inspiration, and there I found Special Collections Curator Kristi Wermager.

THE CURATOR:

When I took over curatorship of Carleton's Special Collections in 1999, I had two immediate impressions: The first was that the collection was a strong one with several remarkable items; the second was that the collection was underutilized. I was convinced that incorporating the use of Special Collections materials into a variety of courses would enrich the Carleton educational experience for students and even, perhaps, for faculty.

The first question that I needed to consider was what curatorship of rare books or special collections might mean in an undergraduate liberal arts setting. As a librarian, I know that my role is to provide access to information regardless of the medium, but the information that rare books and primary materials offer exists as part of the material objects themselves. Curatorship implies careful custodianship of these objects, often in a museum setting. Exhibits have traditionally provided curators a means of sharing this information from their collections with their public, but I wanted a more dynamic interaction, one that was more appropriate for the educational mission of the college.

I came to believe that, in this setting, my role should include responsibility not only for the custodianship of the collection but also for facilitating a series of direct interactions between the students and faculty and the collections. An active Special Collections program working through the curriculum to provide Carleton students with an opportunity to interact directly with the rich collection materials would have value here and my dual role as curator—protecting and sharing rare materials—would be fulfilled.

My own experience, both as a student and as a librarian, had shown me the powerful effect that rare books can have on undergraduates. For the majority of students, a visit to Carleton's Special Collections is their first hands-on exposure to rare, primary materials, and most students are seduced by the experience. Some are fascinated just by the fact that the books are 300 years old; others are struck by the beauty of the bindings or the marbled end-papers; some are drawn to design, page layout, or choice of typeface; still others are interested in the mechanics of how the books were printed. Nearly all of them are struck by an iconic value that seems to emanate from the physical books, whether they are gorgeous old books or exceptionally beautifully printed modern private press editions.

As a curator, my job is to arrange this encounter, and the key to my doing that is collaborating with teaching faculty. On our own, the collection and I can interact with only a handful of highly motivated students. When an instructor brings a class in, however, the interaction extends to students who would never otherwise visit the collection. During a class session in Special Collections, a conversation takes place not only between students and instructor or students and curator but also between students and human beings of another place, time, and culture. The instructor and I are there to facilitate the encounter and to share our knowledge and enthusiasm, but the encounter is the students'. Susan Allen (1999), in her article "Rare Books and the College Library: Current Practices in Marrying Undergraduates to Special Collections," refers to the work of instructor or curator as matchmaking: "Once object and student are brought together, they may be left somewhat on their own for the attraction to occur" (p. 112).

Although the encounter itself can create a passionate relationship between students and books, the preparation that leads to it involves careful collaboration between the curator and the teaching faculty. My first challenge is to find or create interested instructors by telling faculty, often in informal conversations, about the materials in our Special Collections and how they might be used to enrich a class. (And I hope this article might encourage such conversations on many campuses). These instructors must have one or more of the following characteristics: an affinity for the book as object; an interest in introducing new elements, particularly visual and experiential elements, into their course; and a flexible teaching style that enables them to work creatively with unexpected lines of inquiry or with questions to which they have no answers.

Approximately 30 classes have used Special Collections materials in each of the last few years here at Carleton. Faculty members come to me with various goals and hopes, and often these determine the degree of collaboration that takes place. Planning for a class visit is a joint process that begins with a meeting to work through our expectations of one another and of the students. What is the point of the visit? What does the instructor hope the students will get out of the visit? What do I hope the students will get out of the visit? Unless we discuss these questions clearly, we may move forward with different assumptions about where we want to end up. Once we have some agreement on the answers to these questions, we start to discuss possible items from the collection to include in the class session.

It is at this point that the most exciting creative collaboration takes place, for as subject specialist and Special Collections curator we bring different and often complementary backgrounds to the discussion. For some faculty, it is their first visit to Special Collections, and together we troll the collection to brainstorm about possible uses of various texts to meet our goals. If there is a primary text to show, such as the first edition of Samuel Johnson's *Dictionary of the English Language* (1755), we need to think about what it means for the class "to see" or "to use" it. Is the sight of the *Dictionary* itself enough? What could we tell the students about it that would contribute to their understanding or their experience? What other materials might enhance the viewing— later editions, supplementary materials? How much time should we devote to talking about the books as physical objects—for example, the printing and binding process, the paper, the typeface, and page layout?

Once we have settled on what materials we will use, we need to talk about the logistics of the visit. How much contact will the students have with the materials? At Carleton, we want the students to handle the books, turn the pages, and heft the volumes, since touch, feel, and smell are all part of the encounter. Although I start every class visit with a short lecture to the students on handling Special Collections materials, we determine beforehand how much more I should explain about these particular volumes and their care. If there are certain books that cannot be handled, leaves that should not be turned, volumes not lifted, we agree on this ahead of time.

It is also necessary to discuss the role each of us will have during the visit. Who will talk about what, and what will the sequence be? Often what emerges from this discussion is a series of questions or suggestions for observation that the instructor might pass out in order to frame the encounter. Often the best conversations and observations emerge as groups of students gather around to examine and discuss materials while the instructor and I circulate among the groups, answering questions, posing other questions, and pointing out interesting details about individual items.

My experience is that one rarely gets everything right the first time and that the program is most successful when we collaborate through ongoing discussions about what worked well, what didn't, and how we might improve the visit the next time. In such discussions, I bring broader experience with a variety of class visits to Special Collections, along with expertise in the history of printing and the materials in the collection, and the instructor brings subject expertise as well as knowledge of the course goals. Together, we can create a curricular experience with profound effects on student learning.

THE COLLABORATORS:

Our work has been particularly instructive and collaborative, taking place over several years, dealing with a number of classes at different levels that cover various subjects within English literature, and giving us both a chance to develop our interests and skills in joint projects. A central aspect of our collaborative process is what we learn from one another and from the students each time we prepare for and run the class sessions, an exchange that benefits all of us in often surprising ways.

Literature classes at all levels appeal to students from different majors, and these students bring an inevitable interdisciplinarity to our discussions of the cultural materials we display. The visits create an opportunity for students to share their disciplinary knowledge with their classmates as they work together to consider literature in its broader cultural and historical context.

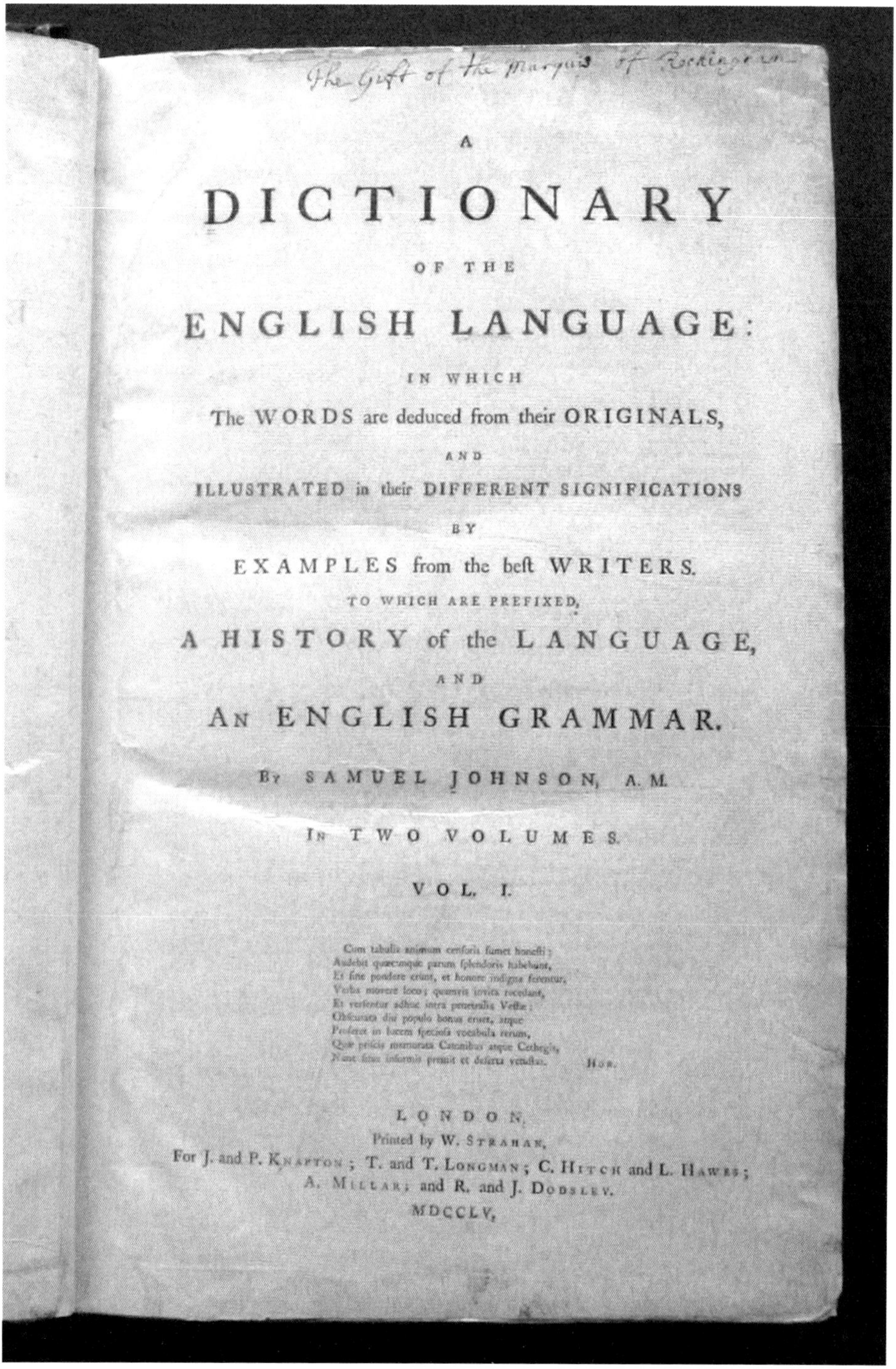

The Gift of the Marquis of Rockingham

A

DICTIONARY

OF THE

ENGLISH LANGUAGE:

IN WHICH

The WORDS are deduced from their ORIGINALS,

AND

ILLUSTRATED in their DIFFERENT SIGNIFICATIONS

BY

EXAMPLES from the best WRITERS.

TO WHICH ARE PREFIXED,

A HISTORY of the LANGUAGE,

AND

AN ENGLISH GRAMMAR.

BY SAMUEL JOHNSON, A.M.

IN TWO VOLUMES.

VOL. I.

Cum tabulis animum cenforis fumet honefti;
Audebit quaecunque parum fplendoris habebunt,
Et fine pondere erunt, et honore indigna ferentur,
Verba movere loco; quamvis invita recedant,
Et verfentur adhuc intra penetralia Veftae:
Obfcurata diu populo bonus eruet, atque
Proferet in lucem fpeciofa vocabula rerum,
Quae prifcis memorata Catonibus atque Cethegis,
Nunc fitus informis premit et deferta vetuftas.   HOR.

LONDON,

Printed by W. STRAHAN,

For J. and P. KNAPTON; T. and T. LONGMAN; C. HITCH and L. HAWES;
A. MILLAR; and R. and J. DODSLEY.

MDCCLV.

Illustration 1. Samuel Johnson's *Dictionary,* 1755 (Special Collections)

Throughout the term, Susan provides information about the authors, their editions and publishing histories, and the broader literary currents of the period. During the visit, Kristi gives details about book production and the book trade at the time, offering observations on the particular books that we will be using, how they were produced and designed, and what their physical qualities suggest about their intended audience. A class can visit Special Collections any time during the term. Depending on the goals and the materials chosen and the overall course syllabus, the visit might come at the beginning as a tantalizing entrée into the material or later when the students have more background knowledge in the field.

THE COLLABORATIONS:

The best way to explain what we have learned and how we share it with students is to show the developing collaborative process through three examples of classes and projects with very diverse goals, time frames, and exercises: an introductory survey, an advanced literature course, and a senior seminar.

Introductory Survey Course

Susan's introductory English Literature survey class, English 111 (Neoclassic, Romantic, and Victorian Literature) comes to Special Collections to do a one-hour focused project with Samuel Johnson's *Dictionary* that nicely illustrates our creative use of primary materials.

Carleton's Special Collections has a beautiful copy of the 1755 first folio edition, a 1778 octavo edition, an 1819 American edition and an 1827 English stereotyped edition. For the class of 25 students, we spread out all four editions (in eight volumes) and ask the students to select an edition and, in small groups, examine it physically, look up words (ranging from common 18th-century words to more contemporary technical words and even slang) to compare Johnson's meanings with current definitions, and finally determine whether the definition changes from edition to edition of Johnson's *Dictionary*. We ask them to call out their discoveries—and within moments, the room is ringing with delighted student voices sharing what they see, moving to other editions to check their ideas, even using the online Oxford English Dictionary to confirm current usages. The exercise allows them to consider questions surrounding the fixity of language and how cultural changes create language changes, which are concerns expressed in Johnson's "Preface" to the *Dictionary*. It also teaches them about books as objects through their hands-on examination of the binding, the title page, typography, and layout. (See Illustration 1, p. 193).

After the first class visited, we recognized that students needed more guidance in order to take advantage of their opportunity to understand these books as cultural, historical, and aesthetic objects. Now, before they examine the editions, we present a brief lecture on the publication history of the *Dictionary* and introduce several topics relevant to the study of the book as object and not always included in literature courses. These include the meaning of *folio, quarto,* and *octavo* in pre-19th-century editions; the diverse materials and ornamentation used in binding and paper-making; issues surrounding author's rights; trans-Atlantic copyright issues; and changes in spelling, alphabetization, and typographical conventions, particularly in the use of the long "s" (see illustration). We continue to work together on the handout for students and the amount of lecture, balancing between guiding their work and allowing them freedom to explore this remarkable first dictionary of the English language, determining how much time and guidance they need in their introduction to Special Collections, rare books, and primary materials.

Advanced Literature Class

A single visit to Special Collections in English 322, The Art of Jane Austen, has evolved, like the survey class, through a process that depicts perfectly the synergistic energy of our collaboration. The course enrolls juniors and seniors from all majors, so students bring widely varied skills and expectations. Since Special Collections does not include any early Austen editions (an obvious starting point) but does have a wealth of materials published during Austen's lifetime, we decided to comb through different parts of the collection for relevant 18th- and early 19th-century books from many fields that would provide a broader context to the world that Austen and her characters inhabited.

We began by discussing issues relevant to one or more of the novels and checking to see what the collection had to offer—a point when Susan's literary knowledge and Kristi's library knowledge were both essential to the result. For example, the concept of decorum is utterly central to Austen's novels. The collection has a number of fascinating conduct books from the period, including some written specifically for young ladies (and one in French, which delighted several of the students fluent in that language). Our unexpected finds included primary historical texts on the topics of slavery and abolitionism, issues that figure in *Mansfield Park*—in fact, one of the books we own is mentioned by Austen's Fanny Price in that novel. More generally, we decided to include a group of travel books from the period, since so many of the novels include touring episodes. The collection has some beautiful folio sets of the 18th-century equivalent of the travel coffee table volume, featuring engravings of grand houses and spectacular views of the Dorset countryside, the kinds of sites and houses that figure prominently in the novels.

As we cast about for other ideas, Susan mentioned William Cowper, Austen's favorite poet and an author whose work we do own in early editions. Since it is difficult to imagine any 18th-century gentleperson without thinking of Johnson's *Dictionary*, we decided to include the 1755 folio edition and ask students to look up words such as *decorum, sensibility,* and *merit.* The students would discover that the meaning of these words, so important in the novels, has changed considerably over the past 200 years. Finally, we would have students look through our collection of the 20th-century *Reports* of the Jane Austen Society in Hampshire, comparing earlier and later article titles in the *Reports* to see if the ways readers and scholars write about Austen's work changed between 1949 and 1985.

In the end, we both immensely enjoyed developing the Austen class visit (see pp. 202–203 for full details on the assignment) and felt that the visit successfully contributed to the students' understanding of Austen's work and time period, as well as exposed them to some enthralling and spectacularly beautiful examples of 18th-century books.

Senior Seminar

Our third example involves a process that extends the collaboration to advanced students as they work with their classmates to understand the role of the book as object in the Victorian period. When Susan first taught an advanced course, Victorian Poetry, in 2000, we brought the students to the Special Collections room for a single session to examine a number of gorgeously printed books from the period. Kristi gave an overview of Special Collections rules and a brief lecture on Victorian developments in fine press editions: William Morris's Kelmscott Press, Doves Press, and the American Roycroft Press. Students examined the library's collection of these beautiful books, and they were moved indeed. Here are two of their comments:

> I think my amazement at these books was quite apparent by my expression! To be able to handle these artworks was almost surreal ... to think that Morris himself could have leafed through these pages!

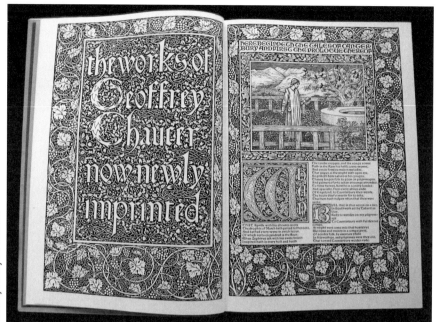

Illustration 2. 2002 Folio Society Facsimile, *The Works of Geoffrey Chaucer Now Newly Imprinted,* Kelmscott Press, 1896 (Special Collections)

Their historical value aside, the care with which these books were assembled reflects the great value placed in them as objects to be treasured. ... To the English major, these are almost holy books! The pages and text unite with synergy, in a way Keats and others reprinted in the *Norton* cannot. Handwritten and hand-printed original editions almost pulse with the authors' spirit. ... It's almost eerie: artworks from a different time and dimension (Mikki Unson, 2000).

At first I thought it would be a somewhat silly exercise, going and looking at old books. After all, a book is a book and I'm not really that into old artifacts and pieces from lost times. And of course what is really important about a book is the story, the text, not the cover or the feel of the pages, and certainly not the smell. But I quickly realized that I was wrong. Holding some of the older books in my hands, feeling their solid covers and textured designs, I began to realize that really a book is not just about the printed words on the page. There is something different about holding a hard back, even leather, sensing the hefty weight and its solid construction that makes the book more than a text, but an object, a possession, to be owned and treasured. Even the feel of the paper made the words on the page somehow more vibrant, more powerful. These books are what the authors envisioned—not some $2.99 paperback throw away from Amazon. ... I came to realize that these "old artifacts" and "pieces from lost times" really are treasures, and that they do affect the ways in which we read our poetry, novels, and texts, transforming words into experience (Kartik Hansen, 2000).

As delightful as the experience was, we wanted more—more than this single aesthetic moment, more intellectual and curricular engagement with the books, and more follow-up collaboration among the students.

In 2002, Susan developed an interdisciplinary senior seminar on the Pre-Raphaelites, an influential group of Victorian writers and visual artists, and we expanded our use of Special Collections in two ways. First, the class visit to Special Collections included a longer, more detailed lecture about books as ob-

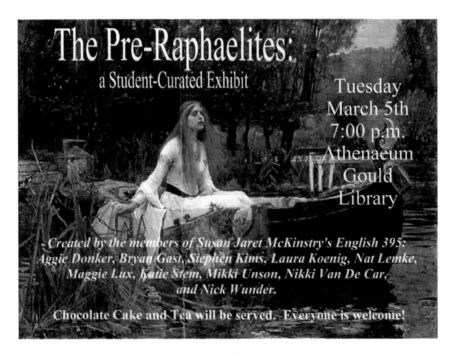

Illustration 3. Poster for Student-Curated Exhibit, 2002

jects, for Susan realized that Kristi's expertise in this area could show students the continuing impact of William Morris's ideas on printing and book design. Morris's Kelmscott Press edition of Chaucer, a collaboration between William Morris and the artist Edward Burne-Jones, expresses this aesthetic perfectly (see Illustration 2, p. 197). The Carleton collection also includes a number of relevant 20th-century illustrated books that we added to the previously used Victorian texts, and we expanded the selection of Victorian materials.

The second step was more ambitious: We asked students to return to Special Collections individually or in small groups and work with Kristi and Susan to select texts for a student-designed library exhibit on the Pre-Raphaelites. What materials could they exhibit to teach the community about the Pre-Raphaelites as artists, poets, and designers?

The result was extraordinary. The students designed the standing exhibit, first working in groups to select more than 40 items to display in cabinets and on the walls, including rare books, art reproductions, and other relevant materials. They devised a visually appealing layout for the display, researched the selected objects and wrote precise, informative, attractive exhibit labels (a difficult genre!), created lovely posters to advertise the exhibit (Illustration 3), and gave a well-attended public lecture in which each student explained his or her contributions to the project. For this small group of students, the books in the library became central aspects of their intellectual and aesthetic understanding of the period, and the exhibit gave them a way to teach what they knew.

In 2005, Susan again taught Victorian Poetry. Clearly the course did not invite the same deep engagement with book printing and art as the Pre-Raphaelite seminar, but we did want to keep the curricular excitement.

In talking over the collection and the syllabus, we realized that the library and Susan together had approximately ten Victorian versions of Dante Gabriel Rossetti's sonnet sequence *The House of Life*, initially published in his first edition of *Poems* (1870) but changed in subsequent editions. The students had read a vituperative 1871 critique of one of the poems in the first edition and knew that Rossetti had altered the sequence over time. In the library session, we let them each select an edition of the *House of Life*—one in the 1870 *Poems*, several in beautifully-bound single editions, several illustrated with prints of Rossetti's drawings and paintings—and comment on the differences they saw. They mentioned the obvious physical details of binding, paper, and design but also dramatic differences in the number, titles, and organization of the poems—including the criticized poem, which Rossetti eliminated after the

Illustration 4. D. G. Rossetti, "The Sonnet" from *The House of Life,* 1904 (Private Collection, Susan Jaret McKinstry)

first edition and later editors included. Together we considered possible reasons for the changes.

Then we went one step farther and asked them to read the unnumbered prefatory poem. They were amazed: Some editions did not include it, one did in its rarely published illustrated form, and several editions had different wording. (See Illustration 4.) This was a profound lesson in the impact of the material book: Rossetti's words were not timeless but altering. For these students, the book had become an essential object of literary study.

The final project in that course involved each student creating an individual Web site to demonstrate his or her understanding of a central aspect of Victorian poetry. Given the explosion of excellent online materials, this seemed a way to combine their knowledge about the material object and poetry analysis with a technological experience. The assignment required the display of at least two visual objects, at least two links to criticisms written during the Victorian period, and a close reading of at least one poem, as well as a link to their own imitation of a Victorian poem. Because of their work with editions of Rossetti's book in Special Collections, students were very attentive to noting physical detail, to finding ways to show the objects of the Victorian world, and to understanding their meaning in relation to the poetry. Learning to use the technology made some of the students nervous initially, but the program was simple and the resulting Web sites were great: Ranging from a study of Victorian handwriting (thanks to scans of original drafts now available on the Victorian Web) to explorations of religion, history, and Queen Victoria, they showed students' learning and their inventiveness in linking these diverse aspects of their education.

In conclusion, we are lucky that we both have expertise in the 18th-19th–century, since books published during that period are both available and affordable, but what we have discovered together is a rich interdisciplinary relationship that translates easily to colleagues in different fields. The collection already includes materials that would enrich courses from a variety of departments. In addition, Internet rare book sites make the acquisition of appropriate texts easy and surprisingly inexpensive.

Aside from the curricular benefits, our collaboration has had individual benefits: It has enriched our professional lives, inspired students to pursue graduate work in fields such as Special Collections librarianship and the history of the book, and encouraged several students to begin their own book collections. This article describes the journey of our collaboration thus far. We hope that our experience will inspire others, at Carleton and at other institutions, to set out on similar journeys.

REFERENCES

Allen, S.M. (1999). Rare books and the college library: Current practices in marrying undergraduates to special collections. *Rare Books & Manuscripts Librarianship, 13(2)*, 110-119.

Hansen, K. (2000, February 3). Untitled, unpublished paper, Carleton College, Northfield, MN.

Landow, G. *The Victorian web*. http://www.victorianweb.org.

McGann, J. *The Rossetti archive*. http://www.rossettiarchive.org.

Morris, W. (1982). The ideal book: A lecture delivered in 1893. In W. S. Peterson (Ed.), *The ideal book: Essays and lectures on the arts of the book* (pp. 67-73). Berkeley, CA: University of California Press.

Mortimer, R. (1983, October). Manuscripts and rare books in an undergraduate library. *Wilson Library Bulletin, 58.* 107-110.

Unson, M. (2000, February 3). Untitled, unpublished paper, Carleton College, Northfield, MN.

ENGLISH 322 / THE ASSIGNMENT:
ART OF JANE AUSTEN SPECIAL COLLECTIONS VISIT

Visit each table in any order and investigate the books listed, using these questions to guide you.

1. **Jane Austen:** Compare the titles of articles in older and more recent copies of the *Reports of the Jane Austen Society*. Is there a change in the way readers talk about Austen's work?

   Texts:

   Austen, Jane. *Plan of a novel according to hints from various quarters.* Oxford,: The Clarendon Press, 1926. "350 copies printed from the originals now in the Pierpont Morgan Library and the British Museum."

   Jane Austen Society. *Reports for the period...* Alton, Hampshire: The Society, 1949-1985.

   Smithers, David Waldron. *Jane Austen in Kent.* Westerham, Kent: Hurtwood, 1981. Library's copy no. 12 of 100 copies.

2. **Conduct Books:** Read a section. Does this view of decorum fit what you have learned from Austen's novels? How does it add to your understanding of decorum?

   Texts:

   Chesterfield, Philip Dormer Stanhope. *Principles of politeness, and of knowing the world.* Portsmouth, NH: Printed by Melcher and Osborne, 1786.

   Du Montier. Madame. *Lettres de Madame Du Montier, a la marquise de ***, sa fille, avec les reponses: ou l'on trouve, avec une lecture amusante, les lecons les plus epurees & conseils les plus delicats d'une mere.* Lyon: Pierre Bruyset Ponthus, 1758.

   Gregory, John. *Father's legacy to his daughters.* Portsmouth, NH: Melcher and Osborne, 1786. In Chesterfield. *Principles of politeness, and of knowing the world.*

   More, Hannah. *Strictures on the modern system of female education: With a view of the principles and conduct prevalent among women of rank and fortune.* Charlestown, MA: Printed by Samuel Etheridge, 1800.

   Pilkington, Mary. *Mentorial tales: For the instruction of young ladies just leaving school and entering upon the theatre of life.* Philadelphia: Published by J. Johnson, 1803.

3. **Slavery:** Read the chapter headings in the *Abstract for the Abolition of the Slave Trade*, and examine the diagrams in the other books. (Look for familiar names on the "history of forerunners and coadjutors"). What do you notice?

Texts:

Great Britain. Parliament. House of Commons. *An abstract of the evidence delivered before a select committee of the House of Commons in the years 1790, and 1791; on the part of the petitioners for the abolition of the slave-trade.* London: Printed by J. Phillips, 1791.

Clarkson, Thomas. *An essay on the impolicy of the African slave trade.* London: Printed and sold by J. Phillips, 1788.

Clarkson, Thomas. *The history of the rise, progress, & accomplishment of the abolition of the African slave-trade by the British parliament.* London: Longman, Hurst, Rees and Orme, 1808.

4. **Travel:** Examine the books. What do you learn about British tourists and local histories?

Texts:

Grose, Francis. *The antiquities of England and Wales.* 4 vols. London: Printed for S. Hooper. 1773-76.

Walpoole, George Augustus. *The new British traveler; or, A complete modern universal display of Great-Britain and Ireland.* London: Printed for A. Hogg, 1784.

5. **William Cowper:** He was Austen's favorite poet. Read a few of his letters or part of his *Memoir.* What do you find interesting here?

Texts:

Cheever, George Barrell. *William Cowper: His life, genius, and insanity.* London: Knight, [1856?]

Cowper, William. *Memoir of the early life of William Cowper.* London: R. Edwards, 1816.

6. **Johnson's Dictionary:** Look up a few essential words—decorum, sensibility, conduct, merit, picturesque, gothic, and so on (use your imagination). How do Johnson's definitions fit with Austen's? Examine the books—including the title page and type. What do you notice about the *Dictionary*?

Text:

Johnson, Samuel. *A dictionary of the English language: In which the words are deduced from their originals, and illustrated in their different significations by examples from the best writers. To which are prefixed, a history of the language, and an English grammar.* 2 vols. London: Printed by W. Strahan, 1755.

"Writing Science" through Student-Produced Journals

Cindy Blaha and Carol Rutz

Too often we hear science and mathematics students ask: "Why do I have to write a paper? This is a science class, not a writing class!" Or "I'm writing this so others in my research area can understand it. Why should I have to worry about whether it is accessible to someone outside my field?" Complaints like these cause a great deal of frustration for students and faculty alike. This frustration prompted us to develop a course called Writing Science aimed at helping students address the unique tasks they face in communicating effectively in mathematics and the sciences.

It's not that students at Carleton College are bad writers. In fact, of those who take the SAT, over 90% enter with SAT verbal scores at or above 600 on an 800-point scale, a score that correlates positively with good grades in college, including grades on written work (Carleton College, *Office of Admissions: Profile of the Class of 2009,* 2005).

Furthermore, Carleton was an early leader in what is now called writing across the curriculum. Anyone who reads the catalog or visits classes cannot escape the emphasis placed on written expression as a key feature of Carleton's pedagogy. In addition, historical data from alumni surveys underscore more recent data from the required sophomore writing portfolio that Carleton students see themselves as improved writers by the time they graduate (Carleton College, *COHFE Alumni Survey,* 2005).

Nevertheless, some of these good—or even outstanding—writers who readily dig into writing assignments in the humanities balk at the idea of writing in the more technical disciplines.

CINDY BLAHA, professor of physics and astronomy, joined the Carleton faculty in 1987. She earned B.S., M.S., and PhD degrees at the University of Minnesota. CAROL RUTZ, lecturer in English and director of the College Writing Program, earned her B.A. degree at Gustavus Adolphus College, her M.A. at Hamline University, and her PhD at the University of Minnesota. She joined the faculty in 1997.

The two of us—Cindy is a professor of astrophysics and Carol is director of Carleton's writing program—decided to team up to offer students interested in science a course that would engage them in both the content and the communication of science. Despite our dissimilar disciplinary affiliations and distinctly different teaching styles, we speculated that our collaboration would help students integrate the content and communicative aspects of the course. We would personally enact the tension and cooperation that characterizes research and publication. Cindy's preparation for class is legendary, despite her modest claims to the contrary. She is well known as the kind of professor who is so engaging that she can coax wary students into solving complex problems while having a great deal of fun along the way. Carol's preparation is generally less elaborate, and she depends on students to generate a great deal of discussion and energy while in class. She then expects them to apply their insights immediately in some sort of writing assignment that will capture that intellectual energy for future development. For each of us, process and product take different forms. The same is true of comfort with our respective disciplines. Carol is easily confounded by sophisticated equations, and Cindy has been known to run screaming from the word "genre." As we found, enacting these tensions to emphasize audience considerations was hardly a strain—we couldn't help ourselves.

> The course methodology, student-produced scientific journals, would offer students a chance to participate in groups with a common purpose—an experience analogous to collaborations among research teams. As an added bonus, students would gain hands-on practice with the intricacies of publication.

The course methodology, student-produced scientific journals, would, in turn, offer students a chance to participate in groups with a common purpose—an experience analogous to collaborations among research teams. As an added bonus, students would gain hands-on practice with the intricacies of publication. A note of clarification: We use "journal" in the course and in this chapter as a generic term for any science-based publication with text, illustrations, and attribution of sources. The specific form of the student-produced journal can vary from the technical to the basic, designed for audiences ranging from novice to expert.

THE PLAN

We embarked on our first Writing Science course in the spring of 2004 with heady excitement about the possibilities for students interested in science. First, we needed to convince students that scientists today communicate in many ways. In addition to writing standard research papers discussing their experimental results, scientists give talks to public audiences and review panels. They also create posters for presentation at professional meetings, write educational materials, and create Web-based information sites for public outreach efforts.

As teachers, we viewed these modes of communication as new pedagogical opportunities to create assignments that would help our students develop skills and gain practice in a variety of forms used by practicing scientists. We designed assignments that required multiple modes of communication, each piece building upon the previous piece with increasing depth of information plus integration of oral and visual presentation techniques.

Choosing a journal-based format for the course gave the students an unusual classroom forum for presenting the results of their research and provided a natural means of writing for a variety of target audiences. It also gave us the opportunity to give students direct experience with the publication cycle. Finally, the journal format gave the students good reason to struggle with the art of effective reviewing.

In developing Writing Science, we began with three major student learning goals: (1) to help students write more effectively in their own disciplines, using writing as a tool to achieve deeper understanding within their field of study; (2) to help students engage in interdisciplinary learning and communicate clearly across disciplines; and (3) to help students communicate more effectively with the broader public by gaining a deeper appreciation of the role that audience plays in shaping the content and style of communication. To accomplish these goals, we decided to challenge students to experiment with the different forms of communication commonly used in the sciences today.

Goal 1: Depth in the Discipline

It seems fairly obvious that we should help our students—even those who have not yet formally declared majors—become more proficient writers in the disciplines they see as their own. Furthermore, an increased emphasis on writing in the disciplines offers students the added bonus of a more sophisticated understanding of their field. Through investing the time in learning to write, students also experience the benefits of writing to learn. When students write up thorough explanations of problem solutions, complete with descriptive prose, equations, and diagrams, they can identify and remedy weaknesses in their explanations and come to a much deeper understanding of the problems and their solutions. Students make the material their own when they read a scholarly article and then write a summary that places it in the context of their learning in classroom and lab. Through use of both critical reading and writing skills, they can claim the information as their own intellectual territory.

Goal 2: Interdisciplinary Learning

Anyone who takes a quick look at the "hot" research topics in the sciences today will immediately realize the importance of communicating across disciplines. Materials science research, nanotechnology (and its biomedical applications), and genetic engineering are but a few of the areas where scientists, mathematicians, computer scientists, and engineers all collaborate to achieve cutting-edge research discoveries. Real world problems such as global warming, the search for renewable energy resources, and the spread of AIDS are all arenas for integrative learning and interdisciplinary cooperation. Neither science nor society can afford to have researchers build walls of disciplinary jargon and unintelligible scientific prose that prevent cross-disciplinary understanding. Writing Science offered students a laboratory for practicing these interdisciplinary communication skills.

Goal 3: Public Communication

Those who have written a grant proposal or given a talk to an elementary school class on their latest research know well that the public or audience is defined differently for every rhetorical situation. The success of any scientific endeavor depends on effective communication with public audiences as well as other researchers in the field. Our students are introduced to the essential techniques of writing in their introductory courses, and within their major sequence, they begin to develop more sophisticated tools for writing within their own discipline. However, they have very little practice with reshaping a written piece to match the needs of a specific audience. Once again, the Writing Science class provided our students with focused opportunities to match their written and oral communication efforts to a variety of target audiences.

ASSIGNMENTS

We were concerned that students interested in science disciplines are often less than savvy about how science is communicated. They read formal articles in peer-reviewed journals, but they are unable to imagine what peer review actually means, much less the many false starts that precede a submission to a scholarly journal. And that's just the writing. Even students who understand the trial and error nature of science itself rarely extend that insight to the communication of new science to various audiences. Perhaps these problems are identical for students who major in the humanities and social sciences as well; regardless, we decided to tackle the problems that were evident among science majors at Carleton.

For Writing Science, we decided to help students sort out the forms, vocabulary, and rhetorical situations that science writers have at their disposal when presenting their work. The best way to explore this variety was to employ as many kinds of science communication as we could manage in one 10-week term. Therefore, our students demonstrated their scientific knowledge through independent research, peer review, oral presentation, a public poster session, interviews, formal review of doctoral research in progress, and production of scientific journals tailored to specific audiences.

All of that in 10 weeks? You bet! Plus assigned readings from *Writing in the Sciences: Exploring Conventions of Scientific Discourse* (Penrose & Katz, 1998) designed to make students aware of the social nature of scientific inquiry.

Penrose and Katz led our students toward the insight offered by Thomas Kuhn (1996) and others that scientific knowledge depends on communication. Data and discoveries do not speak for themselves; they are socially constructed and circulated. Students quickly grasped the connection between collaboration in the laboratory and cooperative communication to the public. Their thinking about audience crystallized as we encouraged them to design custom journals.

To make production of the journals possible, we designed assignments that would generate material that could easily fit into the format of one or more journals, plus the oral presentations and posters. With tongue firmly in cheek, we like to think of this approach to the course as "intelligent design" in the sense that we, as teachers, oversaw controlled chaos throughout the term. Our students wrote so much on so many topics in so many forms that they had copy to burn when it was time to assemble their journals.

The overall flow of our coursework is displayed in Figure 1. After identifying and analyzing a number of information sources, students created pro-

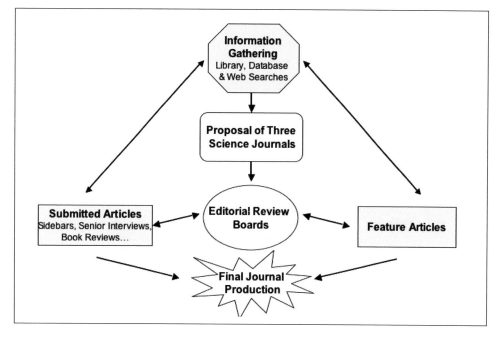

Figure 1. The Flow of Writing Science Assignments During the Production of Class Journals

posals for three science journals and formed editorial boards. Board members chose feature articles for their own journals and solicited additional submissions from the entire class. The editorial boards reviewed submitted articles and provided feedback, which then led to repeated steps of information gathering and resubmission. The finished articles were then gathered and assembled in the final production phase. Briefly, here's what we did.

JOURNAL CREATION

Students analyzed samples of science journals and discussed how the various journals matched the needs of their target audiences. The 13 students separated into three groups or editorial boards. Each group proposed a specific journal and created editorial guidelines to describe the focus, tone, and format of articles to be submitted for their particular journal.

Editorial Matters

To help students understand the duties of an editorial board, we had a guest presentation by two Carleton faculty colleagues who had co-edited a math journal aimed at an undergraduate audience. This presentation and several discussions of reviewing techniques and practices prepared the students to provide constructive feedback on articles submitted to their journals by their peers.

Evolution of Feature Articles

Each student chose a topic for a feature story to be written for her/his own journal and possibly adapted for another journal. The feature article was developed through a set of shorter assignments designed to give students experience with a variety of forms of scientific communication. Figure 2 illustrates the evolution of a feature article. Each assignment step built upon previous work and focused on greater depth of content and integration of visual information.

In every case, the feature article required research. Therefore, our cross-disciplinary collaboration took on a broader campus-wide perspective as we sought advice on information literacy from science librarian Ann Zawistoski. Following a library instruction session and interactive activities, our students became skilled users of Web-based search engines, databases, and bibliographic catalogs as well as print copies of books, journals, and reference resources.

Around midterm, students gave oral presentations on the preliminary research for their feature article, using illustrations and demonstrations as appropriate. Student presenters received feedback on their oral presentations from fellow students as well as instructors.

Our collaboration circle expanded further when we sought assistance from Information and Technology Services (ITS) to prepare students to create

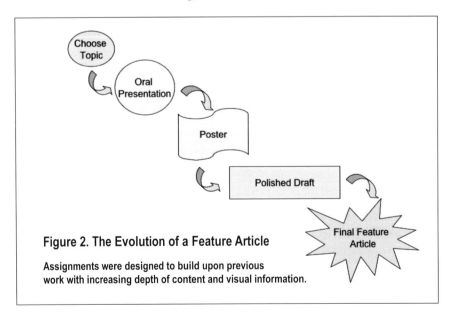

Figure 2. The Evolution of a Feature Article

Assignments were designed to build upon previous work with increasing depth of content and visual information.

posters based on their research for their feature articles. An in-class session on Adobe Illustrator by Doug Foxgrover, our ITS staff advisor, gave students the software experience needed for the poster assignment. The students created full-color posters that were presented in a formal poster session open to the Carleton public.

Additional Writing

Journals are composed of short pieces as well as formal articles, and those short pieces require preparation that is as rigorous as longer pieces. To get students started on a batch of promising topics, we used a technique called a "Web scramble." Topics were assembled from class discussions or personal interest and traded so that groups of two students performed quick research on the Web on a topic they did not invent. They then made two-minute oral reports that were later written and illustrated in the form of short sidebar articles for submission to the class journals.

A "three-source" assignment also served as a source for short sidebar articles. Students chose from a list of teacher-developed topics and conducted research on the topic with a minimum of three sources—an introductory source aimed at a public audience, an intermediate level source targeted at a scientifically literate audience, and a scientific journal article aimed at scholars in the field. Following an in-class discussion of the various communication styles and techniques used by the three types of sources, students wrote short articles for one or more journals and enhanced their textual information with well-chosen images.

Outside of class hours, students conducted interviews of Carleton seniors majoring in various fields who had just completed their capstone projects, also known as "Comps." Information from these interviews formed the basis for short articles or was woven into appropriate sections of the longer feature articles. Senior science majors were flattered to be considered authoritative sources for our students.

In order to help students become more critical consumers and users of imagery and graphics, we used Michael Alley's *The Craft of Scientific Writing* (1996), which includes tips on format and design for tables, charts, graphs, and diagrams. Students employed Alley's techniques to redesign diagrams and adapt images to convey visual information effectively. They then used these techniques to tailor their visuals to suit the needs of their articles.

External Review

Students also gained further experience as external reviewers through their participation in the I-RITE (Integrating Research in the Teaching Environment) program at Stanford University. This program was initiated to help doctoral students communicate their research to a lay public. Since the Stanford graduate students were targeting an undergraduate audience, our students were ideally suited to providing feedback. They gained considerable confidence in their reviewing abilities through participation in this project. Because of calendar considerations, our students' reviews were not received in time for the Stanford graduate students to respond to suggestions during the term they were offered, so our students did not see the fruits of their reviewing labors. Nevertheless, our students took their responsibility as reviewers seriously, and they were impressed with the difficulties attending the communication of high-level new research to undergraduate readers.

Journal Assembly

In order to integrate all of our articles into a "real" journal format, we needed a desktop publishing package. We chose an Adobe product called InDesign and introduced students to use of this layout program through an in-class demonstration. During the final two weeks of the term, classes were held in workshop format, and students were busy with final editing of articles and journal layout and production.

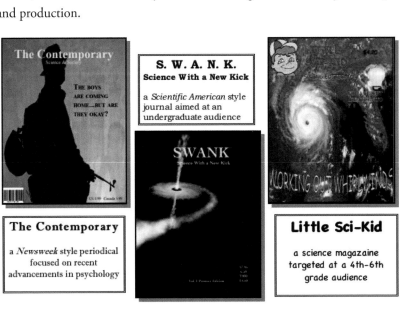

Figure 3. Journal Covers

STUDENT PRODUCTS

The course activities described above resulted in three student-formed editorial groups that proposed three distinctly different journals. All three journals featured formal articles, short sidebars, ads, and pieces derived from interviews. Some groups added book reviews, editorials, or games.

Science with a New Kick, or *S.W.A.N.K.*, was geared toward a college-aged audience interested in new scientific discoveries. The five students in the group ranged from first-year students to seniors, and their interests were reflected in the feature articles on various topics in biology, chemistry, and physics.

Four first-year students designed *Little Sci Kid*, a magazine aimed at 4th-6th graders. Articles on the basics of photosynthesis and inertia ran next to pieces on hurricanes and hybrid automobiles.

The third group, two juniors and two first-year students, was more interested in the social sciences. Consequently, their journal, *The Contemporary*, took on topics that engaged science and society, such as post-traumatic stress syndrome, the role of sleep in human health, and sports psychology. Figure 3 displays the journal covers, and Figure 4 shows a sample table of contents.

STUDENT PERSPECTIVES ON THE COURSE

Consistent with the usual practice at Carleton, we administered course evaluations at midterm and at the end of the course.

At midterm, three related concerns emerged. First, students worried

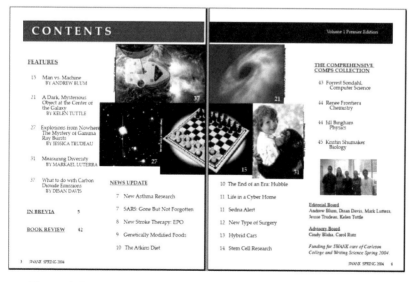

Figure 4. Sample Table of Contents

that they were not writing enough to fill up the three journals. They were also somewhat uncomfortable that the writing they were doing was largely ungraded, even though each of them received a summary of our assessment of their performance at midterm, based on work in progress, participation, and attendance. For those more accustomed to A-F grades on quizzes, exams, and formal papers, this method of grading was suspect. They had trouble making sense of a course where evaluation of the primary products of the course was delayed until the end of the term. Finally, a few students expressed a perception that the course was "informal" or "disorganized," an impression probably based on the way we interacted as teachers. Some students were confused by our deliberate attempts to highlight our disciplinary differences, to play a little good cop/bad cop, to be open about our individual enthusiasms, and to show how we arrived at compromise.

In contrast to these concerns, students appreciated the "applied" nature of the course and the chance to be both writers and editors working toward large projects. For most, the environment was comfortable for discussion and work, despite the age range of students and their—and our—differing disciplinary interests. Attendance was excellent, and students clearly enjoyed one another as well as the writing they were doing.

By the end of the term, the concern about quantity of writing had evaporated, replaced by some frustration about time spent learning new software for the layout phase of the journals. (More on that below.) Some students saw the course as a class in journalism disguised as science writing, which they thought was valuable, but a few found that the journal approach did not meet all of their expectations for learning to write in science. An interesting division appeared: Some students complained that we did not teach them how to write formal lab reports, whereas other students reported using what they had learned about science writing to write strong lab reports in other classes. Unfortunately, we cannot determine from the anonymous evaluations whether that split was along seniority lines, with the younger students wanting instruction and the older students finding immediate application, but that is one hypothesis. In any case, students named and implemented their learning in different ways.

Overall, students expressed enthusiasm for the class and offered thoughtful suggestions for the next iteration, many of which appear below. We were pleased to see genuine appreciation for practice in public speaking as well as the chance to work in teams. The emphasis on peer review produced a group of writers who valued honest criticism aimed at helping them produce the best writing for the occasion. More than one student pointed to the experience of making his or her own decisions in light of multiple critiques (some of them contradictory) as the most valuable part of the course—a way of developing a voice as a writer acting in a community of writers.

FACULTY PERSPECTIVES ON THE COURSE

After our first experience with teaching Writing Science, we can claim success in achieving many of our goals, and we are genuinely proud of our students' achievements. We must also acknowledge a few character-building experiences along the way and consider strategies for next time to enrich the student learning experience—not to mention smooth out the workload and stress level throughout the term. As we reflect on our first class experience, a few highlights (and lowlights) come to mind.

> The choice of a journal-based format for the course was indeed a productive one. The students experienced success, much of it unexpected—by them or, frankly, by us.

The choice of a journal-based format for the course was indeed a productive one. The students experienced success, much of it unexpected—by them or, frankly, by us. We were pleased by the high quality of work exhibited in the final class journals, and through student evaluations and post-class feedback, we found that the students were pleased and proud of their accomplishments. A few of the many benefits we found from producing class journals include:

Literacy skills: By writing for class journals, the students built writing, speaking, and information literacy skills and gained practice at communicating in a wide variety of forms. As they stepped through the evolution of their feature article, the students improved the depth and clarity of their writing, they gained greater comfort with oral presentation skills, and their work demonstrated increased visual impact and appeal.

Audience awareness: Students became keenly aware of audience as they wrote pieces for the three distinct class journals. While *S.W.A.N.K.* was aimed at a scientifically literate campus audience and delivered news about cutting-edge research, *The Contemporary* was targeted at a broader public audience and presented information focused on the intersection of science and society. *Little Sci Kid* was designed to introduce 4th-6th graders to the excitement and wonders of science. By writing articles for all three journals, the students could not help but become attuned to the needs of their various audiences.

Building community: Interviews with senior science and math majors engaged the entire campus scientific community. Through the interviewing process, the students gained practice in asking good questions, listening carefully, and summarizing key ideas. As a bonus, seniors found an interested audience to hear about the results of their Comps research. Both interviewers and interviewees were eager to see their results in print. Our class journals proved to be an exciting new venue for sharing local science expertise here at Carleton.

Reviewing: Our students changed from novice to expert reviewers. Through editorial boards and as outside reviewers for the Stanford graduate student research statements, the students developed conscientious reviewing skills and became more critical editors of their own work. Throughout the term students found their voices as they responded to the work of others. They became adept at providing helpful feedback and writing constructive and thorough reviews. By the end of the term, even the first-year students were confidently supplying the seniors with useful critiques.

Publishing: Students gained experience with the entire journal publication cycle. They were active participants in every stage of journal production: creating a concept for a journal; forming an editorial board and extending a call for papers; researching, writing and editing articles; incorporating effective and eye-catching visuals; and producing glossy full-color spreads. They were genuine science writers, and their finished products were most impressive.

WHAT TO DO NEXT TIME

However, all was not always rosy in the land of journal production. Through a process of trial by fire, we learned that there were definitely some pitfalls to avoid the next time around and new areas of pedagogy to add or improve.

Technology and More Technology

The first of these character-building experiences centers on the use of technology. The next time we teach Writing Science, we plan to introduce the technology aspects of desktop publishing earlier in the term and to package it in bite-sized parcels. We will do this, however, while maintaining our primary focus on writing and clarity of communication.

In order to accomplish all the assignments in the course, students needed to learn a wide variety of software tools to produce their final articles.

During their information gathering stages, students made extensive use of both library and online databases and search engines. After assembling information, students' prose became electronically accessible through word-processing programs and sharing through our campus collaborative network. Next students needed to learn image processing and conversion techniques using Photoshop and Graphic Converter and then integrate images and text into a poster with Illustrator. Along the way they used PowerPoint or Keynote to create their oral presentations.

All of these tools were pedagogically necessary for the final journal production. Students needed to combine text, images, tables, charts, and graphs into full-page spreads using the desktop publishing package InDesign. This software was brand new at the time, and only available on a trial basis, so we all had to scramble to learn new tricks without normal ITS support.

In order to help students achieve these tasks, instructors needed to become familiar with the software. Old instructors had to learn new tricks that did not stick easily in brains accustomed to older technology. Although software tools were introduced throughout the term as students needed to use packages for various assignments, the students were not introduced to InDesign (the most unfamiliar and formidable package) until the end of the term. The final journal production phase was the last week of the term when students were trying to complete their final projects for all their classes. Everyone had too much to do, and stress levels were high.

Collaboration as a Solution

Next time we will enlist more help from our Information and Technology Services staff, both in the use of the varied software packages as well as in managing our information resources. To our chagrin, we learned that collaborative sharing of the large files of integrated text, graphics, and images strained our campus network and file storage systems. We will also employ several student assistants who are skilled in providing feedback on student writing and communication as well as knowledgeable in the use of the journal production software. And we will continue to update our own knowledge of the ever-changing technologies that will help us communicate effectively.

Our own collaborative path had its ups and downs. Despite having been trained in different disciplines, we successfully managed to navigate conflicting ideas and pedagogical differences. For example, one of us learned to adapt her spreadsheet-based grading schema and began to embrace the more subjective, holistic approach of the other. The other learned to accommodate a broader variety of sources and unfamiliar technologies.

However, in class we tried to make our interdisciplinary waters extra turbulent on purpose. We highlighted our disciplinary and pedagogical differences through role-playing and lively discussions/arguments. One of us would erupt with an excited, jargon-filled discussion of a recent discovery while the other would demand clarification. Or one would adopt a pointed review of a sample submission and the other would insist upon a more balanced response. Though we were pleased to hear that our students found our class atmosphere welcoming and jovial, we suspect that some of the "disorganized" and "confusing" comments on evaluations might stem from our purposeful exaggeration of disciplinary differences. Perhaps an open discussion of our pedagogical strategies at the beginning of the course might help students understand what we are up to.

Since our journals were a collaborative effort between students and faculty, the two of us had to relinquish some measure of our usual classroom control. The students created the journals, and so students were responsible for the design, layout, and production stages. We provided suggestions, support, and encouragement from the sidelines. When students proofed the final journals and returned them with a few misspelled words in some articles and headlines,

Figure 5. The Flow of Information, Evaluation, and Analysis During Journal Creation

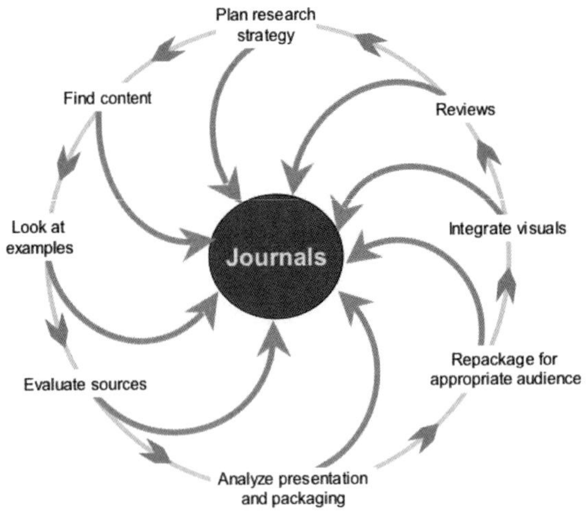

(Figure courtesy of Ann Zawistoski and Heather Tompkins.)

we exercised great restraint in refusing to correct them. The journals needed to be a direct reflection of the students' best work, which required us to allow the errors to appear publicly in print.

Depth in the Major

We would also like to pursue more depth in writing within the disciplines. Although a few of our first-year students had no idea what their major might be, most students had either declared their majors or had definite ideas about which major they would declare. We had hoped to spend time helping students improve their skills in writing lab reports following the standard introduction-methods-results-analysis-discussion (IMRAD) format. But many students had not yet written a full lab report. Perhaps we will provide a common lab experience that could form the basis for a richer discussion of communication of experimental results. The scientific disciplines each have unique ways of writing, review, and citation style. A future exercise might assign teams of students to research the unique styles of various disciplines. An in-class discussion of commonalities and differences would certainly help strengthen our interdisciplinary communication skills.

Visual Rhetoric

Finally, during the next iteration of Writing Science we would like to place more emphasis on the integration and effectiveness of visual forms of communication. Our students have grown up in a world of high-speed Internet access and Web-based information delivery, and we have bred a generation of visual learners. Indeed, we have all become accustomed to gathering our information at a glance. Eye-catching visual imagery, text that is clear, compelling, and concise, and effective use of figures and graphs are all key elements in modern scientific communication. Video, audio, and computer simulations are also employed to explain research at the cutting edge. The bandwidth required for our information superhighway will only continue to grow, and if we hope to be effective science communicators we must be ready for a fast-paced and wild ride.

The path toward journal creation and production was definitely not a linear one. Figure 5, a complex pinwheel, comes close to describing the experience. In practice, the movement among the various categories—information gathering, evaluation, and analysis—was less orderly. The actual steps were more like a spirographic path toward the final journal product, with students making repeated excursions to the tasks named on the rim of Figure 5. In fact the process resembled the orbit of an unsuspecting star spiraling into a black hole. Only in this case, rather than annihilation, the end state was a well-crafted publication aimed at a target audience.

At the end of the term, each of our students left campus for the summer with a CD containing complete copies of all three journals in .pdf form. While all of us were pleased with this accomplishment, the journals did not become "real" until they appeared in print the following fall. The final steps toward print production were both time-consuming and expensive, but they were well worth the effort. There is something infinitely more satisfying about a printed journal that can be left on a coffee table or passed around the dorm. We all felt an enormous sense of accomplishment once we held the journals in our hands. Instead of collecting dust in a professor's office, the students felt that their writing now had a life of its own and a real audience.

The fruits of our labor are now featured on coffee tables all over campus, and copies have been requested by colleagues across the country. Using a publication approach to a writing course is nothing new (e.g., Graves, Shine), but we have discovered that applying that pedagogy to science writing is unusual. If our initial experience is any indicator, this approach is effective, productive, and fun. We have our students to thank for the delight we experienced during the first iteration, and we look forward to teaching the course regularly over the next few years.

REFERENCES

Alley, M. (1996). *The craft of scientific writing* (3rd ed.). New York: Springer.

Carleton College. (2005). *Office of admissions: Profile of the class of 2009.* Northfield, MN.

Carleton College. (2005). *COHFE alumni survey* (Unpublished results). Northfield, MN.

Graves, R. L. (1981). Using writing models from across the curriculum. *English Quarterly, 14,* 31-40.

Kuhn, T. S. (1996). *The structure of scientific revolutions* (3rd ed.). Chicago: University of Chicago Press.

Penrose, A., & Katz, S. (1998). *Writing in the sciences: Exploring conventions of scientific discourse.* Boston: Bedford/St. Martin.

Shine, M. (1983). Motivating university students to write and publish. In C. Thaiss (Ed.), *Writing to learn: Essays and reflections on writing across the curriculum* (pp. 135-139). Dubuque, IA: Kendall Hunt.

Collaborations in Classics and Classics as Collaboration

Clara Shaw Hardy and Chico Zimmerman

I t all began when we stopped believing in mythology. This is the story of how the Classics Department at Carleton College stumbled into major curricular change. It is about collaboration among faculty within our department, as well as many other levels of collaboration both throughout the college and in the classroom. It is also about exorcising seductive myths about the glories of autonomy in teaching, learning, and scholarship.

MYTHOLOGIES

Despite its perennial popularity, the course Classical Myth, offered by our department for years, no longer seemed to fit rationally into our departmental offerings as faculty members retired and new faculty joined the department. For generations of Carleton students, mythology was the only contact they ever had with our department, yet "mythology" does not even describe an actual area of scholarly study in classics—nor is it a term the ancients would recognize. The material taught under the rubric of "mythology" was a mixture of literary and religious texts, delivered in translation for the purpose of "knowing the players" and providing a background for allusions

> A single scholar with a set of texts may have an interesting idea, but it isn't until that idea is shared and discussed among peers that the full implications emerge. Knowledge is, as Socrates understood, essentially a social phenomenon.

CLARA SHAW HARDY, professor of classical languages, joined the Carleton faculty in 1990. She earned her B.A. at Oberlin and her PhD at Brown University. CHICO ZIMMERMAN, the Humphrey Doermann Professor of Liberal Learning, professor of classical languages, and coordinator of the Perlman Center for Learning and Teaching, joined the Carleton faculty in 1989. He earned his B.A. at Duke University and his M.A. and PhD degrees at University of North Carolina, Chapel Hill.

to these stories in later writing. Despite the intrinsic fascination people have had for these stories throughout the centuries, the incredible range of sources made it impossible to present the material in a way that revealed its social, historical, and religious contexts. Consequently, the mythology course sat uncomfortably spread out across boundaries more natural to the field.

We wanted the opportunity to teach these wonderful texts in their various natural environments instead of artificially uprooted and packaged together as a "subject." Additionally, we felt we needed a better "gateway" into our department than the mythology course. As we considered how our colleagues elsewhere in the college managed this goal, we began to wonder if we, too, could design an "Introduction to..." course of the type offered by many departments in the sciences and social sciences.

> As we write this, our e-mail delivers an invitation to an upcoming lecture described as integrating "archaeology, written data, and social psychology, in the attempt to show how the physical environment at the Roman amphitheater contributed to the psychological state of the spectators." Classical scholarship itself is a collaboration, and we felt that students should see this in action.

The discipline of classics, however, is made up of several discrete sub-disciplines with greatly varying methodologies and areas of specialization. What they share is the history and language of the time period and people of the classical past. We wanted the introductory course to reflect both the rich content and the enormous range of sub-disciplines that shelter under the umbrella term "classics." Such an introduction would give students a more accurate picture of what it is that classicists do. Indeed (again in language we were hearing from colleagues outside our department), it would try to get them "doing classics" or "thinking like a classicist" by the end of a term.

The mythology course we wanted to replace had served two somewhat different populations of students: those who were already interested in the field, many of whom would go on to take more courses and perhaps major, and those who were looking for an interesting course to take as a distribution requirement. Both sets of students, we felt, could be better served by some kind of introduction to the field than simply by a familiarity with a range of entertaining stories.

A COURSE IS BORN, SORT OF

While the general idea of creating a new introductory course was clear, little else was when our department of four sat down for a week one summer to hammer it out. No other institution we could find had attempted to construct a "gateway" course of the type we were considering. Models based purely on content, comprehensive surveys of Greek and Roman history and culture, were too much for a single course, especially given Carleton's 10-week trimester. But we also wanted the course to provide an overview of the various approaches to this vast content.

These two goals clearly comprised too vast an area for an introductory course. There needed to be some way of prioritizing what we wanted students to know, and that was where the bulk of our departmental collaboration took place.

We knew that students should learn some content from both the Greek and the Roman world—the "what" of our discipline. We felt that students who would take no other courses in classics ever again should become familiar with the classical material that they would be most likely to come in contact with in other contexts of their education. This was an interesting discussion, since a case can be made by classicists that *all* the material is vitally important. But in the end it seemed clear to us that 5th century Athens and Imperial Rome were the essential periods for our students to learn about. Those who were inspired to seek broader exposure to classics would find it in our other courses.

In addition to the "what," we also wanted students to get a sense of the "how." How do classicists know what they do about the ancient world? What constitutes convincing evidence? Where does one look for this evidence? These were exciting questions to formulate and discuss, and they gave us a set of working guidelines for what would be the actual syllabus of a 10-week course. A final desire we had was for the course to introduce the various faculty members in our department and their own areas of expertise to the students. We conceived of the course as being team-taught, with guest appearances from all members of the department during the term. This seemed like an especially good strategy, since it reflected the reality of our discipline: No single classicist has command of all the material or all the approaches to the material, in spite of the myth of the lone (19th-century German) omniscient scholar. In addition, the powerful fiction of the New Critics—that careful attention to the language of texts alone could produce understanding of them with no knowledge of their context—has gradually given way to more interdisciplinary approaches to the content of the ancient world. As we write this, our e-mail delivers an invitation to an upcoming lecture at the local university described as integrating "archaeology, written data, and social psychology, in the attempt to show how the physical environment at the Roman amphitheater contributed to the psychological state of the spectators." Classical scholarship itself is a collaboration, and we felt that students should see this in action.

COURSE REALITIES

At the end of our departmental discussions about the introductory course (which we decided to call Classics 110), we had a clear sense of what the course should accomplish, and roughly what we thought we should cover. Specific content choices, however, were left up to the two faculty members who would be teaching the course for the first time.

Making our general principles work "on the ground" involved another level of intense collaboration on the part of the teaching team. The first iteration of the course had, as one could predict, too much material: Content was still seen as the primary expression of our desire for students to understand the classical world and how scholars reconstruct it. In subsequent years, the content has been steadily winnowed, allowing the students more opportunity to digest and compare material and to explore new, related material on their own. We have hit upon the working concepts of "better-informed encounters with the past" and "texts in context" to express our overall learning goal and method for the course. These two ideas drive the changes we have made to our original design. Gratifyingly, over six years of tinkering, the learning experience has come to resemble what we thought we wanted in the first place.

Interestingly, one of the main goals we set for the course has proved to be unnecessary. We originally wanted the introductory course to address common misconceptions about classical antiquity and classical scholars. Consequently we had allowed significant class time for lessons that would accomplish this. In the actual event, it turned out that students at the turn of the millennium had very few notions about classics at all! So one of the shortcomings of our collaborative efforts was that it did not include a member of the target audience who could give us a sense of what students do and do not already know.

Team-teaching Classics 110 has been a completely different experience from any other sort of team-teaching we had done in the past. Collaboration with faculty outside of classics is highly stimulating but generally involves independent preparation of the classes or portions of classes having to do with our specialty, as well as independent writing and evaluating of assignments.

With 110, however, we discuss every aspect of the course extensively. Before the term starts we hash out the syllabus (which changes more or less from year to year); during the term we discuss the material for each class both before and often after we teach it. We collaborate on assignment design and evaluation standards: While we do split up the papers rather than each reading all of them, we often share and discuss those most difficult to evaluate.

The pay-offs of this system, both for us and the students, are substantial. There is a real difference in our own engagement with and approaches to the material when we walk into class having just discussed it with a colleague. In a sense our process enacts for students, in a small way, the manner in which ideas actually take shape in the field: A single scholar with a set of texts may have an interesting idea, but it isn't until that idea is shared and discussed among peers that the full implications emerge. Knowledge is, as Socrates understood, essentially a social phenomenon. Nothing can convey this more powerfully to students than a course that is a product of—and structured around—dialogue.

One of the ways that we try to have students enact this collaborative construction of knowledge is through the final project in the course. In the "Roman" half of the course, we focus on events of the year 65 CE. Students work in research groups that will produce a poster or presentation on some aspect of Roman life that pertains to the material we are covering. The water supply of Rome, the demographics of the population, and the role of public religion are a few of the areas researched. At the end of the Roman half of the term, there is a poster session at which students present their research findings. Each group, therefore, represents a small group of "experts" with specialized knowledge that can inform the rest of the course material. Through class presentations, the rest of the students gain access to this information, though they are dependent upon other "scholars" for it. This process gives the students a glimpse (albeit a very cursory one) of how the world of classical scholarship is collaboratively constructed by sharing information.

Of course there are challenges as well. Time is the major one. While it may seem as if two professors would each spend half the time teaching a single course that they do alone, in fact the collaborative preparation and teaching end up taking more time rather than less. We have now taught the course together for six years, and our views on much of the material have increasingly converged with the time we've spent discussing it. Thus, in some senses, in order to maintain the excitement of the dialogue we necessarily have to continually tinker with the format and material. We do not always succeed in replicating in class the moments of discovery we shared in preparation. And, practically speaking, it is not easy for a small department to continue to devote 2 FTE (full-time equivalents, i.e., two faculty members) to one course; it will not be surprising if one or the other of us has to take over sole responsibility for it soon.

Even in the face of all these challenges, though, the introductory course is a case-study of collaboration on the various levels of planning and pedagogy. This process mirrors the larger processes of scholarship in which collaboration is essential and energizing.

UNFORESEEN CONSEQUENCES

As mentioned above, the discussions that we had regarding learning goals for the introductory course had broader implications. We were forced to think about our learning goals in other parts of the curriculum as well, so that the new gateway would "lead" somewhere.

This is not to say that our courses did not have learning goals before, but the collaboration on the introductory course made us realize that we could be more intentional in coordinating the learning experience of our students. Our curriculum at this point was a product of the interests of individual faculty members and a vague sense of what was "important" to cover in the field. Although we were a very collegial department that talked frequently about pedagogical issues, our department culture had traditionally placed a high premium on faculty autonomy. New courses came and went erratically, almost always based upon (possibly idiosyncratic) individual faculty interests. We had only vague ideas about our curriculum as a collaborative effort, a vehicle to deliver conscious educational goals beyond the "coverage" of the material.

In a way there were several mythologies here about how a department operates, how faculty teach, and what students need to know, and how one "learns" classics. While dissatisfaction with mythology was our starting point, therefore, this became the catalyst for systematic curricular changes. It was like

> Collaboration on the introductory course made us realize that we could be more intentional in coordinating the learning experience of our students. Our curriculum at this point was a product of the interests of individual faculty members and a vague sense of what was "important" to cover in the field.

clearing a path in an overgrown garden. In fact, such intentionality made everyone's jobs easier, as we planned syllabi for our own individual courses. There were agreed upon principles in circulation now that could inform choices we were making in designing other courses. These principles centered on helping our students learn how to gain access to other scholars' voices and begin to understand how knowledge is generated in our field.

A LUCKY COINCIDENCE

In 1999, Carleton's library invited all department chairs to participate in a three-year Mellon Grant it had won to integrate information literacy into the curriculum. The grant would provide up to $5,000 over three years for each of five pilot departments to work in collaboration with library staff on this project, with the expectation that they would then share the wisdom they had acquired with other departments. The Classics Department, already interested in giving some time to thinking about our majors' research skills—and never flush with cash—hopped aboard.

Our fellow pilot departments in the grant were the Departments of Economics, English, Geology, and History. The library assigns a "liaison" reference librarian to each academic division. These three librarians, plus representatives from each of the participating departments, formed a steering committee that met regularly through the three-year period. Thus we had throughout a clear idea of what the other departments were doing with their grants and could use or modify their ideas as we felt appropriate.

But the real action happened during the departmental retreats, which (for the Classics Department) occurred over several days in each summer and each December break of the granting period. In these retreats our entire department, often with the addition of temporary leave-replacement faculty, as well as our liaison librarian, met and discussed what we wanted our majors to know, how best we thought our curriculum could deliver it, and how we would assess whether or not students were actually succeeding.

As we had found in our 110 discussions, there is something energizing about starting at such a basic level, and having the full department's participation was a great advantage. While we all consider ourselves generalists, as is typical for a small liberal-arts program, we each brought a different perspective to the discussion based on our own experiences and tastes.

At the outset we set ourselves the task of defining "information literacy" in our field, and even this preliminary exercise developed into a fascinating and

Curricular Matrix for the Classics Major

Analecta Technica (Classics 295, "Junior Skills Portfolio")

CHECK-OFF SHEET: Check boxes if you have taken (or will take, during your junior year) the courses specified for each of the required reference and search tools below.

You must document experience in **all** of the following **tools in boldface** as well as **any three others**. If you have not taken the courses specified, indicate the course in which you did get experience with the given reference or search tool and get the faculty member's signature.

Reference Tools			
Basic Reference Tools for the Languages:			
Tool		Course (fill in the course in which you used the tool)	Check-off (faculty signature)
Lexicons		Greek or Latin 204	
Grammars		Greek or Latin 103	
Thesaurus Linguae Graecae (TLG)			
Indices Verborum			
Basic Reference Tools for Texts:			
Commentaries		2 and 300-level language courses	
General Reference Tools:			
Oxford Classical Dictionary (OCD)		Classics 110	
Perseus		Greek or Latin 204	
Pauly Wissowa, The New Pauly			
Specific Reference Tools:			
History:	Cambridge Ancient History (also Perseus)	Greek History	
Mythology:	Lexicon Iconographicum Mythologiae Classicae (LIMC)	Ancient Epic	
Art and Archaeology:	Princeton Encyclopedia of Classical Sites (also LIMC, Perseus)	Greek History	
Geography:	**New Barrington Atlas**	Greek History	

Search Tools		
General Library Tools:		
Library Organization	Tutorials provided by Heather Tompkins: indicate in which course this occurred, if appropriate. If you haven't had one in the context of a course, please arrange a session with her while you are putting together your bibliography for item d	
General Library Search Engines (Bridge, JSTOR)		
Bibliographic Software (e.g., Endnote)		
Search Tools Specific to Classics:		
L'annee Philologique	300-level language courses	
TOCS-IN	300-level language courses	
Purposeful, Physical Browsing of Shelves	Classics 110	
Footnotes and Bibliographies of Published Works	300-level language courses	
Citation Indexes		
Subject-oriented Search Tools:		
Nestor		
Diotima	Gender and Sexuality	
Published Subject Bibliographies		
Bryn Mawr Classical Review		

valuable discussion of both the basic bones of our subject area and the skills appropriate to an undergraduate major in it. While none of us individually would have come up with the definition that emerged from the initial retreat, all of us agreed on the final product and were convinced that the process would help us improve the education our majors receive.

In the retreats that followed this preliminary discussion, we borrowed an idea from the Geology Department and developed a curricular matrix, showing which courses would provide students with which elements we had agreed they should be exposed to in advance of the work we wanted to require of them in their senior year. Since our new introductory course was the only specific one required for the major, it was necessary that we spread many of the skills we had articulated more broadly through our curriculum. While we couldn't be sure that all our majors would take the Virgil seminar, for instance, we did know that all of them would, at some point, take a 200- or a 300-level course in Latin or Greek. If we agreed that every 200-level language course would teach a certain set of skills, we could be confident our seniors would not only have had a brush with them but some practice as well. Of course this kind of curricular plan required us to give up a degree of freedom in designing our courses and in particular to ensure that visiting faculty understand what is required of them. But this seemed to all of us a small price for the pay-off of a set of well-prepared seniors.

A CAPSTONE IS BORN

After we had filled out the curricular matrix and devoted some time to crafting specific assignments, we turned to the senior capstone experience itself. All Carleton students are required to engage in some discipline-specific capstone experience during the senior year. In classics, as in many other departments, this requirement was for many years satisfied by a year-long independent study which culminated in a long research paper (20-30 pages) and a public talk. This experience (once it was over) was clearly valuable for many of our students. But in process it felt inordinately painful for many and required a large amount of work for faculty on top of their regular course load.

The major problem with the old system, we came to feel, was that it imposed on undergraduate students the model of a graduate dissertation. Even our best majors lacked the preparation to really do this kind of research, which requires not only a greater facility with the ancient languages than they can yet have, but also reading knowledge of other modern languages, a much more specialized library than Carleton has, and faculty expert in the particular area they are investigating. Our students, on the other hand, were free to choose topics that none of the faculty specialized in and that the library collection might or might not reasonably support.

From the faculty side of things, directing senior research (for which Carleton awards no teaching credit) was like running numerous independent studies in widely varying areas on top of our normal course load. Sometimes a student would happen to choose a topic on which we could be helpful and directive, but frequently we were exploring almost as much as they. While the subject areas differed widely, we were also working to help each of them separately with essentially the same general problems of finding a feasibly narrowed area to work in, locating productive primary and secondary sources, and articulating a good thesis. Finally, while we tried a number of ways to foster some real discussion of the papers when the students gave their talks, the idiosyncratic individual topics meant that they almost never were able to really comment upon their peers' work.

> After extensive discussion, we decided to shift the structure of the senior research requirement from an independent project to one modeled more closely on the way scholars operate in our field: Starting with a call for papers on a specified topic, students submit an abstract, then give a conference paper at a festive symposium, and finally revise this paper into a short article, which is printed along with all the work submitted that year in a journal format for all the seniors. Students work together through much of the process.

In fact, we came to believe that the model of a graduate dissertation perpetuates the myth of a scholar working in isolation that we were in the process of exploding in the context of our introductory course. Serendipitously, it was just at this moment that our department became involved with an institutional initiative that gave us the opportunity we needed for further collaboration around the problems we had identified with our senior projects.

The particular retreat during which we started discussions of the capstone happened to follow directly on a Carleton Writing Program workshop in which two of us had participated. This workshop had focused on helping students to define problems to address in research papers, rather than vague topics or areas. The coincidence of this particular workshop is probably responsible for our initial focus in that retreat on the invention phase (always the most problematic) of our students' research. We started wondering how the process would look if we specified a large topic for everyone to research together, rather than allowing students to choose independently and wallow in isolation. Once again, in fact, we were thinking about trading autonomy for a collective goal.

After extensive discussion, we decided to shift the structure of the senior research requirement from an independent project to one modeled more closely on the way scholars operate in our field: Starting with a call for papers on a specified topic, students submit an abstract, then give a conference paper at a festive symposium, and finally revise this paper into a short article, which is printed along with all the work submitted that year in a journal format for all the seniors. Students work together through much of the process. As juniors they are involved as a group in the choice of a topic for the conference. Over the summer they read a recent book in the area and use that as a jumping-off point for their discussions of the specific call for papers, which they craft collaboratively. During the term in which students complete their preliminary research and write their abstract, they meet once a week with all faculty in a seminar format, commenting on each others' work and sharing sources and ideas.

We used our final installment of the Mellon Grant to investigate number of possible topics for the first run of this new system: Each of us researched and reported on a potential area. We wanted to make sure that whatever area we designated would appeal to students interested in either Greece or Rome and would offer potential topics in literature, political or social history, or material culture. After considering a number of possibilities, we settled on the topic of "Food and Dining in the Ancient World" for our first run of the new system.

Students will always balk at the loss of choice, and we must admit that our first set of seniors was, at least to begin with, balky. But, to their credit, they were a game bunch, and the notion that they were really going to do "what classicists do" had an appeal for them. We spent the first session of the senior seminar brainstorming the range of specific topics that could appropriately fall under the aegis of "food and dining" and soon the board was covered with possibilities, including agricultural practice, trade, religious regulation of dining—even child eating as a recurring pattern in, yes, mythology!

We learned a great deal taking the seniors through the process in that first year, and we will continue to massage the system in various ways to improve their educational experiences. But even in its first run the process was a success. At an afternoon symposium in February we heard papers on (among other things) ritual sacrifice, breast-feeding, vegetarianism, man-eating monsters, changing fashions in Roman dining-room structure, poisoning under the Julio-Claudians, and the figure of the cook in Roman comedy.

We can't claim that the new system magically transformed all of our seniors into professional classicists. It did, however, give them a degree of intellectual community our old system never delivered. After the symposium we had a dinner for all the junior and senior majors and all the faculty. As some 20 of us balanced plates in our laps, conversations bubbled up all around the room about food and Greece and Rome, about successes and failures in research, about classics. The juniors began talking with real excitement about what they wanted to do at their symposium next year. The myth of the scholar toiling alone was starting to lose its appeal.

OBSTACLES

Inevitably there were challenges and difficulties along the way from the old system to the new. Most difficult during the Mellon Grant was communications with the library staff. The position of humanities liaison (working with both the History and Classics Departments on the grant) turned over three times in the course of the grant period, and each time we needed to start from scratch with the new person. In addition, faculty were simply not accustomed to, and frankly somewhat suspicious about, collaborating with staff on curricular matters. While we can't say that we ever entirely got over this hurdle, the best progress came about through developing personal relations and being willing to experiment. The fact that three of the participating pilot departments had excellent and productive relationships with their liaisons gave us motivation to utilize our own more fully and faith that in the long run such collaboration could really be helpful to us and our students.

The other major difficulty we encountered was simply in keeping track of our own process and communicating with each other. While we are a small (four permanent faculty) and generally collegial department, our administrative skills vary widely. Whenever we began a new retreat we inevitably had to spend a certain amount of time reminding each other what it was we had agreed upon at the last one. It never occurred to us that inviting the departmental assistant to the retreats would have helped us keep track of the discussions. Scheduling retreats when all four of us would be in town and available also proved difficult. (In fact, we were the only one of the five participating departments whose activities regularly included all permanent faculty.) But having all department members present was extremely important in the process. The program we had designed would never work without full faculty buy-in, and this was impossible without full faculty participation in the invention process.

Our new capstone experience is a product of collaboration at a number of levels (department faculty, library, and other departments participating in the Mellon Grant program). It is based upon and will continue to require departmental collaboration in integrating research skills into the major curriculum to ensure that students are prepared to do the work required in the senior year. It also folds student-student collaboration into the research process in an entirely different manner from our old and more traditional system. In the future we hope to expand the circles of collaboration outwards as we engage an external scholar to give a keynote address or response to papers at the symposium.

CONCLUSION

The preceding narrative makes the whole process and its outcome seem very tidy and straightforward. The actual path to curricular change, however, was much more circuitous and involved a great deal of discussion, false starts, dead ends, and open questions. In short, it required good faith collaboration. The discussions our department began in designing a new introductory course for our curriculum set the stage for future, farther-reaching discussions which we continue to have. So this is really a story about collaborations that continue and that continue to bear fruit.

Collaboration, in fact, extends beyond the borders of our department. For example, some of the members of our department were heavily involved in the ongoing development of the use of portfolios to assess the college's writing requirement. Our interactions with faculty from other departments and disciplines as the portfolio was being designed caused us to realize that writing, specifically, was not deployed in an intentional manner in our department's curriculum, although we all regularly asked students to write in our courses. The collaboration with faculty members in other departments on the writing portfolio also drove home the fact that our courses were part of the larger offerings of the college and as such should further, where possible, the broader aims of the overall curriculum.

These considerations led to the further application for funds to develop writing assignments for the new introductory course as well as a writing composition course to be taught in our department based on classical rhetorical theory. Both courses would now have assignments that invoked the goals of the writing portfolio, though tailored to the needs of our department courses. In this way we managed to leverage the collaboration we had had outside the department into an outcome that was useful to ourselves and the college as a whole.

Outside of writing concerns, we hear from our colleagues by our participation in and presence at events sponsored by Carleton's Learning and Teaching Center. Frequently, we have found inspiration in topics that are not directly intended for us but can be adapted for a problem or a situation that we face in our discipline. Finally, several members of our department participate in interdisciplinary programs and college-wide committees. This extended connection with other areas of the college draws us out of the narrower concerns of classics into the larger life of the college.

> Collaboration needs fuel to burn, beyond good faith (even when this is in good supply), and our department took the critical step of securing funds in order to give a definite shape and time frame to our discussions. The money itself was not a tremendous financial gain, but even small, token amounts serve as a catalyst for converting our ideas into actualities. It made us accountable and gave our collaboration a sense of urgency.

But collaboration needs fuel to burn, beyond good faith (even when this is in good supply), and our department took the critical step of securing funds in order to give a definite shape and time frame to our discussions. The money itself was not a tremendous financial gain, but even small, token amounts serve as a catalyst for converting our ideas into actualities. It made us accountable and gave our collaboration a sense of urgency. Because we were being paid for our time, we had just the prod we needed to make difficult decisions or secure compromise on issues we were in disagreement about. Without the funds, it would have been too easy to put off discussion when intellectual exhaustion set in. Furthermore, the granting of the funds was also a public acknowledgment from the college that it valued our efforts to keep the curriculum current and vital. These gestures matter.

WHAT WE HAVE LEARNED

Collaboration is energizing. All teachers experience the frustration of the class that doesn't go well, the assignment that doesn't work, or the course that fails to produce the results one wanted. Scholars get stuck in similar ways as well. Too often they look for answers within the narrow confines of their own experience or expectations. Collaboration helps to get us "unstuck," and the corresponding rush is exhilarating and productive. One cannot predict when, how, or why collaboration will do these things, but that, of course, is why we should seek out as many opportunities as possible to work with others.

Collaboration is exhausting. Working with others requires a good deal of patience and an appetite for compromise. Successful collaboration requires more "exploration" time and more effort invested in securing agreement. This can be especially tiring for faculty who do not usually engage in shared enterprise. Good leadership and division of labor help, but these things must be collaboratively worked out as well. Sacrificing some autonomy is necessary, but it can feel inefficient and laborious.

Collaboration happens on lots of different levels (and needs to). In the narrative we have provided above, one can see faculty working with faculty within a department, faculty working with faculty (and administrative staff) outside the department, faculty working with students, and students working with each other. Even within these broad categories there are subdivisions that require collaboration. But such a broad range of collaborations has helped us to balance departmental goals with college goals. This is, in fact, the payoff for the college's generous—and necessary—provision of development funds. The money keeps us honest and focused; it provides a space for faculty sharing ideas, fears, hopes, and dreams.

In the final analysis, there is nothing exceptional in any of the collaborative steps we have taken along the way to re-imagining our department's curriculum. By simply being willing to utilize the opportunities for collaboration that fortunately exist in abundance on our campus, our department has positioned itself to manage future curricular change in a sensible way and has reaffirmed the limits of scholarly autonomy and the power of collegial cooperation.

Administrators as Collaborators in Support of Faculty Collaboration

Scott Bierman and Elizabeth Ciner

Among faculty or administrators, we expect the following story will be familiar. A long-time faculty member, one who has earned the deep respect of her colleagues through careful listening, good judgment, and effective leadership, has just been assigned an administrative position as a dean or associate dean. The first sidewalk conversation, the first e-mail, the first congratulatory phone all start with the exact same sentence: "I see you have decided to move over to the dark side." While intended as a joke, the comment serves as a serious warning that prompts these questions: What inclinations and actions can an academic administrator employ to help ensure that she is a collaborator with faculty? How can one be viewed as an enabler of good faculty curricular initiatives, rather than someone who is seen as an impediment or a force to be overcome with political shrewdness or guile?

> What inclinations and actions can an academic administrator employ to help ensure that she is a collaborator with faculty? How can one be viewed as an enabler of faculty curricular initiatives, rather than someone who is seen as an impediment or a force to be overcome with political shrewdness or guile?

Perhaps it is our view of ourselves as faculty first and administrators second—as professionals who have chosen a path that veers away from the classroom and toward roles that empower faculty in their work—that accounts for our collaborative

H. SCOTT BIERMAN, professor of economics and the dean of the college, joined the Carleton faculty in 1982. He earned his B.A. degree at Bates College and his PhD degree at the University of Virginia. ELIZABETH CINER, associate dean of the college and senior lecturer in English, earned her B.A. degree at the University of Pennsylvania and her M.A. and PhD degrees at the University of Washington. She joined the Carleton faculty in 1982.

approach to intellectual community. Of course, we are fortunate to be deans at an institution with an environment that invites collaboration in a number of ways. First, Carleton is small enough that people in various academic and administrative units know one another. Proximity through office and classroom locations, committee service, the recreation center, and community activities all contribute toward the development of relationships. Like all kinds of community, intellectual community depends on relationships, and past deans at Carleton have engendered a strong sense of trust among the faculty. While there is no shortage of mistakes both previous deans and we have made, it is relatively rare that faculty question our motives. We feel free to talk openly and candidly about our opinions, and faculty feel equally free to challenge us. And we rarely insult each other in these exchanges.

Second, since 1992, Carleton has turned to the Perlman Center for Learning and Teaching (LTC)—whose coordinator is always drawn from the faculty on a three-year term with a half-time teaching load—as a locus of communication, institutional planning, faculty development, and outreach to all constituencies on campus. From a week-long workshop for new faculty to a library of pedagogical materials to weekly lunchtime gatherings open to all faculty and staff, the LTC serves as a venue where faculty can test new ideas, confess to mistakes, and talk openly about their teaching in a congenial, supportive context. The collegiality fostered by the LTC has been transformative for faculty and staff alike, transcending administrative boundaries and traditional job roles to promote the kind of communication that need not depend on formal work assignments to be successful and rewarding. The LTC works closely with the dean's office to set a yearly agenda, but it is seen accurately by the community as ultimately working toward the benefit of the faculty.

Third, we occupy a dean's office that has traditionally taken seriously its mission to support faculty, a mission made possible by an organizational position with a broader field of vision than any individual or department can perceive. Support for faculty takes many forms: money, creative thinking, sympathy, willingness to solve problems, and the promise to keep looking for the resources faculty need to do their best work. This volume speaks directly (see the Hardy-Zimmerman chapter) and indirectly (see almost all of the others) to the work we do both on stage and behind the scenes to do our part in building the kind of community that yields the wonderful teaching, research, scholarship, service, and above all, student learning that characterizes a fine liberal arts college.

At the risk of revealing tricks of our trade, we offer the following principles that speak to our separate and shared senses of the work we do to support faculty. We present these principles in our own voices, addressing readers who want to know how we work. Liz begins with the principle and Scott follows with a key expectation implied or imposed by that principle. We also offer, in parentheses, our *sotto voce* advice to faculty who want to advance these principles via active collaboration with us.

PRINCIPLE 1

Elizabeth Ciner: Be there for faculty. Make yourself available to faculty, a natural choice for them to consult about their ideas, worries, and frustrations. Respond supportively to faculty curiosity and show your own. Brainstorming about a problem or complaint may be the first vital step toward a true breakthrough.

Scott Bierman: Expect the dean's office to be patient, because issues are complicated, resources are scarce and cannot be wasted, and getting it right is important. To be nurturing and helpful does not equate with rushing into a new initiative nor does it imply the dean is dragging her feet. Indeed, the dean should be openly optimistic as long as the initiative continues to show good promise. (Try to keep a regularly updated timetable in front of all concerned. If people can see the expected steps of getting from here to there, they are often less apt to see a dean as holding things up. The timetable also provides a remarkably helpful record of the many times that developing initiatives veer in new directions—a living testimony to the value of patience.)

PRINCIPLE 2

EC: Support a faculty development initiative that brings faculty together in a low-stakes environment. A first encounter may be better termed a conversation than a meeting. Informality is the friend of interpersonal experimentation. At Carleton, an accident of campus geography has produced a decentralized administration;

administrators are not herded together all in one building that is insulated from the students and faculty. In contrast, Carleton administrators, including the president and the deans, are located among classrooms and faculty offices, which means that the accidental meetings in the halls, on the stairs, and on the sidewalks can yield positive interactions that accumulate into consistent communication.

SB: Expect a dean's office to participate regularly, in both official and unofficial capacities. Our ability to bring people together who have expressed similar ideas or concerns requires that we are invited into multiple conversations at the earliest stages. Our ability to help a president and a board understand the importance of a new initiative is made far easier and more effective if we have participated in the conversations that have shaped the initiative. (Make sure there are agendas and programs that take good advantage of everyone's time, including those in the dean's office.)

PRINCIPLE 3

EC: Listen to faculty: Keep your ear to the ground, roam around, connect, consult. Create opportunities for serendipitous meetings. Faculty complaints are particularly helpful in this regard, as there is nothing like a disgruntled faculty member as a source of available energy. If in any one month three faculty complain to me about the college's foot-dragging on a sustainability program, or about how poor their students are at clear communication, or how dismal their students' quantitative skills are, I can begin to test their understandings with other faculty with whom I am in conversation and organize a meeting of faculty with mutual concerns.

SB: Expect the dean's office to be able to articulate an informed institutional perspective. Articulation of a common purpose that is internally aligned with institutional goals makes faculty-dean collaboration a unifying and satisfying experience. Where possible, a dean should think about ways to integrate ideas that seem to be about separate initiatives—to imagine Venn diagrams and work to develop the overlap that joins constituencies. When our social scientists who were interested in developing a quantitative reasoning program wanted to explore the use of a writing assessment to sample student work for their purposes, the dean's office was delighted to help them try it. Now a grant-funded program in quantitative reasoning is conceptually joined with a writing-across-the-curriculum program to the greater benefit of both efforts. (Make sure you have something important to say that has been tested with other faculty and staff. While it is often the case that an idea starts with a complaint, spending some time thinking about ways to proactively address the complaint helps to mitigate defensiveness and emotional exhaustion.)

PRINCIPLE 4

EC: Do something. Be a matchmaker. Tell Professor X you have had a conversation with Professor Y. E-mail X, Y, and Z and suggest you all connect over coffee.

SB: Expect a dean to help you secure a presence in well-regarded institutional structures and to help with academic support once you have an idea that can be developed. We have already noted the central importance at Carleton of the Perlman Center for Learning and Teaching and the role that the dean's office plays in shaping its agenda. But, we have also had terrific success with engineering time for initiative leaders to meet with the president and the board. There is no good substitute for demonstrating to the decision-makers the passion and energy that busy faculty are willing to bring to a new initiative. (However, often you can do much of the ground work yourself. For example, you can invite speakers to campus who connect to your initiative and also to faculty who have not gotten as involved as you would have liked. Or, you can reach out to other more established initiatives or programs for a collaborative opportunity.)

PRINCIPLE 5

EC: Do more. Offering logistical support is not inconsequential in the very busy lives of faculty. Help out if someone needs to find a meeting time and place; send out invitations; get a first meeting off the ground. This support is not only important for what it can buy directly, but often it sends a credible signal about deanly interest that has enormous indirect benefits. Faculty want to be recognized for the creative and important work they are doing and a financially inexpensive recognition often provides disproportionate satisfaction. Validating a faculty member's concerns is vitally important in an environment where almost everyone has a complaint or a terrific idea or two once or twice a week. Offer to bring in a speaker, look for grant opportunities, or organize that second meeting. Be willing to be hooked by the issue and become part of the team.

SB: Expect a dean to be supportive with money, food, and visible opportunities if the dean really is supportive of your issue, but honest with you if not. (Try to leverage a dean's support with support you find elsewhere—the expressed commitment of time and energy by busy faculty speaks volumes.) Furthermore, expect a dean to help provide leadership in locating appropriate curricular ownership. The leadership locus for an initiative is not always obvious, can often require a surprisingly complicated structure, and is regularly fraught with political difficulties at multiple levels. The reality is that finding the right group of people in the right curricular areas with the political and relational skills to move a program from an idea into a reality is fundamentally important and not easy. (In some cases, you may want to deliver your idea and advice and get out of the way.)

PRINCIPLE 6

EC: Pat Hutchings of the Carnegie Foundation for the Advancement of College Teaching talks about bringing our skills, values, and habits as scholars to our work as teachers, but it is also wonderful to make it possible for faculty be students again. A dean's office can help to create occasions for faculty to learn together by offering to bring in external speakers, fund (or organize) reading groups, and sponsor workshops. (You may also find that powerful change agents are right on your own campus.) Intangible benefits include increased understanding and appreciation among faculty members of what they are doing as well as opportunities to connect over issues more substantive than complaints about the administration! Tangible benefits may be as simple as deciding to use similar terminology (or discovering that faculty in different disciplines are using similar terminology to mean different things) or as complex as identifying and coming up with cross-disciplinary solutions to common problems. Faculty working hard together are simply more effective than faculty working hard in isolation from one another. Moreover, because faculty development is actually about teaching—and any faculty development session must be as carefully planned and delivered as any classroom session—innovative pedagogy can be modeled and once modeled may be picked up and deployed creatively by faculty. Remember, the inoculation model does not work for either students or faculty. Iterative approaches and learning communities are good for faculty as well as students. Faculty are superb learners, and they deserve the very best we have to offer.

SB: One of the places that a dean's office can be most helpful is finding ways to connect faculty exploring a new idea to external communities that are working in similar areas. We have found it particularly valuable to challenge our faculty, while providing lots of support, to seek external funding. Independent of whether or not we receive the grant, this exercise invariably sharpens the faculty's thinking, exposes them to what other schools are doing, and usually requires them to think seriously about assessment. We are careful not to limit our external connections to peer institutions. Indeed, we often learn more from schools that are fundamentally different from us (community colleges, professional schools) than we do from schools with a similar mission. (In addition to bringing in speakers and holding workshops, you should be making connections with other schools, participating in national groups interested in your curricular initiative, and learning about grant opportunities.)

PRINCIPLE 7

EC: Cultivate faculty leadership. Some promising initiatives get off the ground but never become more than boutique operations at an institution. When their originators are no longer present or run out of energy, the initiative dies. Someone—often a dean—has to take the long view and think about bringing in new blood.

SB: Expect a dean to help identify leaders to carry the initiative forward. This probably best happens at the point when the initiative has some real clarity. (Your perspective will be important here, but remember that the program after a year's conversation is likely different than the program when it was first conceived. In the interval, faculty and other stakeholders will have revealed themselves in unpredictable ways.)

PRINCIPLE 8

EC: Be on hand to break up log jams by articulating common purposes. Keeping a shared vision in focus is a healthy way to build consensus and community.

SB: There will always be challenging moments when it appears that the momentum is dying. In the worst of these moments it may appear that the dean's office has lost interest. At that point a direct face-to-face with the dean is the best way to gauge where you are. But expect a dean to be unhappy if you go through the back door to the president or board when you get frustrated. This is not the same thing as saying that you should never be talking directly with the president, just that the dean should not be surprised when you do it. (By and large, you are far better off to go through the dean to the president and the board. Any responsible president will take your conversation back to the dean anyway, and you want that moment to be met with a knowing smile rather than a surprised frown. You also want to be honest with a dean who is honest with you.)

PRINCIPLE 9

EC: Be the voice of reason. Time and money are in short supply everywhere, so make sure that faculty, in their idealism, are not putting in place something they simply cannot sustain.

SB: Amen. It is easy for faculty excited by a new program to engage in a type of benefit-benefit analysis (i.e., one that completely ignores the cost in time, money, and energy). But deans also have an historical perspective that alerts them to models that characterize the institution, its constituencies, and its best work. If curricular change has been advanced through faculty development and assessment, expect that a similar program, suitably adapted, may be worth applying to the next initiative. This is not to say that all institutional change is patterned, but where a reliable wheel has been invented, it should be employed as often as it fits the need. To be sure, collaboration depends on shared goals. Collaboration also depends on shared administrative machinery to accomplish those goals. (Update the dean regularly and listen to feedback.)

PRINCIPLE 10

EC: Remember assessment, which should always be paired with faculty development. Even an unwelcome mandate for assessment can be a faculty development bonanza. Put the work of compiling and analyzing data back into the curriculum and give faculty credit for their efforts.

SB: Expect a dean to want to pilot, test, and assess before committing the college to a new program. The dean, like you, will want everyone to be successful and look really good. As mentioned earlier, an application for external funding can be a way of using an external agency to require a thoughtful assessment program without ever having that thorny issue arise internally. (You can help the dean by working with faculty to understand the importance of this feature of collaboration.)

BACK TO COLLABORATION

These principles can best be employed when certain attitudes and dispositions characterize the key administrators. Being an optimist with the patience to take the long view always pays. We well remember the example of faculty from the Physics and Astronomy Department who were slowly won over to the writing-across-the-curriculum program through patient, friendly overtures over lunch for a period of three years before they agreed to participate in a faculty workshop. That entire department is now a showcase for writing to learn, an outcome that may have surprised them but did not surprise the deans. A similar movement toward rethinking writing in the major is also occurring in the Economics Department. In both cases, faculty are doing the hard work of taking stock and making change; the dean's office is delighted to support their efforts and praise them for their results.

We return, however, to the core principle that began this chapter. Being collaborative among faculty and academic administrators is best accomplished if the dark side jokes are simply jokes and not thinly veiled descriptions of reality. In a busy day filled with administrative duties and great pressures, it is very easy to lose sight of the fundamental mission of any academic dean: to support the work of the faculty. It is time to hand over the keys to the office the day you begin to develop an "us versus them" mentality or if you begin to get angry about faculty frustration over not getting enough of your attention. Helping faculty realize their vision in a world of constrained resources is an art best accomplished with skills that derive far more from Yoda than from Darth Vader. May the Force be with us.

Dedicated to the Memory of Shelby J. Boardman, Colleague, Leader, and Friend

November 7, 1944–January 19, 2007

As this book was prepared for production, the Carleton community was stunned by the news of Shelby Boardman's unexpected death from natural causes. A committed faculty member since 1971, Shelby was the Charles L. Denison Professor of Geology. He also served as associate dean of the college from 1994 to 1997, as acting dean of the college in 1997, and as dean of the college from 2002 to 2005. His leadership influenced many of the scholarly, classroom, and administrative projects described in these pages.

We at Carleton miss Shelby greatly, and we remember him here in the context of other wonderful colleagues, past and present, who inform our work together.

The Editors

Reflections on Learning as Teachers

$17.95, 6 x 9, paperback, 240 pages

Richard M. Reis (executive director, Alliance for Innovative Manufacturing, Stanford
University; moderator of *Tomorrow's Professor*, a faculty development listserv):

Hearing from teachers as they reflect on their own learning and that of their
students is inspiring and of considerable practical value as we all look for ways to
make our daily efforts more meaningful...